Suddenly something cracked in front of me. Jerking up, still trying to hold the girl, I reached for my rifle. In the first split second I saw an enemy uniform. In the next fraction of a second I saw a woman, her eyes flashing darkly at me. My God, it was her! I knew it was, even though her hair was pinned under her cap. I couldn't move. She stood there pointing a rifle at my chest, eyes darting from me to the girl. With arms outstretched in either direction, I knelt frozen—mesmerized by a distant recognition. I didn't even think about the danger I was in. This was the woman! This was her! She stared back, not pulling the trigger. My God, she could kill me!

She stood there silently as I mouthed, "Who are you?" Then her hand went to her head. Her other arm kept the rifle leveled on me. She let her hair drop. It cascaded to her waist. A slight breeze gently curled it around her uniform. Then her lips parted, and she said, *"Be Dau."*

BLOOD ON THE LOTUS

Lawrence C. Vetter, Jr.

IVY BOOKS • NEW YORK

Ivy Books
Published by Ballantine Books
Copyright © 1990 by Lawrence C. Vetter, Jr.

Grateful acknowledgment is made to the following for permission to reprint previously published material:
C.J. Berkman: Excerpt from "Ex-Bull Rider" from *No More Dues to Pay* . . . (Saddle Tramp Press, 7615 Stone Crop Lane, San Antonio, Texas, 1985). Copyright © 1985 by C.J. Berkman. Reprinted by permission of the author.
Foreign Languages Publishing House: Poem excerpted from THE NARROW STRIP OF LAND by Tran Mai Nam, 1969. Reprinted by permission of the publisher.
Henry Holt and Company, Inc.: Excerpts from *We the Vietnamese: Voices from Vietnam* edited by Francois Sully. Copyright © 1971 by Praeger Publishers, Inc., Reprinted by permission of Henry Holt and Company, Inc.
Charles Scribner's Sons: Excerpt from *Ho Chi Minh* by Charles Fenn. Copyright © 1973 by Charles Fenn. Reprinted by permission of Charles Scribner's Sons, an imprint of Macmillan Publishing Company.

Library of Congress Catalog Card Number: 90-93057

ISBN-0-8041-0614-2

Manufactured in the United States of America

First Edition: September 1990

There is no question to whom this book is dedicated. The cover carries my father's name, Lawrence C. Vetter. He speaks quietly, but throughout his life, he has established a long and respected reputation in Seguin, Texas. I'll never forget one of the first checks that I ever wrote on my first bank account. When the store owner looked at my identification, he said, "You're Lawrence Vetter's son—your check is good." He was a low-paid teacher and coach, but his word was and is his honor.

However, Dad, please step aside, because your wife of fifty years deserves the spotlight. Thanks, Mom. Thanks for the countless rosaries, masses, and endless prayers that helped to see me through my two and one-half year involvement in the Vietnam War. In spite of the long hours you spent in your dual profession of schoolteacher and mother, you never stopped praying me home. I love you.

This book is dedicated to Elizabeth and Lawrence Vetter, both heroes of the Vietnam conflict and much more.

ACKNOWLEDGMENTS

To those Marines who helped me with information, maps, and friendship that has spanned more than two decades, I gratefully say, "Thanks"—Tim Huff, David Burkhardt, Greg Buccellato, and Justin Bridges.

To the family of Patrick Blagg, I want to send my special thanks—Marjorie, Robert, Kenny, Kathy, Terry, Tanya, Sam, and Bitsy.

To my friends who read the manuscript and encouraged me offering smiles, advice, and critique, I would like to insure that they know that their encouragement meant more than I can adequately describe—my wife Deborah, Jane Clausen and Terry Kaiser, Joyce Spence, Nancy Collier, Caroline Bakes, Karol Brown, the managing editor of the *Kerrville Daily Times*—Wanda Garner Cash, Kathie and Mike Walker, Julie and Richard Aquan, and Randy and Michelle Lindner.

Finally, I would like to thank Dr. Tran Qui Phiet. His home used to be in Hue, Vietnam, but now he is a professor at Schreiner College in Kerrville, Texas. He gave me advice concerning Vietnamese names and words, and he has also written a monograph on the most famous of Vietnamese epic poems that I quote throughout this book: *The Tale of Kieu* by Nguyen Du.

AUTHOR'S NOTE

In this story, I have used an old and special Vietnamese saying on several occasions. The words are *Be Dau*, and literally it could be translated ''sea and mulberry,'' but more fully it means that the sea now rolls where mulberry trees once grew. Colloquially, it has grown to mean an extreme agitation, disorder, or radical change in the concerns of mankind or in nature.

For the past one hundred years such has been the case on a scale that is unprecedented in this country whose culture existed before the time of Jesus. Monk Thich Nhat Hanh wrote of his country:

> ''. . . Viet Nam, land of tears . . .
> Tears and blood flowing everywhere
> Brothers killing each other
> For alien seducers . . .''

As my *compañero*, C. J. Berkman, has said in his poetry *No More Dues to Pay*:

> What's the past?
> only a series
> of serious mistakes
> we really didn't
> learn from.

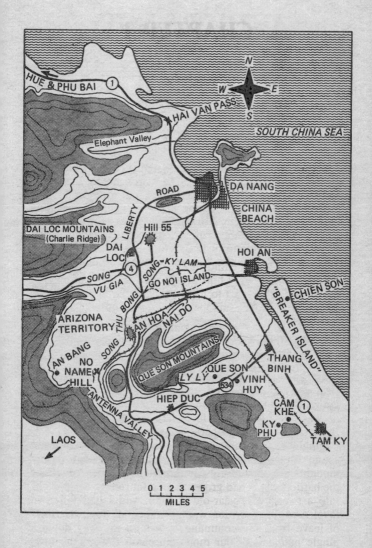

CHAPTER 1

By lamplight turn these scented leaves and read a tale
of love recorded in old books.
— Nguyen Du, *The Tale of Kieu*

I heard the dog behind me again. Wheeling around, I put my hands on my hips and looked down at him. Trying with all my heart to look angry, I glared at him and, stamping my foot, said, "Muc, you go home, you miserable animal. Three times now I have scolded you, and twice I have sent you running with a slap to your backside. You cannot come with me!"

He just stood still, his tail wagging, and his great, gentle eyes staring at me out of his foolish-looking face. I sat down on a log and stared back at him. His tongue hung out the side of his mouth, and he was panting like he was near death. His face, half white and half black, sadly tried to win sympathy from me.

Jungle bushes surrounded the two of us, but with the sound of a distant explosion, I began to drift in my thoughts away from my panting friend. In the middle of the battlefields, I had grown from a fourteen-year-old girl into a twenty-five-year-old woman, and I had fallen in love! And this morning was very special. With five days of leave from my command, I was on my way down a jungle path out of our mountain camp toward the low-

lands. It was hard to really believe. I was on my way to
be married.

Shafts of sunlight knifed through the tall jungle trees
and lightened the early gray morning. The heavy rains
were recently past and the warmth of this April day felt
wonderful. A Vietnamese spring was a time to love and
to try to forget. And though it was not possible to do it
completely, I tried to take my mind off the killing. The
man I loved was coming to meet me, and for just a short
time, to take me away from the bloody and battered into
our own private world of peace and love. A warm feeling
circled me as I thought of Van Thi's touch and loving
words. He had entered my life in the worst of times. My
brother, Ba Can, was the only one left from my family,
but he had grown away from me. Without those who had
been close and so deeply a part of my life, I had relied
on Tran Van Thi more and more with each passing year.
I was six years younger than he was, and he treated me
with such gentle understanding that sometimes he seemed
to have my grandfather's wisdom that had nurtured my
life in days gone by.

Finally, I cut short my daydreams and looked back at
the dog, considering the problem of stopping him from
following me. I sternly focused on him and said, "What
am I to do with you?" His eyes were about level with
my knees, and he cocked his face to one side like he
really wanted to understand me. How could anyone get
mad at him?

"You know Ba Can," I continued, "the one who is
my brother, your master, and commander of our battalion and the camp I have just left?"

"Yes, him," I mocked, pretending I could hear his
answer.

"Ba Can likes to have you around to kick and would
not like it if you were gone."

"What? You want to be in my wedding!" I teased.
"You're really lacking intelligence, Muc. Those people
down in the valleys may be hungry and eat you."

With my hands I molded a surprised look on his face,
and said, "Yes, they most certainly might. Up at camp
no one will eat you because you belong to Ba Can. Elsewhere, they may sneak up on you and capture you just

like any other dumb dog. Not that you are a dumb dog you understand, but believe me, there are thousands out there in the world. And as much as Ba Can feeds you, you'd probably taste good as charcoaled meatballs served by the *nem nuong* vendors. And covered in roasted onions and *nuoc mam* sauce.''

The dog just cocked his head to the other side, and those big, sad eyes continued to gaze at me. He was frustrating and lovable, but I slowly began to feel my concerns again and began to pour them out on my friend. ''Oh, Muc,'' I said, ''sometimes I have so many doubts about myself. After eleven years of war, I feel so dirty and plain. How could Van Thi really love me as he says? The dust, mud, heat, sweat, and blood of the battle leave me so often feeling like an overworked and underfed cow coming from pulling the plow. How could anyone see anything beautiful in me? How could he love me? And I am too old. Tell me, Muc, aren't women married long before they reach their twenty-fifth year? Sometimes people comment about how I have sacrificed my womanhood for the revolution. They may be well intentioned, but it stabs at my heart. Look at me. Am I not a woman? Even though I fight for the revolution, I have the same needs, aches, pains and feelings that any woman has.''

I paused and looked at the dog, who just stood where he was watching me. ''I can't believe that I'm talking to you like this. I hope that no one has seen me spending so much time talking to a dog.''

Then, I jumped at him and yelled, ''They're going to catch and eat you.'' I swatted him and sent him running back up the trail. He disappeared through the bushes, looking back like he thought I was crazy.

Dreaming and doubting, I continued to walk down the path. I again imagined Van Thi's touch. Although I stood taller than the average woman, Van Thi was still a hand above me. I could see him looking down with love in his eyes, stroking my hair, and saying how he liked it flowing long, almost to my waist. Then his hand would hold mine—his soft, light brown skin belying the fact that he endlessly toiled for the revolution. His dark eyes mirrored mine, and I could sense his need for me—

unspoken but reaching out through the expression on his face and the tenderness of his hands.

With thoughts of my lover as my companion, I continued alone down the trail. The dog seemed to be gone now. I walked past shoulder-high plants and vines that brushed my clothes. The morning sun, barely able to be seen through the thick forest overhead, stole brief glances at me. I knew that if I were ten times taller, my reach would be only to the middle level of these great trees.

A vine clawed at my hat, knocking it to the ground. I picked it up and thought about myself marching to my marriage with my hair rolled and pinned under an army hat. Instead of the beautiful *ao dai* with its high mandarin collar and a skirt split to the waist over long silk pants, I wore the irregular black and tan mixed uniform parts of our army. The hat was black, floppy, and had a wide brim. My shirt was light brown, and I had found a green scarf to wear around my neck. My black pants and sandals were the only things I wore that could be considered normal. Then there was the rifle. Gently I rubbed the polished wood of this dear friend. Like a faithful companion, it had saved my life more than once.

Was I the picture of a woman loved and about to be married? It was hard to believe. At least I had hope that my friend Xuan Hoa awaited me with a beautiful dress. She had written that she found one made in heaven just for me. I had read the letter several times, impatiently trying to imagine what the dress looked like.

Then, ahead, I noticed the sun shining more brightly, and I continued down the mountain with my rifle cradled in my arms. Six-hour journey or not, today was the beginning of several happy days, and I gladly let the anticipation lift my spirit.

An hour's walk brought me to the lower slopes of the mountains. But suddenly, like I had been slapped in the face, as I rounded a bend in the trail my pathway ended, crushed by trees. The great lords and kings of the jungles had been ripped apart, uprooted, and scattered like toys. Here and there, large boulders lay split asunder, and everywhere the ground was cratered. I stood still and clenched my teeth.

The American bombers! I hated them. Years of war

were destroying my homeland. Tears of frustration welled up within my eyes. Anger again kindled fires in my soul and pushed aside my thoughts of love. I leaned my rifle against a rock, knelt on one knee, and picked up an orchid which hung limply, dying. Beside me, the jagged metal of a large bomb fragment protruded from one of the splintered forest giants, forever an emblem of the rape of my land by an enemy without mercy. The joy and anticipation that I had felt for the last days faded, and I remembered the words my mother had spoken eleven years ago: America has been seduced into bed with a sick, French whore, and now she also is becoming diseased.

I glanced at the orchid lying in my hand. Then I crawled up on a fallen tree and looked ahead at the hillside so horribly scarred. The smell of death drifted around me. For a moment, the flower I still so carefully held felt like my life, delicate and vulnerable. Memories came back of my parents and grandparents with their lives torn from them. Tears touched my cheeks, and anger tied a knot around my heart. My gaze returned to the orchid lying limply in my hand. Then I knew that the two-thousand-year-old culture of my country was, like the flower, exposed, shattered, and dying.

A nightmarish picture then seared my mind: a two-headed dragon swooped out of the sky to devour my people. The dragon seemed all-powerful. The larger head was strong, vicious, and armor-plated, while the smaller was much like a spoiled child, trying to loudly imitate its parent. The fire from the larger one's nostrils was like molten metal. It rained destruction across the earth and burned the souls of my countrymen. Standing on the broken remains of this grand old man of the forest, I trembled with rage watching this scene unfold and prayed to be shown a weakness in the dragon's armor. He had to be killed.

Then, the vision was gone, and I stood alone again in this forest graveyard. Trees like giant bones littered an area for a thousand yards. I decided to move around the edge of this tangled mass of shattered jungle, but had gone only a short distance when I noticed a paper nailed to a broken tree stump and walked over to it. Written in the note was a poem:

> With rice paddies as battlefields,
> Two-wheeled carts and hoes for arms,
> The peasants are fighters.
> Even if the bombs kill us,
> The people will have food to eat!
> We must answer the call of Uncle Ho!

I recognized the first three lines as a poem of Uncle Ho's, but the last three must have been written by an anonymous traveler, as he in his own small way expressed his anger and resolution in the face of the American bombing. I felt a surging pride for that person and all the people of my province of Quang Nam who fought against the two-headed devil: the Americans and their Saigon puppets. Our people were fighting, whether quietly in their villages or actively in the People's Liberation Army. I saw the beast again, only this time it faced thirty million Vietnamese who had staffs and machetes.

I hated the American soldiers and wished that I could be with Van Thi. Compared with him, the Americans were crude people. While he was filled with compassion and tenderness, they had killing in their hearts. Their eyes reflected a feeling from within them that spoke of their own arrogance and sense of superiority over our race.

Then as I stood and looked again across the bombed and devastated land around me, a battlefield within my mind came to life. I saw dead foreign soldiers. As the trees in front of me were scattered everywhere, so were they. But then suddenly like a ghost, one rose from among the others. I felt a slight tremor shake my body, for like a spirit from years past, he faced me. I stared, unable to take my eyes off him, for I had seen his face again and again in my dreams. I knew him! He was American, but he was different.

Leaning against a shattered tree I felt nightmares reach out of past years. I closed my eyes and gripped a branch of the tree, frightened at what my life could have been. Then I felt myself drifting back across the years, remembering old terrors. The French were gone, but their Vietnamese lackeys remained in command. I saw my mother taken. Screaming and kicking, I fought them, but she disappeared into an unknown death of a faraway prison. Then a year later they had come for me. I was thrown in with other women destined for the private brothel of the government's elite. It was as if it were 1956 again.

I huddled in the corner of our assigned chambers: a fifteen-year-old girl, terrified and filled with hate. For a week, although not beaten, I had to endure the looks and laughs of the officer in charge. He was no more than my height but much older. His body was beginning to show signs of an easy life. His uniform bulged from too many fat meals and a lazy routine. His eyes would narrow into wide slits when he laughed with more than a hint of his evil nature exposing itself.

We were bathed, fed, groomed, and clothed in French-style dresses. Two older women waited on us and tried to assure us that we would be taken care of as long as we obeyed our new master. Confused, I withdrew into myself, horrified at the thought of my fate; I soon learned what obedience meant. I never uttered a sound, but within myself, the realization of what awaited me wrenched from my soul a lonely scream.

After a week, one by one, the women began to be called. Finally, it was my turn. I thought, this cannot be real. It's not really happening. My hair had been washed, perfumed, and rolled on top of my head. I was given a red dress to wear. The officer in charge brought me out, smiled crudely, and patted me saying, "You are a prized one: a virgin, still tight and firm." Frightened, I had tried to pull away, but his hand gripped my arm and squeezed to the bone.

"A sorry state of affairs," he added, "your first night is with an American." He spat on the floor, and we continued down the dimly lit corridor in silence. I prayed and naively hoped for a way to escape but found myself, instead, escorted into a large room. A Vietnamese colonel and two Americans sat there laughing and drinking.

A table set with food for rich men rested in front of them. So much food was still uneaten, yet they seemed to have finished. The room was filled with windows revealing the darkness of the late evening. But lights, lit by the electric power that the French had brought, brightened the room.

The colonel was not at all like the officer who had been in charge of us. He seemed tall, even though he sat on a couch. His attitude displayed a certain dignity, and his smile was polite. The two Americans were strange. I had never been in the presence of one before. Both had been drinking, and the one with dark hair laughed loudly and was becoming drunk. The other, with short blond hair, also drank but was quieter. Confused, I stood there feeling like a foreigner, an alien in my own country. Not able to understand the American language, I shivered, knowing they were talking about me but unable to comprehend.

Finally, the colonel broke into laughter and got up from the couch and walked to me. He looked me in the eyes and spoke softly in Vietnamese, "My young maiden, they do not understand our language so do not fear that they know what I say. Obey me, and I will take care of your needs. Until you are an old woman, you will have a soft bed, good food, and clothes. You will not face the difficulties that so many of our countrymen do. However, you must honor me by going with this young American. This is your first time, and he has assured me that he will be gentle with you. Do what he wants. If he hurts you, tell me later. I will see to him. Remember your life, your future, rests upon the words I speak. Now go."

Thrown into confusion by his almost gentle attitude, I felt like he had just given me a nice bed and silk sheets with the comforting assurance of a father. However, the walls of my prison rose with a quiet, foreboding picture of my future. My life was not my own.

The blond-haired one rose to his feet and looked at me. His eyes searched me, and I glanced away. The other American laughed, slapped him on the back, and spoke to him in their own language. I looked away from the lustful glare of the second one. Fearfully, I prayed for a way to escape but felt tears on my cheek knowing there was none. Anger and fear tied knots in my stomach. I glanced up again at the blond American. He was speaking with the colonel. I could see his blue eyes and no-

ticed that he stood even taller than the colonel. His cheeks
were slightly red, but still, his attitude was more controlled than his friend. His eyes again rested on me with
a questioning look.

The colonel called a maid of the house. She came and
seemed to have been waiting, knowing what she was to
do. He then looked at me again and quietly said, "Go
with the woman. All will be well. Trust me."

The woman led me and the American out of the room
down one and then another hallway lit only by a few
lamps. The scent of perfumes touched me, and somewhere in the distance a person, hidden by walls, played
on a guitar. Occasional laughter could be heard from behind the same walls as we walked past. I closed my eyes
as darkness gripped my heart, and my body trembled
with a lonely, captive fear.

A hand on my arm startled me, and the maid directed
me into a room. Hesitating, I glanced first at her and
then him. Then she gently but firmly led me in, saying,
"My daughter, do as they say. The pay is good, and there
is food and shelter. Outside these walls, many die. Here
you will have a chance to live well. I will be nearby."
She did not leave the small, dim room yet, but I moved
to the side wall and stared first at the American and then
at the floor. Fear, anger, and embarrassment crushed my
ability to think. It took great effort to keep my body from
shaking.

He sat on the bed and just looked at me, still searching
for something. Words came to his mouth that I didn't
understand. But then he rose and walked up to me. I was
petrified, frozen in place. He placed his hands on either
side of my face and looked closely into my eyes and then
at the maid who still waited.

Waves of fear shook me, and I remembered the horrible stories my mother had told. Then in spite of the
fear, I felt a surge of my mother's pride. I looked at his
face and memorized it. His blue eyes, almost green in
the lamplight, stared into mine. Thick, blond eyebrows,
and a nose that was straight framed his eyes. He tried to
smile showing teeth that were even and very white, and
his face was almost burnt by the sun. I could smell the

beer on his breath and stepped back as the maid came forward.

She motioned him to sit. Then her hands unbuttoned my dress, and again, I felt I was drowning in total hopelessness. I stared through the wall into nothing. Slowly I tried to forget where I was. I began to dream of my mother—it was she who undressed me for bed.

Vaguely then, I realized that my clothes were nestled around my feet. Then I was lifted in arms and laid on the bed. My mother drifted as in a vision, clouding my thoughts. Suddenly, I saw the soldiers taking her again, and I cried, "No, please, no!"

The sound of my voice startled me, and my eyes burst open like I was waking from a nightmare. The maid was gone, and the American sat beside me. I lay on a pillow and glanced at my nakedness. I started to cry in embarrassment and fear, and without thinking I rolled on my side facing the wall and held myself.

Then I felt a sheet pulled over my body. Slowly, I turned over not understanding what was happening. He stood beside the bed. His look was one of confusion and sympathy. Then he knelt beside me. He spoke and his words were soft. His hand gently wiped away my tears, and stroked and combed my hair so that it framed my face and shoulders.

Now he no longer seemed to be drunk. His attitude had suddenly changed, and for a moment he looked out the window. His brow wrinkled in thought. Still kneeling by the bed, he turned back to me, smiled, and put his finger to his lips as a sign to be quiet. Then he rose to his feet, while motioning me to stay. Quietly, he walked to the door, opened it, and glanced back at me. Once more he smiled and motioned me to stay. Then he was gone and the door closed.

I was alone, lying naked under a sheet in a strange bed. I wanted to get up and to put on my clothes, but the red dress was a symbol of evil, and I remained clinging to my sheet.

In a few minutes he returned, but the maid was with him. He smiled at me and again put his finger to his lips. He whispered to the maid and gave her some money. She then opened a bag and handed me the clothes of a peasant woman: the clothes of my people.

Quietly, she said, "The American lieutenant says he did not violate you and wishes you to be free. He has asked me to bring you these clothes and to help you escape out beyond the walls. He will make an excuse. You are to return to your home or wherever you wish."

I was dazed. Then he whispered to her again. She repeated his words, "The lieutenant knows only a few words of our language. However, he remembers one old saying of our country: 'The sea now rolls where mulberry trees once grew.' He says his gift for you is that the sea will return to its former shores, and the trees will again grow where they did before. In our language he says, *be dau*." Slowly, I turned my head to look at him. I knew that I could never forget his face. It was more than that, though. He was different.

Suddenly a blast of thunder shocked me back to the present. It was the sound of an aircraft flying fast and low, shattering the silence of the jungle. Then it was gone as fast as it had come. I held onto the tree. The horror of what my life could have been shifted into some back part of my mind by the crushing sounds of the American airplane as it flew just above the treetops. But I saw the American's face once more as it drifted in time and then disappeared. I would never forget it. Why? Why had he who had intended to rape me become my rescuer instead?

I had known other Americans. Years after my escape from the colonel's house of whores, I was trained in English by our National Liberation Front and was placed in a job with an American military office. They never realized that I was also a secret agent for our army. I even became a translator for them! But I often found myself comparing the others to him, or to what I imagined him to be. At first I would even look for his face thinking that he might return. Then I realized that most of the Americans counted the days until they could return to their homeland and get out of their army. I knew that he would not come back.

With mixed emotions I continued my journey. Some-

times I needed to talk my soul out to someone. More
than ever I felt the need to be with Van Thi. My headquarters lay in the Que Son Mountains, while Van Thi
was located with his regiment in the mountains above
Dai Loc about twelve miles away. The villages and fields
between the two sets of mountains had been secured by
our 5th and 20th Battalions. The village of An Hoa with
its neighboring coal mines was not far from where I now
stood, and my path would take me across the rice paddies
north of it. We had many local village cadres throughout
the towns and hamlets, and I expected to see many new
and old friends on my way to be married.

I worked around the tangled mass of trees and on down
toward the rice fields. My path led toward the base of the
mountains and a narrow secluded valley where the small
hamlet of Phu Loc lay. It consisted of only four homes
hidden on the edge of the rice paddies in a cluster of
trees. Coming down from the hills cratered by the bombs,
I came to the rear of these homes which somehow had
been preserved from the air raid.

I walked into a clearing under the trees where the
farmers kept pigs and chickens. I smiled at a dozen little,
yellow, fuzzy chicks as they scurried behind their mother
and out of my path. The pigs took no notice of me and
continued to root some distance away.

Coming to the doorway, I was met by the friendly faces
of Mr. and Mrs. Trinh, two of my old friends. Quickly,
as was their custom, they served me some food. Today
it was a bowl of *hu tieu*, and it smelled delicious. The
pork had been slowly cooked and mixed in a light broth
with rice noodles, onions, and sweet-smelling herbs.

It was nice to rest for a moment. As I ate, they excitedly showed me how they had reinforced their home to
protect it from the bombing. Then they proudly pointed
to their children studying at a table and said that neither
the Americans nor the South Vietnamese government
could keep them from teaching their children. I hugged
them, loving the spirit of my people, but I needed to
finish and get back on my journey.

After the meal, Mrs. Trinh showed me to the bedroom
where I changed my clothes so I could walk the open rice
fields dressed as a peasant, not an officer in the army. I

also borrowed a pole and two baskets to carry over my shoulders, within which, covered by vegetables, would be my uniform and rifle.

Minutes later, I was boldly walking into the fields across both broad and narrow paddy dikes. The sun shone down uninterrupted by the great forests that now lay behind me. Rice blossomed as the time of our second harvest neared. Squares of rice fields flooded with brown water were framed by the dikes across which I walked. More and more I thought of Van Thi. Would he be waiting for me, or would I get to An Bang before him?

When we had planned our marriage three months before, he and I had decided on the village of An Bang because it was about midway between our two headquarters and we each had friends there. It was a small beautiful village nestled at the foot of the mountains. But I wondered whether the arrival of the 2nd Division from the north had delayed him. I had recently heard that they had liberated the A Shau Valley from the Americans and their puppet troops last month and now had arrived above Dai Loc.

By midafternoon, I was near the village. Gradually, I could make out one lonely figure on top of a small hill. Then it jumped up and began waving at me. It was my friend, Xuan Hoa. I smiled and waved back. She ran down the hill, while I continued to walk up carrying my baskets. I dropped my pole and baskets, and she almost ran me over in a great hug. She was smaller and slimmer, and I swung her around in my arms. Oh, it was so nice to see her and to finally be here.

She began to speak rapidly, her face beaming with excitement, "Oh, Kim Lan, I'm so glad that you are well. I want you to forget your warrior responsibilities. Let me take care of you until Van Thi arrives. He is not here yet. Here, let me carry your baskets."

"Thank you, my dear friend," I replied and began to relax. "I would like to forget many things for a few days. First, I will let you take me to that beautiful stream of yours. It is hot and dusty, and I need to bathe before Van Thi places his arms around me."

Suddenly, before we could leave the hilltop, we were surprised by a swarm of enemy helicopters as they de-

scended like a cloud of insects into the rice fields near
the Song Thu Bon, three miles behind me. Anger rose
within me as I stood and watched. I felt that I needed to
be in the villages under attack; I had just come through
those hamlets and talked with my friends there.

Xuan Hoa came close and held my arm. We stood together watching the assault from our distant hilltop. Then
she pulled me away saying, "I will take you to the
stream. Come, you must forget for just a while. Your
chance to seek revenge will come later."

That night, after bathing and eating, I lay in a hammock in Xuan Hoa's home and wrestled with my angry
frustration before exhaustion finally overcame me, and I
fell asleep.

The next day was a hurried rush of activity. Although
marriages could no longer be celebrated with the tradi-
tional series of banquets, a good dinner and drinks
needed to be prepared. Through it all, I expectantly
awaited Van Thi.

He would be skirting the edge of the hills, having
crossed the Song Vu Gia about four or five miles north
of here. Several times during the day, I walked to a hill
just east of the village and watched the comings and
goings of the American helicopters a few miles away.
They did not seem to be moving any closer. Although I
still felt guilty for not being with our people fighting the
foreign invader, I quietly hoped for a couple of days of
leave to be with my husband.

On one trip back from the hill in the early evening, I
met Xuan Hoa rushing toward me, announcing, "Van
Thi is here! Van Thi has come!" I hurriedly walked back
with my friend, giggling.

Then I saw him, walking tall, straight, and proud. His
uniform was light brown, and he carried a pistol at his
side. His short, black hair was uncovered, and his dark
eyes danced happily. When we at last came together, I
shyly glanced down and felt my heart racing.

He hesitated a moment while my whole being wanted
him to take me in his arms and fill me with his love.
Finally, he said, "Kim Lan, it is so good to at last be
with you."

My eyes shyly darted back up to his, while he silently

looked at me. He then came close and our arms wrapped around one another instinctively. Holding me close, he softly said, "I love you so much. You are so beautiful."

I felt love pulsing through my veins. His lips were at my ear, and his neck caressed my face. Oh, how I had missed him and needed him. I whispered in his ear, "And I love you, Van Thi. I am eager to be your wife and have your children."

He then leaned back from me, looked quietly into my eyes, and said, "I am so proud of you. Your name is well known. In all the reports from your district you are mentioned as a great fighter."

I glanced into his eyes, my heart still pounding its beat wildly within my breast. My tongue was unable to speak.

He said, "It is hard to believe that you can be so shy when you are such a great warrior." I looked at him questioningly, and he continued, "I have read the accounts of the actions in your district, and I am very proud of you. You are held in high regard. When I told people in my headquarters that we were to be married, they said, 'Ah, but Co Kim Lan must be one of the Trung sisters returned to help our revolution. How can you marry one who is destined to become a national heroine? She can never be at home.'

"But I simply replied, 'The Trung sisters lived two thousand years ago and fought the Chinese but did not sustain their victories. My woman lives today and together we fight the Americans and their puppets. This time we shall prevail and so shall our marriage.' "

Laughing and now relaxing in happiness, he said, "Remind me later to tell you about the attack the fifth Battalion is planning on the Americans."

His arms encircled me again, and he pulled me close. It had been three months since I had seen him, and I felt the womanhood within me burning warm. Tomorrow would be too long coming.

That night, for a long time, I lay in the thatch hut without sleeping. Van Thi slept nearby in the home of one of his friends. I wanted to be sleeping with him, and I imagined his body next to mine. I gently, softly, stroked my skin with my fingertips, believing for a moment that

they were his. My body tingled in the pleasure I antici-
pated. But I would have to wait another day.

Then my thoughts drifted slowly back in time. Why
couldn't my mother have been here? I wept thinking of
her. I wanted so much to be able to share tomorrow with
her. I remembered the times of laughter, and I almost
felt her hand in mine. When she had returned from the
war with the French, we had so many days of joy. Why
couldn't it still be so? But the bitterness and sorrow over-
shadowed so much. Our enemies had taken almost all my
family, including her, from me. They had become a part
of the stream of life, returning to the earth which had
given them nurture.

Restlessly I got out of my hammock and quietly walked
past my sleeping friend and through the doorway. Standing in the front yard, I looked up into the sky and watched
the stars. The clouds drifted on a gentle current of air,
reshaping themselves in the moon's glorious light. The
nearby fields of rice rippled easily in the breeze, and I
began to sense the spirits of my parents, my grandparents, and their fathers and mothers before. They all
seemed to be calling to me from the fields.

I needed to walk. I needed to think. Slowly, I followed
a path to a small hilltop. Far away American flares lit
up their part of the dark sky and gave the night an eerie
edge of distant danger.

I could, however, almost touch the blossoming fields
of rice becoming ripe like a woman with child. In front
of me, the small stream sparkled in the bright moonlight
circled like a glistening ring across the wide expanse of
rice fields.

The simplicity, the naturalness, and the peacefulness,
all touched and soothed my mind, and the sounds and
sights of war receded to a remote place and time as if
they were part of another world. I took a deep breath and
gradually felt at rest and at peace within myself. Gently
my hammock called me. I walked back to Xuan's Hoa's
hut, and lying down I closed my eyes and breathed deeply
and slowly.

The next morning was a whirlwind of excitement and
confusion. I found myself desperately wanting to be alone
with Van Thi, but that wasn't going to be possible until

later. More and more I thought about our wedding night. Most women my age had been married for several years, and more than one of my friends had offered advice to make my wedding evening more pleasurable. I sat in my friend's backyard thinking of the hundred different things that whirled around my life.

Xuan Hoa found me meditating and quickly rushed me into the house, scolding me for not getting ready. She was already dressed in a sleeveless black tunic with red stripes that made her look so pretty. "Xuan Hoa," I said. "You should be the one getting married. You are beautiful. You are as beautiful as your name, 'Spring Flower.' "

A shy smile crept across her face, but she suddenly laughed and loudly informed me, "Nguyen Kim Lan, I have traveled through many villages trying to find the perfect dress in your size. A dear friend has been so nice to loan this one to me, and in it you will be as the sun, and I no brighter than its distant reflection in the stream. Your name means 'Golden Orchid,' but it would take one thousand of those beautiful flowers to equal your beauty. This is your day, and now I certainly hope that you can get yourself ready without me having to push and yell at you to do it." Then we laughed together.

The dress was indeed beautiful. It had three pieces that included a white skirt with pink trim and a pink silk shirt covered with a white jacket embroidered with pink flowers. Xuan Hoa had washed and cut my hair so that it fell in a straight black line across the middle of the jacket. After I dressed she appeared with a fresh pink orchid and set it into one side of my hair. Then she stepped back and looked at me. Clasping her hands together at her mouth, her eyes glistened, and she said, "Come, before I soak my tunic in tears."

It was time for the ceremony. I saw Van Thi, so handsomely dressed in a soldier's uniform, tall, lean, and strong. He and I came together and stood before the people ready to speak our vows. Xuan Hoa unwrapped her small guitar and played a soft and beautiful song of love. Tears flowed down my face, and my eyes silently spoke words of appreciation to my friend who had worked so hard to make this day one of love and happiness for me.

Then both Van Thi and I spoke our vows to each other facing the assembled village. We pledged our lives, not only to each other, but also to the revolution. The people all cheered and shouted.

We then led our friends to the banquet tables set outside. Joyously, we all shared the meal and drinks. I held my husband's arm, and he never left my side until it was time for us to leave. I quietly slipped away to Xuan Hoa's home. Quickly, I changed clothes and readied my bag with all that I needed for the short time that Van Thi and I would have before we had to part again.

My husband then appeared at the rear door and said, "Let's hurry and still make the most of this day."

I blushed, and Xuan Hoa hugged and kissed me saying, "Do not worry about our friends. They will eat and drink until dark. Tomorrow the village of An Bang will have a giant headache." We laughed, and I hugged and thanked her with tears beginning again.

Then Van Thi and I went unnoticed out of the west end of the village, and he led me on the two-mile trek toward the place about which he had told me earlier. It was not long before he stopped and pointed up a narrow, almost hidden trail, branching off our main path and said, "Only about a half-mile up there and we can rest in our little paradise." He smiled and added, "The fifth battalion will be using this very trail to attack the Americans. They will be through here tomorrow morning early but will never know two lovers are nearby."

We walked up the trail a distance to a point where the trees stopped abruptly, and the afternoon sun shone brightly into a clearing. Van Thi halted and said, "It is only a very short distance ahead now. Listen, you can hear the water." He paused before adding, "You go on. It is totally secluded. I have left a bag near here that I want to get. I'll join you in just a moment."

I walked alone down the narrow path and then emerged from the jungle into a large clearing covered by grass. A lake lined with flowering lotus reached from just in front of me to a great waterfall that rushed and tumbled over a cliff that was the height of three elephants. The white water sprayed and sparkled in the bright sunlight of mid-afternoon. Standing in the clearing, I paused, watching a rainbow glistening in the floating mist. Just to my right, a small stream, not more than a-hop-across-it wide, sang to me as it splashed down its path to the lake. A short walk away that little run of water gushed from the top of a rock shelf that was just more than head high. I walked across the grass which grew with the softness and richness of deep-piled silk and knelt beside the stream.

I felt that I had stepped into a dream. The memories of the bone-soaking rains and sticky sandal-sucking muds of the monsoon season were fading, and I stood feeling the warm beauty of the sun's heat. In the quiet beauty of this private garden, I felt the beginning of an overwhelming sense of peace and love that had so far eluded me. It was as if the world of war was evaporating around me. I turned and looked longingly at the shower created by the stream where it splashed over the rocks.

I walked over and slowly took off my clothes. The heat of the sun touched and kissed my skin, and I slowly ran my hands up my sides. Touching my breasts, I shyly and fearfully hoped that Van Thi would love my body as he loved my soul. Then I stepped in, and the streamlet cascaded over my head. The coolness of the water mixed with the heat of the sun and wrapped itself around me like a fresh bouquet of flowers.

I stood with my eyes closed with the water pulsating over me. When again my eyes opened, I saw my husband standing at the trail's end on the edge of the pond. He stared at me. Clothed only by sunlight and dancing waters, I saw his look of love and desire. I glanced down blushing but not moving. My whole being ached for him, but I stood unable to move or speak. My eyes were fixed on the water around my feet as I heard him come forward.

Then I saw his feet and watched from the corners of my eyes as he quietly dropped his clothes on the grass near mine. Briefly, I caught glimpses of his smooth, almond-colored body as he stepped into the water behind me. I felt his body near mine, and my heart raced, wildly beating its song of love.

"I love you," he whispered. Then his hands touched my body. They slowly caressed my shoulders, and I felt his lips kiss both sides of my neck. His fingers stroked my skin and muscles and firmly but smoothly slid slowly down my back working their magic. His hands moved back and forth from my neck to the middle of my back.

My body trembled as I felt him kneel in the water showering around us. His fingers pressed deeply into my lower back and teased and plied their way around my hips. His thumbs pressed even more deeply into my back, and my flesh pleaded for more. Then his arms circled my waist, and he kissed my hips and hugged me tightly from behind. My body was on fire, and I could hardly stand on my feet any longer.

Then his hands smoothly slid up and down both sides of each leg. The muscles in my legs rippled, and my nerves tingled, longing for more of his touch. As his hands pressed high into my thighs, I could no longer stand where I was. My body burned hot, and I quickly turned into the water. As the stream splashed around my head and shoulders, I knelt with Van Thi in our small sunlit waterfall. I no longer felt embarrassment as I threw my arms around his neck, pressing my lips to his. He kissed me hungrily, and his body pressed harder against mine. I felt his tongue. Slowly his mouth circled my lips and then the side of my cheek. He kissed my ear, and I felt the touch of his teeth. With my eyes closed, I burrowed my face into his shoulder and held him tightly, passionately, desiringly.

Then he was lifting me, carrying me to the soft, thick grass which carpeted the sides of our small stream. He laid me gently in the warmness of our place of love. For a moment he stood beside me, and my eyes shyly, but longingly, consumed the fullness of his body. He knelt, and I reached up and ran my fingers along his chest. Leaning forward he kissed me on the lips, on the eyes, and on the forehead. I closed my eyes and heard a moan come from my lips as his fingers moved over and around and lightly squeezed my breasts. Then I felt his lips kiss my nipples, and the touch of his tongue and teeth shot shivers of pleasure throughout my body.

Then he reached out and put both hands on the sides of my head and pulled my lips to his, kissing me hard. He pulled me over in the grass and rolled my body on top of his. My shyness was consumed in a passion I had never before known.

I kissed his lips, his face, his ears, his neck, and we rolled over on one side. I quickly stole a glance at his body; I wanted him but couldn't say a thing. His leg moved over the top of mine, and I slid my arm under his and moved closely against him. I felt his body tremble ever so slightly. Slowly, our bodies began to stroke each other. I felt his manhood pulsate against me. He moaned and brought my body hard to his, kissing me and locking me hard within his embrace.

Passion burst from every pore of my body, as he pushed me over in the grass. His lips seared my skin and his hardness throbbed between my legs. Then his hand moved down, and he placed himself, hard and warm, into me, penetrating slowly. I felt him slide into my own warm and moist body. There was a slight pain, but my body arched eagerly seeking pleasures that I had never known. Moving together, I felt him within me, hurrying more deeply, and I found myself beginning to cry out. Then a sheer, sensual, consuming fire burst in and up, to explode throughout my whole body.

My arms were tightly circled around his back and tears flooded my eyes as I felt my husband moving even more rapidly within me. Then with a moaning cry, he shuddered. Gradually the rhythm of his body slowed. Still I moved with him, feeling the continuing, tingling pleasure with him in me. Tears rolled down the side of my face. I did not want to let him go and clung tightly to him, wiping my tears on his shoulders.

He kissed me on the side of the face and whispered, "I love you, Kim Lan, I love you." The tears streamed down, and I couldn't speak.

Slowly, I relaxed and laid back with Van Thi still on top of and within me. My arms still held him as he raised his shoulders and head to look lovingly into my face. Then I touched his chest with one hand and with the other lightly caressed his face. Finally, I was able to speak and say, "I love you, my husband, more than words can ever express. I love you, I love you, I love you."

Then easily he pulled back and out of me to lie in the grass. The moment he withdrew, my body felt a twinge

of incompleteness; I wanted him back, filling me. Rolling on my side, I put one arm over his chest and pulled
close to him. I felt the warmth of his seed on my leg and
again shivered in love.

We lay together on our carpet of grass, listening to the
calls of birds and the chattering of monkeys and feeling
the peace of total love in our hidden garden. Not since
my mother had come home, before she was taken from
us, had I allowed myself to be so completely vulnerable.
My whole inner being was exposed and placed in the
hands of another.

After a long time just quietly lying on our bed, my
husband, with his arms around me, lifted me and rose
to his feet. Then he walked into the pond, smiled, and
said, "Let's swim to the falls." He was watching my
eyes, waiting for a response.

I smiled, touched his nose with a finger, and teased,
"Do you think you can beat me there?"

"I'll give you a five-second head start and still beat
you."

"Is there a wager?" I asked.

"If you beat me," he said, "any wish is yours."

"And so for you," I said, smiling, flirting with my
eyes.

He set me down in the water, waist-deep. I looked at
the falls which were about two hundred yards away. There
was a rock shelf on the right side of it and I said, "The
race shall be to the flat rock on the right, and remember
to count five seconds fully!"

I dove into the water and was off, swimming and feeling strong. Within seconds, I heard Van Thi yell as he
dove after me. Pushing hard, I swam as I had learned to
swim in the sea. I was determined not to lose, regardless
of the bet. As I sensed my husband starting to gain on
me, I redoubled my efforts. There was only one hundred
yards left when he seemed at my heels. Forcing myself
for all I could, I kept pace, stroke for stroke. He never
got any closer as I grabbed the rock first.

We both were laughing and exhausted. Lifting ourselves onto the large rock, we lay there, naked and shimmering in the sunlight. Occasionally, one of us would

laugh and the other would uncontrollably join in. He asked, "What is your request? It is my command."

I replied as I stood, "Oh, I don't know just yet. I'll let you know when I am ready." I then smiled at him and walked toward the nearby falls. It towered over us about twenty feet and created a minor thunderstorm where I stood. Van Thi then walked past me and around the back of the wall of water, and I followed. We found and explored a small cave shielded by the falls.

We sat, holding hands, leaning against the walls of the cave. He then moved over and knelt between my legs and pulled my lips to his. He kissed me for a long, long time, and then said, "Regardless of what happens outside of this paradise, I have now experienced Heaven, and no one can take that from me."

I put my fingers on his lips and said, "Hush, this is the real world. You and I together make our own world, regardless of the troubles beyond here. This day, however, is too special to think of the times beyond this place. Come, let's see if we can find any flowers on our way back."

Slowly we arose and walked back to the rock shelf. There Van Thi took me in his arms again and kissed me sweetly. I gazed into his eyes as we leaned slightly apart, still with our arms around one another.

There were flowers at the water's edge, and Van Thi picked them for me. As we got back to our little clearing beside the streamlet, I spread out a blanket he had brought, sat down, and said, "The wager that I have won comes in two parts."

He laughed and said, "I'm not so sure that I can agree to a 'two-part' bet."

"I want you to braid my hair and weave flowers in it. You will circle my head with the braid, and it will be my wedding crown."

He smiled and asked, "How do you know that I can braid hair?"

"I once saw you braiding a small girl's hair."

So he sat behind me and began to stroke and work with my hair. I couldn't remember ever feeling like this. He took a long time to braid the thick long hair, but finally finished. Then methodically, he circled my head with his handiwork, and with a deft tuck, the hair was in place.

He said, "Now for your rainbow," and he placed the flowers.

Finally, I turned. His eyes opened wide, and he said, "Never has there graced this land a woman more beautiful. If you were a poem, your poetry would rise as perfume to give beauty to the clouds and winds of heaven. If you were a flower, no artist could ever capture your beauty. Say now the second part of your wager, and if it is that you want the moon, I shall win it from the sky."

I smiled and moved close to him. "The next part of my winnings," I said, "is much closer than the moon."

I placed my arms around his neck and kissed him, and he pulled me over on our blanket. I laid on top of him, and we looked into each others eyes for a long moment. Then we kissed again, and he rolled back on top of me. Slowly, his lips explored my body from my head to my feet. I thrilled in the excitement of his hunger for me.

He leaned back and said, "This is better than the moon, and the sun, and all that is."

The afternoon sun passed its zenith, and as it began to descend, we loved and loved again. Later, in the warmth of the early night, I lay on our bed listening to the birds and monkeys calling to one another. Van Thi had fallen asleep beside me. Momentarily, I remembered my husband speaking of the attack that our battalion would be making tomorrow from near here. Emotions collided and thoughts of war battled sensations of love.

Then I glanced at my sleeping husband and felt overwhelmed in security, fulfillment, and love. I began to drift away in dreamy images of long ago memories. Our little garden faded, and slowly my thoughts focused in the past. The present became the hazy periphery of my vision. I remembered again how close I came to being enslaved in prostitution when I was but fifteen.

Another dream then touched me from a further distant place. I was warm and happy. It was my thirteenth year, and I was experiencing the love of my mother who had returned from the war of independence. Yet, even then a threatening cloud had overhung us all, and again I felt the pain of her betrayal and humiliation.

CHAPTER 2

The white-faced soldier, armed, equipped, and trained
as he is, is not a suitable guerrilla fighter for Asian
forests and jungles.

—General Maxwell Taylor (1965)

*T*hese guys were Marines: a bunch of prideful, hard-
headed, screaming assholes maybe, but I loved 'em all.
The engineer battalion had been great, but this was special. Recon Marines had a camaraderie all their own.
When I decided to reenlist, the guys I knew as a civilian
thought I was a goddamn stupid jarhead. "Why should
you go back in?" they asked. "You've got it all. You're
free and living good in California. Why the hell do you
want to go back in the fucking Marines? You've been out
for five years! You'll get your ass blown off!" They had
seen the surface of my life, but none of them had to look
into my mirror. I saw deeply inside myself, and no
fucking, nose-picking civilian could ever understand the
love-hate affair between the US Marines and one former
Lieutenant Ryan Michael Collins. I had friends still in
the Corps and risking their butts in war for me. Shit, I
could never have enjoyed the free, fun, and easy life as
long as that crap was happening. The hardest explanation
though had been to Julie.

We had been dating for four months, and our relation-
ship was beginning to get serious. I lived in San Diego

near the beach, and she had half her clothes in my bedroom. She had been reluctant to completely move in and
maintained her independent life-style apart from that with
me.

After I told her that I was rejoining the Corps and
going to war, she stood shocked, looking at me with her
beautiful eyes wide with disbelief. She stood by the end
of the kitchen bar in my apartment, finally asking,
"Why?" I felt the knife blade slicing down my side with
that one simple word, but one that was cutting in building
fury. I couldn't answer and looked down at nothing on
the floor.

"Why?" she pressed me. "Is it that you have to go
defend the United States against communism? Do you
really feel that they are a threat to us in some stupid little
country halfway around the world? Why?"

Then wiping away tears she walked to the window
looking out over the world of blond surfers and Chevy
vans and burst into anger. "Goddamn you, Collins. I was
just beginning to tear down the wall I had built since the
last asshole I fell for. I thought I could trust you. For the
first time in a long time, I was beginning to feel that
someone could really love me. Shit, Collins, why?"

I walked over, put my hands on her shoulders and
gently turned her around. Softly, I said, "Julie, I'm sorry,
but it's hard to explain. Maybe there's some of the fighting communism business in it, but mostly it's something
else. I'm healthy and still in good shape, and there's Marines in some other land dying for me and all of us. How
can I walk around here living good and knowing that?
Hell, I could never be a lifer—the Marine Corps is a
chicken-shit outfit. But this is different. I know people
over there. Some have been shot. I got a letter from a
friend last month in a hospital in Okinawa.

"You know some people say, 'God, Country, and
Corps,' but that's wrong, it's the other way around. The
Corps is first. Their time in hell is on this earth, and I
need to be with them."

Her steady gaze remained unmoved, and it hurt. My
anger started to build. Why couldn't she understand? I
walked out onto the open balcony, and stared at kids playing on the beach without really seeing anything. Behind

me I heard her say, "Collins, I hope you make it back safely, but don't give me your forwarding address. I'll be back to get my clothes and leave the key while you're at work. Good-bye." The door slammed, and I refused to turn around and look.

But that was a long time ago. Thirty days later I was in uniform and on a plane flying over the Pacific. Now I felt a smile slowly crack my face as I lay in the jungles and thought, "Boy am I really back in the green machine: the Third Reconnaissance Battalion, Third Marine Division."

For a moment longer I daydreamed about soft beds, hamburgers, and beautiful round-eyes. Then silently I cursed as the camouflage greasepaint slowly ran down my face and sweat flowed from all my pores. The stifling, humid, jungle heat wet-baked our US Marine Corps hides. Trying to ignore the hundred and one insect bites and all the aches and pains, I carefully parted the brush in front of me and watched the trails for Charlie. In the distance the grunts were kicking ass near the Song Thu Bon, and all of us were in a new neighborhood. We were beating the bush in the hills near the Arizona Territory. These were virgin jungles for us. Another twelve or so miles beyond the Song Thu Bon, faintly reflecting the sun which dominated the day, was the South China Sea. I remembered my first trip to Vietnam when I spent some time out near there. Some ten years before, as a young lieutenant, I had been assigned to help advise a South Vietnamese Army unit for a month at a place called Hoi An—shit, it was there that some South Vietnamese colonel almost had my throat slit!

But then I reminded myself, hell, Collins, quit your damned daydreaming and come back to real life! You'll get your ass blown off with your mind in another world from ten years ago.

God, it's miserable! I complained silently as reality began to weigh me down. It was another "quadruple nut" day: temperature 100 degrees and 100 percent humidity—four fucking zeros. At least that's the way it felt. My skin itched from three days bathing in insect repellent, sweat, and dirt. Cuts, scratches, and bites competed for attention, and I longed for a dip in a cool stream.

Something thumped against my head, and I looked down at a pebble as it rolled on the ground in front of my face. Glancing at Corporal Alexander, my squad leader, I saw a shit-eating grin spread across his face. He whispered, "Lieutenant, you're supposed to be watching the trails, not daydreaming."

"Alexander," I replied, "you remember the clearing by that little lake that we set as our pickup LZ yesterday? Well, I've been thinking. It's only a half-mile off, and the patrol's almost over. Maybe we could go back there and set up around that water for the night and sneak a little dip."

"Whataya think our luck would be?" he whispered.

"If we snuck back there this evening? Probably World War Three will break loose down in the paddies, and the general and colonel will be asking where the fuck we were, and why didn't we warn 'em."

"Do you believe the G-2, Lieutenant? Do you think Charlie's got a battalion somewhere around here that might try to come outta these mountains and hit the infantry from behind?"

"Fuck, I don't know. This is all new country for us. We're the first round-eyes to ever beat this bush. No telling what we'll find. We've only seen three small groups of Charlie heading south. Maybe they were going to the party in that little village called An Bang this afternoon. We were so close to that one that we shoulda got invited. But hell, what do you think? Maybe they're moving in at night. Think we should go down there and set-up there this evening and watch the trail?"

The corporal didn't answer, but just looked back down below at the clearing we had been scrutinizing. Then without turning his head, he grabbed my arm quietly urging me, "Look!"

Two hundred meters below us, five enemy soldiers moved quickly across the small open space and disappeared into the jungle. "Same direction," Alexander said. "Lieutenant, maybe we should go down there tonight. Maybe we'll find that five-hundred-man battalion intelligence is worried about."

I answered, "We probably should go down there and set an ambush, but fuck if I want to find the whole damn battalion. But I tell you, I bet the grunts got that battalion running scared out there in the paddies, and all we got around here is a few leftovers. Maybe we can set-up so that we can pull an ambush if another small group of Charlie comes by in the morning before the choppers come in to get us.''

''It'll be risky, Lieutenant.''

''Yeah, maybe, but if we go down there, we might as well try to make the most of it. Why don't you get everybody ready, while I try to figure out the map and some routes.''

He muffled a laugh as I got hung up trying to roll over on my back, forgetting about the seventy-pound pack that clung to my backside like a fat giant leech. With a lot of clumsy effort, I slipped out of it and began to study the maps. This is stupid, a little inner voice said. Suppose that battalion is coming down the trail. Fuck! Those little communist cocksuckers are no slouches. If they get between us and our landing zone back uphill, we're in a world of deep shit. We could stay here. We don't have to take the chance. I don't need to put this undersized squad down there where we could run into that many fucking enemy. Slowly I could feel a bit of fatalism creep in, and the stronger voice responded, Oh, fuck it anyway! That motherfucking VC battalion is trying to avoid the grunts out there in the villages and rivers. We're not gonna find five hundred Charlie up here.

At 0800 the next morning the choppers were due to pick us up near that pond, and I needed to plan this business so I could get all nine of us back to the LZ. I damn sure didn't want to run uphill under these packs with Charlie shooting at our asses.

The sun was sliding down the backside of the mountains when we began to snake our way in the shadows toward the paddies. That little village was only about two miles away. We had been close enough to hear music coming from there yesterday, and I wanted to be careful. We planned that all we would do that night would be to lie quietly and watch. At first light if an opportunity showed itself, we'd try to pull an ambush and then slide through the jungles like unseen banshees back up to our

LZ, jump on our perfectly timed choppers, and fly off with no problems.

Nervously we moved down; there could be absolutely no noise. We couldn't climb down the fifty-foot drop in front of us without sounding like a group of noisy rock apes, so we crawled, walked, and scooted on our butts around to the north. Any metal, including dog tags, had been black taped to help muffle any inadvertent clanging of metal against rock, and to stop any reflection of either sun or moonlight. We swung in an arc back toward the open space we had been watching. When we found it, we noticed that the trail did a double dog-leg just after crossing the twenty-foot clearing. We set ourselves in the corner of that double-bend in the trail, and I hoped that we had positioned ourselves well. It was becoming too dark to know for sure. We cleared away the leaves to keep the leeches off and to reduce noise. Then we made like snakes hiding behind the rotting wood of the lower jungles.

Corporal Alexander had the three-man point team on my right. Doc, Red my radio operator, and I were in the middle looking directly up the trail before it cut sharply around Alexander's team. The rear team was to the left. We connected all teams by a slim rope, hardly more than a string, which we could pull to alert each other. As darkness engulfed us, the day's hard heat slowly evaporated to a level that was just plain uncomfortable.

The night was slow. Now that I was down here, I felt even less confident about this idea. I remembered my first platoon sergeant saying, "Lieutenant, hardly a fucking patrol goes by when I don't find myself feeling like a fat, juicy rat surrounded by four-hundred-pound cats." I was beginning to feel that way now. I hoped the night would hide us like a dark blanket, but I still worried that the morning sun would reveal that we were in a very vulnerable position. I finished my last watch at 0300 and dozed off.

Suddenly my eyes opened as someone grabbed my arm. I froze. It was Red. Not daring to move, I lay on my side. I glanced at my radio man. The skies were much lighter; dawn was close. I could see Red's eyes darting back and forth from me to somewhere out front. The camouflage paint hid his dark freckles, but anxiousness was etched into his eyes.

Carefully, I rolled on my stomach and inched closer to him. Jungle plants covered us like an umbrella. Except for small openings through which we watched, we were pretty well hidden. Red pointed to the front and then cupped his hand around an ear. No one spoke. I listened. A light fog was lifting but still drifted higher in the trees.

Then out there not very far away, I heard it. Indistinct voices were coming in our direction. I jerked the two ropes tied to each of the other teams. Glancing in their directions, I saw my Marines silently position themselves.

Looking around in the faint light while lying next to Red, I tried to evaluate our situation. Slowly, I began to fear that the jungle undergrowth, which was hiding us fairly well, would do shit for stopping a bullet. We were only fifteen to twenty feet off the trail, and I felt very uneasy. I found myself hoping that whatever was coming wasn't very big.

The first Charlie came into view just in front of my nose. Son of a bitch, he's got a good-looking uniform for this jungle, I thought as I watched him quickly move across the short open area, his rifle riding easy in his arms. The early morning gray was turning almost blue now. We waited.

The first man, obviously walking point, moved past us quickly. To my knowledge, our patrol was the first ever west of the Arizona Territory, and it was obvious that this Charlie was not overly concerned about the possibility of Marines in this, his neck of the woods.

He made the second turn in the dog-leg as he went past Alexander, who glanced at me. I looked back to the front. Then the second, third, fourth, and more came. Jesus, Mary, and Joseph, I thought, these are the real McCoys. No black pajamas in this gang.

I began to count, thinking we might be able to pull off a major ambush. There must be a couple of dozen of 'em, I thought.

My count continued. I was trying to estimate the center of the enemy unit. A minute had gone by. Good

God, I thought, fifty fucking Charlie, and the little assholes are still coming.

One of the shitheads spit in my direction, and I almost
ducked. Sweat dripped off the end of my nose. I was
afraid to blink. I prayed none of my Marines would
choke, cough, fart, or move—not even a little finger. In
another agonizing minute, one hundred of those slant-
eyed Charlies, armed to their motherfucking teeth, had
marched past us. From what I could tell, it looked and
sounded like another hundred were still coming.

A stream of epithets exploded through my mind—Holy
shit. Lieutenant Ryan Michael Collins, you are one dead
son of a bitch! Enemy by the shitload was in front of and
behind us. We all lay frozen on the damp jungle floor.

I forced my shaking hand to inch over to the radio
handset hooked to Red's backpack strap. Red didn't
move. With his rifle in front of him, he was afraid to
even look at me. Slowly, I brought the handset back.
Dear God, I prayed, make everyone of those cocksuckers
deaf. Please Lord!

Then I began to whisper into the handset, which I had
almost buried in the leaves and dirt. Last evening, I had
preplanned an artillery strike named ''alpha one'' just in
front of us about fifty meters. It hadn't been fired; just
set on paper. Normally, the 105 howitzers were pretty
accurate—after you got the first rounds out and adjusted
them. A chilling panic was about ready to take over my
body and soul, and I thought, I gotta call for a ''fire-for-
effect'' first shot out. Please, God, I'll find a chaplain
Sunday and go to church, but please help!

The motherfucking Charlie were still coming, as I quietly radioed the battery, ''Brown Bomber, Brown
Bomber, this is Charlie Brown, over.'' I waited for a
two-second eternity before they answered. Glancing
around, scared to death the enemy would hear, I whispered back, ''Brown Bomber, this is Charlie Brown.
We've got Victor Charlie out the ass. Target is one hundred and fifty or more Victor Charlie. We're in the middle of 'em. Fire mission alpha one. Repeat: fire mission
alpha one. Fire for effect. I say again: target one hundred
and fifty Victor Charlie; fire mission alpha one; fire for
effect.''

The artillery radio operator read the fire mission back to me, and I confirmed it as quietly as I could. Then I pulled gently on the ropes to try to get everybody's attention. Shit, I couldn't speak, and I couldn't signal! I just had to hope that they would all understand we were about to make a move. There was so much adrenaline racing through my body, I was ready to do a ten-flat hundred uphill in boots carrying a pack, and that's exactly what I planned for us all. I whispered to Red to tell Doc to haul ass uphill when I gave the signal.

Then I heard 'em. A low whistle at first, and then roaring kamikazes blitzing out of the rising sun. In one frozen second of time, I watched a series of events and prepared to leap into them, running for my life. The enemy column became still for just that one second as the sound of incoming artillery tore through the clouds. As that second ended, Charlie scattered, and the 105s ripped the treetops, and exploded like a freight train crashing into and heaving the ground, throwing and slamming us. At one and one-half seconds, I was screaming at my patrol, "Let's go!"

The 105s had blasted just ahead of us, and the call for fire-for-effect was working. Barrage after barrage was following one on top of the other. The shockwaves almost knocked me off my feet as I rushed my Marines under the giant trees, tearing through the bush. Thorny vines grabbed and tried to hold a body. Scared shitless, I ran, bringing up the rear. I watched for enemy—all fucking two hundred or so of 'em!—who were also running in all directions.

Screaming, I heard screaming! To my right. Not more than thirty feet away two enemy soldiers dragged one of their buddies. It looked like he was a dead, bloody mess. *Run Collins! Run you dumb shit*, was all I could think!

I pulled myself behind a tree and saw Alexander just ahead. Three Charlie broke out of the bush just to his right. I had to do a double take as they looked so much like us in the uniforms they were wearing. I screamed, "Alexander, to your right." Rifle at my hip, I fired as Alexander spun and did the same. The three gooks were blown backward as if they had just been hit by a sledgehammer. They still didn't know we were in the big fucking middle of 'em. I ran. Breathless, and almost unable to speak, I caught up with Alexander. The deafening thunder of the artillery devastating the jungles continued less than a quarter-mile away. I had no idea how many Charlie ran in the same direction as we had. We could still be surrounded. Crouching in the jungle under shoulder-high bushes, I directed Alexander, "Get the squad squared away. Let's get our shit together and move over this rise. We've got thirty minutes to find the LZ, and then the choppers will be here. Man, we better not miss our motherfucking ride. We got sixty seconds to get our act together. You do that, and I'll report in to the battalion. They're probably shitting green apples right now wondering what's happening out here."

"*They're* shitting green apples." Alexander responded, "Charlie's gonna have to slip through nine bad cases of the shits to get to us."

He then ran low from one person to the next getting everyone reorganized while I called our headquarters and quickly explained what was happening and that we were moving to the landing zone. Then we shoved off like nine nervous monkeys. Our camouflage paint had washed away in nervous sweat.

With jungle brush whipping our faces, we managed to cover a half-mile in twenty minutes. The artillery had lasted for only about ten, and now we were trying to make the last hundred meters to our LZ without being seen or heard. The landing zone was a small clearing on the south side of a waterfall we had passed two days before. As we carefully made our way to it, I motioned to Alexander to hold the patrol inside the jungle. We positioned the teams as safely as we could to watch all directions. I carefully crawled forward and parted the last bushes to check out the place. It was quiet. There was nothing moving.

Red moved up and grabbed me saying, "Birds are on their way. Should be over our heads in a minute." I sat down, took the handset, and listened. We were just inside the jungle, and I prayed that Charlie hadn't come up here, too.

Then the choppers were there, rotor blades wopping out of the clouds. As quickly as I heard them, they were overhead. We moved out of the trees, and Alexander popped a smoke grenade. Quickly the LZ was decorated by a green plume. I talked 'em down: three UH-34s. Three men would go in each bird. I would be last.

One, two, three, one after the other, the birds came down sucking up each of my teams in turn. I ran and jumped in the wide hatch of the last chopper. Dropping my pack, I threw down my cap and placed my face at the open portside window. The crew chief watched the starboard side over the sights of his machine gun. We surveyed the clearing anxiously, as the bird seemed to take fucking forever to get into the air.

My rifle was ready to fire at anything. The crew chief was alert with his M-60 on the other side. For a moment though, in spite of my nervousness, I noticed the beauty of the place. A small rainbow arched over the little waterfall and flowers grew around the edge of the lake.

Then the bird bounced once trying to rise, and I regained my focus. Suddenly, I caught a glimpse of someone dashing out of the jungle to my left front. I quickly half-turned and raised my rifle, but hesitated, not believing what I was seeing.

It was a woman. She stood almost in spitting distance, a rifle in her hands, and clothed only by sunlight. I watched her long black hair being whipped around her body by the prop wash of the helicopter. Mesmerized, I saw her throw the rifle to her shoulder. It was pointed at my face, and I couldn't move. Her body was a naked bronze. The sun shown down on the verdant landscape, but my eyes were riveted on her. She didn't fire, and we climbed out of range. As my eyes remained fixed on her, she became only a speck in the distance. Still, in my mind's eye, I saw the waist-length, carbon-black hair only partially clothing her naked body. She had stood there and challenged us but had lowered the rifle never firing a shot. Something inside my memory teased me with a clue to the mystery, and I racked my brain trying to figure it out. Who the hell was she? It was like I knew her!

Fifteen minutes later back at Camp Reasoner, Corporal Alexander and myself went through a debriefing for the better part of an hour. Division had sent a major from

the hill to sit in—there was a lot to talk about. The final
outcome was that everyone felt that we had found the
better part of Charlie's 5th Battalion preparing to move
down on our infantry. Small observation planes were still
out there searching. We had broken up their plans and
knocked off more than a few of the enemy. However, I
held one thing back. No one else had noticed that woman,
not even Alexander, and for some reason that I didn't
understand, I reported nothing about her. Still, I couldn't
get her off my mind.

Early that evening I grabbed Lt. John Meyers, the motor transport officer of the Third Recon Battalion, and
said, "Give me a fucking jeep man, I gotta go work off
some steam."

"Shit, old buddy," he replied, "let's both go. I know
where the best ass in town is located."

"Fuck, John," I had to answer, "you've had four cases
of the clap in six months. I think I'll pick my own
women. Do you think we can get into the MACV club
downtown?"

"Just lock and load man. We're on our motherfucking
way."

John Meyers was a little taller than I, maybe 6 feet 1
inch, and about twenty pounds heavier. Being a "Motor
T" officer, he stayed back in the camp area and knew
every damn alley and whorehouse in Da Nang. He was
invaluable for a little R&R between patrols. Of course, I
had to put up with an endless stream of his New York
bullshit.

Dusk was settling around the town as the two of us
made our normal unauthorized visit to off-limits places.
How the hell could a person help it? There were fancy
bars in town and even a few round-eyed women.

"There." I grabbed John's arm. "The Paris Steam
Baths. God, I've got to have some hot water poured on
me and my aching muscles pounded and soothed by the
prettiest slant-eyed bitch in the place."

"Whatever the doc's ordered," John replied. Tires
squealed, and he sharply turned into an alley and around
behind a piss-ant Vietnamese version of an Oriental pleasure palace beckoning to tired, lonely, or just plain horny
American males.

It was artificial as hell, but so is war. The absurd stupidity of slipping through the shadows so the MPs wouldn't see you, and wondering if the VC were hiding in the next shadows from the same MPs. What the fuck anyway?

We slipped in the side door. John sneaked up and grabbed Mama-san from behind yelling, "Hey, Mama-san, you got time for this horny Marine? You Number One ass in town, Mama. When you gonna do me?"

Mama-san had about jumped out of her skivvies. She turned around and yelled, "John-boy, what kinda dumb shit you think I am? Man, I take you money, not you sick prick."

"Oh, Mama," John lamented, "I'm so big and hard for you, it makes me cry. But if I gotta live without you, I guess it just goes to show you don't really love me. Hey, but you got pretty virgin for me, Mama?"

I leaned against the wall and smiled at the repartee and glanced around the dimly lit room. If there were any other customers, they were already in back rooms. Two young women walked in. One I recognized from before; the other was new. She smiled.

"I think I just fell in love, John. Mama-san, your price the same for a bath and massage?" I asked.

" 'Rum-and-Coke man' asks if the price the same. Hell, yeah! What you think I am? Think I try to screw you? No, man!"

"Well, Mama," I said, "here's the five bucks for this girl, and I need a rum-and-Coke to go for this here picture of George Washington."

"Fifty more cents for the drink," she said.

"Mama, behind those stained black teeth beats the heart of a born liar." I laughed at her. "Girl's the same, but the drink goes to a buck-fifty. Since I got no change, here's two more dollars and give me a drink for each hand, and let's get this show on the road."

As I drank the first rum-and-Coke in one swallow and John made his deal, my sweet young thing led me to a back room. I watched her walk in front of me down the barely lit hallway. She was tall, her waist slim and hips just right. Inside the tight black skirt, her tush arched

beautifully in my direction. Her black hair was pulled
tight and pinned in a bun on top of her head.

She stopped at a door, turned, and smiled again. I
walked into the door frame on my way through. What a
beautiful woman! She had high cheekbones and looked
almost like a gorgeous American Indian. At least like the
ones I had seen in the movies.

One small lamp lit the room. There was a couch, and
something of an open shower stall to one side. A cur-
tained window overlooked the dark alley. I turned around,
and she stood there, door closed behind her. Sitting on
the couch, I watched her slowly remove her skirt and
blouse. Then she walked over to me wearing black silk
panties and bra and the most enticing smile I could ever
remember. It was very possible that she was the most
beautiful woman I had ever seen.

Warmly, she said, "Let me help you take off you
clothes." While I sat, she took off my boots and socks.
Then as I stood, she slipped off my shirt and trousers.
That was it, since the miserable climate of this country
had forced me to stop wearing skivvies. She motioned to
a stool in the "shower." Naked, I walked over and sat
down on the little seat in the open, concrete slab that had
one drain in the floor.

Then she grabbed a bucket, filled it with hot water,
and slowly poured it over me. Oh, God, I thought, this
is heaven. I had been in-country for nine months without
hot water, except at the Paris Steam Baths. My body
began to disintegrate as her hands worked on tight and
tired muscles. Then she poured more water, hot and
steaming, over me from head to foot. She soaped me off,
washed me, and teased me just so much with a little extra
massage. Then she whispered in my ear, "Come over to
the couch where I can give you very good massage."

For the next fifteen minutes, I think her hands managed to isolate and knead every muscle in my body.
Slowly she worked oil into my skin, and her silken hands
glided over me from the bottom of my feet to my shoulders, and then she worked around my face. I didn't want
it to ever end.

I wasn't able to take my eyes off that gorgeous body
and watched as she stepped back and slipped out of her

bra. My breath stopped! Good Lord, she was beautiful. She bent over pulling down her panties, and before she raised back up to face me, unpinned her hair. It cascaded to the floor like a coal black waterfall. Then she stood up.

Shocked, I sat bolt upright. Speechless, my mouth opened in a fool's confusion. She stood in front of me with her light brown body gleaming like a bronze suntanned goddess. Her hair fell to her waist partially covering her nakedness, and I saw a rifle in her hands. Spellbound, I sat transfixed.

There was jungle all around, and a waterfall was to my left. I saw the morning sun glisten off her naked body as she ran in slow motion into the clearing. Slowly, the rifle went to her shoulder. Her breasts clothed only by long black hair, her face proud, she laid down her challenge. I could almost see flashes erupt from the barrel.

"Marine, you okay?" I heard a voice say. Looking around, I saw the jungle was gone, and Mama-san's girl in front of me. She asked again, "Marine, you okay?"

My mind stared through her, past her, and I heard myself answer, "Where did you come from? Were you about twenty miles south of here this morning?" Then I shook my head and tried to come back. Man, I needed some R&R. I looked back at her and wanted to reach out and hold her. She still stood there with questions in her eyes.

Suddenly, the pounding of boots echoed down the hallway. Instinctively, I ran. In a second I had my clothes in one hand, my pistol in the other, and I had vaulted halfway through the window as the door almost crashed off its hinges. I sat on the windowsill, the dark of the moon silhouetting my naked body, as John Meyers bolted into the room. My momentum was carrying me through the opening when I caught myself. John's whisper was rushed. "The fucking MPs man! Get out the goddamn window."

I was gone, trying to pull up my pants on the run down the alley. Meyers was behind me. At least he had all his clothes on, except his shirt. We both leaped into the jeep with John driving.

"Goddamn it," he yelled, "they're coming up the

alley." He floored the accelerator and smashed through
a chicken coop by a little shack of a house behind
Mama's, bounced across its yard and down the next
street. I threw a not-so-dead chicken off my lap and tried
to finish getting my clothes on as I brushed away feathers.

As we headed out of town, I looked at John while I
laced up my boots, tried to laugh, and said, "Son of a
fucking bitch, Meyers, why don't you knock?"

However, for the next few minutes, I leaned back in
the passenger seat and took a few deep breaths. John
asked, "You okay, Collins?"

"Yeah, I'm okay. This rear-area shit is bad for my
psyche. All I need is a couple of days to get drunk, get
a hot bath, and then go back to the motherfucking bush.
Things are simple out there. Let's stop by Shore Party
so's I can get me about a dozen rum-and-Cokes." All I
could really think about though was that woman with the
rifle, and whatever the hell it all meant.

I watched the headlights probe the dark, gravel road
as we bumped our way toward the Shore Party compound, but I could see only her. I had been over here for
the better part of a year and nothing like this had happened. I had worked in the engineers, and then Third
Recon had sent me from the Hai Van Pass and Elephant
Valley to the Dai Loc Mountains. I had shot and been
shot at, but now we go down into this new south country,
and I run into a naked Viet Cong goddess with a rifle
pointed at my running lights. Why the fuck hadn't she
killed me? Why couldn't I get her off my damn mind?

Then I felt John's eyes on me.

"Collins," he finally said. "You need some goddamn
R&R. You've been in 'Nam too damn long. Why the hell
do you push yourself?"

CHAPTER 3

Red and white tracers thunder everywhere. "Be quiet," she says, "don't be afraid," . . . Valiant image, valiant girl, in future battles come with us.

—Giang Nam, *Night Crossing*

My dreamworld turned vividly real. It was again June 1954. I was a thirteen-year-old girl. The excitement of our defeat of the French was still fresh, and my village was a happy place. Early one evening, I walked along the beach which was just a short distance from our home. The warm, wet sand felt wonderful. The evening sun was setting behind me to the west, and I found a spot to sit just short of the last reach of the foamy waves. Watching the bugs burrow in the wet sand, my mind wandered. I felt the beauty of the ocean with the diminishing rays of the sun warming my back. As I sat there with my mind drifting on the waves, I vaguely heard someone calling my name, but I didn't turn to look. I just wanted to sit by myself awhile. The voice grew louder, and I heard the sound of someone running. I turned and looked over my shoulder. It was a woman. Then in an instant I was on my feet running for all my life toward the outstretched arms of my mother who never slowed in her race toward me.

Although at thirteen I was almost as tall as she, I leaped into her arms. She held me and swung me around. We were embracing and tears flowed like rivers. We fell

together on the sand, laughing, crying, and not knowing
what to say. Then Grandfather, Grandmother, and my
brother came. She had already been to the house, and all
four had come to find me. We all sat and knelt in the
sand, while we hugged, cried, and made foolish attempts
to make conversation.

As we walked back toward home, I had one arm firmly
around Mother's waist, and I made a vow to myself that
I would never again leave her while in this life. I looked
at her; she was about two inches taller than I. Her body
felt tough and strong. Her arms were muscled, and her
hair, although wrapped in a bun on the top of her head
when I first saw her, had fallen down and hung about
midway between her shoulders and her waist. To me, she
was all I could ever have wanted to see.

That evening we sat around the teapot catching up on
so many things. Although she still wore a Viet Minh
uniform, she said she was to put on the clothes of a peasant and work for the coming political campaign to set up
a new government. She told us about a big meeting in
some faraway land that was intended to bring peace to
our country. Like children listening to a mysterious tale,
we clung to her every word. At the battle for Dien Bien
Phu, she had commanded a battalion that had been responsible for much of the tunnelling and hand-carrying
and backpacking of food, ammunition, guns, and other
supplies to the front-line infantry. We all sat enthralled,
listening late into the evening to any and all stories that
she could relate.

Grandfather then asked, "Do you think we shall really
have peace and freedom? I heard news reports all during
the war about America helping France, and I still hear
disturbing news even though we've defeated the French."

Mother stared out the window, lost for a moment in
some distant thought. From the look on her face, whatever thoughts she had were causing her pain. When her
attention returned to Grandfather, she leaned forward and
became angry. She said, "I do not understand America.
Ten years ago I left this home to begin my career with
our army and was sent north, near the border with China.
At that time, the French cooperated with the Japanese.
We fought against them both. I was with a guerrilla unit

that rescued an American flyer. I remember his name, Lieutenant Shawyer, and how we hid him from the searching Japanese patrols. We took him to Pham Van Dong's office which was in a mountain cave and provided him with protection while we safely outmaneuvered the Japanese patrols to put him in American hands across the border. I knew of several other downed American flyers that other of our units rescued. Even Americans from their special intelligence forces worked with us. They helped with training and supplies, while we helped provide them with information about Japanese locations and intentions. We worked well together fighting the Japanese from guerrilla bases in the mountains.

"Then with the end of the war in 1945, things quickly changed, and America began to help the French. It has always angered me. In our political education classes there has been some discussion about this. We have been told that America's change happened as a result of the death of a great president who died shortly before the end of the war. Their new one did not understand our situation and had close ties to the French. Our instructors have been careful to attempt to teach us that although the American government may have turned against us, that our government's policy should not condemn the American people, but strive to establish favor with the American people. Sooner or later, they can be made to believe in our destiny to unite and rule our country free from foreign domination just as they themselves fought for their freedom. But now our job is a political one. I can only hope that the French and Americans will not make us take up arms again, but we will if we have to."

Although we wanted to talk longer, it was very late, and we all reluctantly went to bed. The next days were like a beautiful dream to me. However, I wanted to know more about my mother's secret life away from here. Then one day the opportunity came, and as we walked together out of our home, I led her down the well-swept dirt path leading from the front door. The whitewashed rocks that lined the path, the banana trees, and betel palm tree, all surrounded by a live sugar cane and bamboo fence, always gave me a sense of security and comfort. I felt at home, and there were so many things that I wanted to

share with my mother. I wanted to hold her and talk with
her, and finally I could. Images of the two of us, side-
by-side, being able to work in the garden, or in the rice
paddies, were becoming reality. I glanced at the corner
of the yard where a thick finger of cane had grown away
from the fence and had reached out to touch the palm.
These had formed a little secluded place in the corner of
the yard—my favorite childhood secret place. In there I
dreamed, laughed, and had my own world which no one
could enter without my permission. Sometimes I would
dream of visiting my cousins in the big city of Da Nang
with Mother. Although, in reality, I had no *ao dai*, in
my secret place, my mother and I would stroll together,
both of us wearing these beautiful dresses. Mine was
white with a high Mandarin collar, a close-fitting bodice,
and front and back panels that were gently blown by the
sea breezes over my black silk pants. I could smell the
sea and catch of the boats as we walked along the river-
front. The Han River with its boats and ships were just
along one side of the wide street. Small round sampans
mixed with larger square-sailed boats in which families
lived and worked. The river was at its widest point here
in the city and entered the bay only a short distance away.
Lining the other side of the street were many three-story
brick buildings where government offices were to be
found. The street was so wide that down its center was
a wide strip of grass with trees that ran the entire length
of the roadway. People on the fishing boats passed by
and looked twice as did those in the tall brick buildings
across the boulevard. For a moment, I could feel like a
princess from the old capital of Hue city visiting the big
seaport.

Within my secret place I could dream these dreams,
but it was always by myself. I now stopped and prepared
to invite Mother to sit with me there, where we could
share a little time. But I was anxious. Maybe she would
think it too childish.

I looked into the face of this woman who was part
mother, part stranger, and part idol to me. She said,
"What is it, Kim Lan?"

I glanced down and back up again, finally saying,

"Mother, if you would, I would like to talk with you—just you and me."

She hugged me and said, "Is that all? You were so serious, I was beginning to worry. Let's do it! Where can we sit?"

"Over here," I eagerly said, and half pulled her to my nook.

We sat down on the earth tucked inside curtains of cane and bamboo. She looked at me, smiled, and reached out to hold my hand. Slowly, I relaxed and said, "Mother, I have seen you so seldom. My head is bursting with questions. I love you so, and I need to know more about you."

She leaned back against the tree, smiled lovingly at me, and asked, "There is so much that we need to share with each other, but what is it that you'd like to know?"

"There are so many things, but maybe the thing that is most in my mind is how did you get involved in the war in the first place? Why is it that you've been gone from my life since I was a baby? Grandmother and Grandfather have reared Ba Can and me, and you only came to see us once in a long while. Why? I know about the war, the French, and all that they did to us. But why you?"

There was a moment of silence, and she looked intently at me. Then I saw a tear, but she quickly wiped it away. Turning her head she gazed off somewhere beyond me. I sat still, fearful that I had asked a bad question. Her brow wrinkled, and her eyes seemed to glaze over.

"You deserve to know, and you're old enough, but the story is often an ugly one." She watched me questioningly, as if she was afraid to continue.

I said, "Please go ahead. I want to know. I know it's behind us now, but I need to know what has kept us apart."

Then continuing, she said, "It was during what they called World War Two. Times were very, very difficult, and food scarce. Your father worked hard, but we had, like so many others, become tenant farmers. The French had taken our land away and given it to the landlord, Vo Van Mon. Each year, we had to contract with one of the landlord's agents to deliver over to him a predetermined quantity of rice equal to one-half of the expected rice crop. Additionally, we had to pay all costs. If crops were poor, we still had to turn over the agreed upon quantity. During the last years of this war, in addition to all other difficulties, there were two years of drought. There was never enough food and many people died. But we kept going and believed that if we worked hard, were frugal, saved a little money, and were patient, no matter the conditions, good would eventually come. Even in the worst times, we made sure that the young and old had at least one meal of greens and one of rice gruel each day. This, however, meant that occasionally, a healthy adult would go with only one meal, and often this was very skimpy. Neighbors tried to help one another, but most people endured the same hardships, and there was precious little to share.''

I watched her, intently listening and feeling the pain reflected in her face. Looking at the ground, she continued, ''However, these last years of their war were very bad, as bad as I can remember. Your father had a five-year-old son and a two-year-old daughter. He worked at part-time jobs after a full day in the fields, often working with only one meal to nourish his body. In 1943, an illness overcame him, and his body did not have the strength to survive. There was no finer man than your father, but after his death, if it were possible for things to get worse, I believe they did. The whole village, except for Van Mon and his friends, suffered greatly, and no one could help much. Then one day when you were almost two years old, your grandfather and I were in the market in Hoi An, and we encountered three of our countrymen singing songs about working on the rubber plantations in the south. They showed pictures of a beautiful place with nice homes, good medical care, and excited us with stories of good salaries. We stopped to listen. They said that they were recruiters here to hire workers for the plantations and told us of benefits such as vacations and extra money to send home to help those left behind. Finally, a small advance pay was offered as a sign of good faith. We asked how long we had to make a decision, and they said that we should be back the next day before noon.

"That evening, we sat around the table drinking tea in our home discussing and arguing after you and your brother had been put to bed. Your grandfather was fifty-six and your grandmother forty-eight, and while they were in good health, neither of them felt that we should try such an adventure. But I argued that it was my responsibility to take the job and to send the desperately needed money home. They felt that there might be better alternatives available closer to home.

'I guess I was always too stubborn for my own good, and I decided to go if they would take care of my children. I knew that I could earn more in one year than we could here in three, and then I would be able to return home. The next day, having firmly decided, I gave you all many hugs and kisses, and with tears being shed by all, I left. I promised to write soon and often, but after that morning, it was as if I simply disappeared into hell."

As I listened, it was as if I were being absorbed into an unfolding tragedy. There was a sense of foreboding as I sat silently at her feet and listened as she continued talking to me. "The story is full of tragedy and cruelty, and Kim Lan, I want to remind you that I am alive, well, and home again now. So please remember that as I tell you what happened."

She reached out to hold my hand and then said, "All the recruitment stories were lies. Once they had us on the trucks, their attitudes quickly changed. We had become low-paid prisoners. We were hauled the long distance to the French overlords of the plantation. They worked us from four A.M. to seven P.M. We were severely beaten for the slightest error. Housing and medical care were poor, and the pay was only a fraction of that which was promised. I remember seeing a pregnant woman miscarry in the street while being beaten. One out of every three or four workers died, and we called the place 'Hell on Earth.' "

I felt her grip tighten on my hand.

Looking down she paused, and when again she raised her head, staring off again at some dark and distant thought, I saw a flash of anger, even hatred, on her face. I had not yet seen her act like this, and for a brief instant it frightened me. I waited and feared what could cause such a reaction. I wanted to tell her to not go on, but she continued.

"One day, some of the plantation guards came. It was early yet, and I had three hundred trees to tap for the latex, and the light was still dim. They grabbed me, held me, and one by one they . . ." Tears rolled down her face. I knelt in front of her, and she hugged me, holding me tightly. Then it dawned on me what she was trying to say. I was repulsed, confused, and felt rapidly growing within me an anger and need to strike out. My mother had always been to me a heroine, almost sacred—how could this have happened? I felt the anger and tears I saw in her face. I wanted to run and scream, but I still found myself kneeling at her feet. I felt immobilized with my hand on her knee, unable to move. It was as if a horrible nightmare had engulfed me, and though I wanted to run from it, neither my legs nor any part of my body would cooperate. I knelt looking, staring into her face. She clenched her teeth and then reached out to hold me again. Then she went on. "They cut my hair short and told me that the close-cropped hair would be the mark of my whoredom for all to see. They laughed and left. I cried and was bleeding as I lay behind the trees that were my daily responsibility. That wasn't the end. The guard assigned to that section came along and beat me, forced me to get up and to finish working. He yelled at me, 'If you want to play the whore, do it in the evening, not on company time.' "

It was as if a thousand worms were crawling within my stomach. I wanted to vomit. I wanted to run and hide, but I stayed kneeling, frozen where I was.

Her story continued. "After this, I knew that I would never live to see my family again. Given a chance, I would either kill a guard and then myself be killed, or I would die while trying to escape."

Tears rolled down my face, and I found myself not wanting to listen but, at the same time, unable to stop.

"Conditions were tyrannical in the camp. Life was strictly regulated by guards and overlords. If anyone tried to voice his complaints about living or working conditions, he was labeled a communist and could be shot on the spot, which was legal according to French law. I decided that I would patiently wait for my opportunity.

"Finally, it came, and I and three men were able to kill a guard and escape the plantation. We made our way for about a mile through the forest before deciding to split into pairs in the hope of a better chance to escape pursuit. It was the beginning of the rainy season, but for the first few miles we made our way with ease, although with the fear that we had left too many signs of our trail. My companion and I crossed a stream and climbed a rocky, moss-covered cliff. The skies were heavy with dark clouds, and it began to rain. Just short of the top, we hid on a shelf to watch and listen. It was here that we had to helplessly watch the other pair be recaptured a short distance down the stream. We saw them brutally murdered. We lay hiding on that cliff side as the rains fell more heavily."

I felt myself lying on that cliff, soaked to the bone in rain and mud, frightened beyond description. Every step my mother took, I took with her. Trembling, I hung on her every word.

She paused and looked tenderly at me and asked, "This is too much, isn't it?" She reached out and hugged me saying, "I'm so sorry."

"Mother," I replied, "I love you. I want to be a part of your life. I have to hear the bad and the good. Now, you have to finish your story."

She held me tightly for a little longer and then leaned back again. She then reached out to touch my face before continuing. "On two occasions, we heard guards nearby and feared to move. We shivered in the cold, rain, and mud on that narrow flat ledge overlooking the stream. We were miserable, but knew that the rain was a blessing. It frustrated attempts to find us. The rain fell without stop for about six hours. When it slowed to a steady drizzle, we carefully climbed the last several feet to the top and were able to work our way a few miles through the jungle, slipping and sloshing in mud and pools of water. Then we parted and went in separate directions, and this was the last I saw of any of those who escaped with me.

"I walked another day before encountering a small

group of young people who were leaving their homes to join the new League for the Independence of Vietnam. It was organizing the various resistance movements to rid our country of the French and controlled the mountains and a growing number of villages. They offered me assistance and a respite during which time I was able to become healthy and feel free again. I stayed with them and learned their organization and objectives and was finally able, with their assistance, to come back home. However, I was by then labeled a murderer and communist.''

I began to now fully realize that I had been separated all these years from my mother by the cowardly dictators who ruled our country. It was as if my feelings of randomly flowing anger were now focusing on those local tyrants, both French and Vietnamese. I listened even more intently to Mother as her story continued.

''I knew that I had no choice left. My home now was with the League, which was being called the Viet Minh, and the sooner we could drive the French from our shores, the sooner I could come home to stay. And so, I had to accept the joy and intimacy of my family's company on a very infrequent basis.'' She paused, smiled at me, and said, ''Remember those times when I could visit and would hold you? Tears always flooded my eyes. I looked forward to those visits more than I can ever describe. But I know you never understood why I came only at night and had to leave so quickly.''

I held her hand tightly, and she looked lovingly at me. Her words had filled me with fear, anger, and anxiety. I was shocked by the rape of my mother, and yet I angrily fought with her to escape from her hell. I had always disliked the French and the few of our countrymen who helped them. Now my dislike was becoming much more.

Her story seemed to end, and she stared at her sandal-clad feet, while I sat by them on the earth. Slowly, a smile worked its way across her face. She looked into my eyes and said, ''But we have won the final battle! I am home! We are together forever! So come, let's walk over to the beach and forget the past. Let's plan a beautiful future.''

* * *

Then suddenly, out of another world, the ground rolled and thunder shocked me awake. I sat upright, stunned out of my dreams, eyes wide open. Trying to shake the sleepy fog from my mind, I struggled to understand the cause of the crashing shockwaves. I heard Van Thi say, "Kim Lan, lie down, be still." I was back again. My husband was beside me, and it was again 1966, and the day of my marriage.

My dreams now gone, my mind sobered, I was fully back to reality. "Enemy artillery," I said. "What do you think?"

"Yes," he responded. Speaking over the noise of the artillery, he added, "We have slept through the night, and it is now early morning. Our fifth battalion is sched-uled to be moving on that trail now. Somehow they must have been seen."

"We can't stay here. We have to help," I said.

"Yes," he said, "but let's think a moment. Do you hear any gunshots? Are there any enemy troops involved or is this just an artillery barrage?"

We listened. The thunder of the artillery was so loud that we probably couldn't have heard gunshots had there been any. The violence was occurring on the other side of a small hill nearby. Then we heard two short bursts of automatic weapons fire. That was all, no more.

Van Thi said, "Get inside the jungle. Come."

He pulled me with him into the jungle cover. Then he said as he slipped into his pants, "I'm going to quietly look around, you watch this clearing." He left me with a rifle and quietly moved off.

I knelt, clothed only with my weapon, and watched. My pants, shirt, and blanket lay by the water, but I waited out of sight.

Maybe fifteen or twenty minutes went by, and Van Thi was still gone. The artillery had stopped now. I listened and watched. Then I heard the noise of helicopters. They were coming overhead. Suddenly green smoke rose in a column only a short distance from me. Nine soldiers jumped out of the jungle, watching the helicopters and the clearing I just left. They were Americans, and they were very close. Quietly, I watched and waited. Then their aircraft came down, and one by one the enemy jumped into each of the helicopters.

Two helicopters were quickly gone, and the last was down and then trying to leap into the air like a frightened animal. I had to at least try to stop them. I rushed into the clearing with my rifle. A face appeared at a side window of the American helicopter, less than a short stone's throw from me. I raised my rifle to kill as he did his, but my eyes fixed on his face, and he hesitated as well. So close, but he just stared at me. Something kept me from shooting, and then I knew.

No! It couldn't be real! Ghosts are only for dark dreams, not reality! But it was. I knew it. I could never forget that face. It was the American. It was him. I saw his short blond hair, and his sunburned skin. His blue eyes stared with an unspoken question. It was him.

I was frozen in place; his face framed by my rifle sights. Then, as his eyes stayed fixed on me, his look searching me with questions, the helicopter roared across the grass and lifted into the air. I was whipped by its windstorm, and as I lowered my rifle, I felt a shiver run the length of my body. I watched him disappear beyond the treetops. His eyes had never left me. I couldn't move or think.

CHAPTER 4

> We need to fight the way they fight . . . but no one is
> quite sure how they fight.
> —Lederer and Burdick, *The Ugly American*

*T*welve inches of fine dirt kicked up into the hot, sticky
air with each footstep. Clouds of dust chased after every
vehicle. The Marines had landed. Back twenty miles
south again, we were to find and destroy the 5th Vietcong
Battalion. Our base camp was called An Hoa, and it rose
like a dusty wart out of the last of almost endless miles
of rice paddies. The barren backside of this poor excuse
for a hill was now polluted by dirty tents and a pisspot
full of war machines.

In the last week since our aborted ambush, the grunts
had moved to An Hoa from their attempts to find Charlie
in the villages near the Song Thu Bon. This was the first
time in the year since Marines had landed in Vietnam
that we had established a permanent post this far south
of Da Nang. Still, the elusive 5th Vietcong Battalion, like
shadows, patrolled the nights. Every hill, village, and
rice paddy, a threat during the day, became death at night.
Yet my job was to find that enemy battalion; the 2nd
Battalion, 5th Marines, was to destroy them.

Intelligence from our battalion S-2 had also reported
that a key figure in the communist insurrection in this
area was a woman. Her name was reported to be Nguyen

53

Kim Lan. She was very active in organizing village resistance and, in addition, had led small unit attacks against the government. All of our units in this area had been ordered to watch for her and, if possible, to capture her.

Our camp was tucked into the southwest corner of the most productive rice fields in Quang Nam province. However, towering above An Hoa in an L-shape from the southeast to the southwest and west was a range of mountains that rose from almost sea level in the paddies to just short of five thousand feet. Tropical jungles blanketed them, and wild animals and enemy soldiers called them home. My patrol was to go after Charlie in the lower foothills. At least we were going to try to find him, and then let the grunts "go after" him. I stood in the middle of our makeshift hillside fortress as the sun lowered itself beyond the mountains on this evening of our first day in the camp. Tomorrow we'd be shoving off on our first patrol for the 2/5. I grabbed a hot beer on my way back to the men and my tent.

We had to be packed for possibly a longer patrol than normal, and after a couple of hours of cussing and discussing the next five days in the mountains, I left the men and straggled back to my tent. My little canvas bungalow greeted me with the odor of hot, clammy dust. My only piece of furniture was a lonely cot. Sheetless, it stared at me. I sat down on it and slapped the taut canvas mattress to beat off the dirt. A small cloud of the inevitable dust rose up and settled back down. I lay down anyway and aimlessly studied the not quite as dusty ceiling under the light of one sixty-watt bulb. Before I pulled the chain on the light, I watched a spider scramble across my ceiling but was too tired to give a damn where he intended to go. The light out, I listened in the darkness to sounds of the green machine calming down for the night. A small pop in the distance preceded an illumination flare sputtering to life. Out of the tent's side flap, I watched the thing. It looked like a large, lonely, flickering streetlight drifting over the neighboring hamlet.

The next morning, before the sun had yet risen, we nine Marines, using the call sign of "Charlie Brown," were waiting for our birds at the An Hoa LZ. The adrenal glands were pumping their little hearts out. I looked around at my men. A few wore wide-brimmed bush hats, but most had the Marine Corps issue soft utility cap pulled low on their foreheads. With painted faces and bulky packs crammed with extra ammunition, we quietly waited as the darkness evaporated around us. A few smoked, but no one spoke.

From this flat plain, we could see the helicopters coming from miles away, as they flew high with pink-bottomed clouds as their backdrop. We waited in the shadows below. The smokers took their last drags and buried their butts. Everybody got to their feet and moved to group in their three-man teams, each ready to run aboard one of the three 34s.

Then they were on top of us, burying us all in a tornado of dust that shotgunned its way past uniforms, saturating every pore with stinging, dirty filth. While each team jumped aboard its respective bird, I scrambled up the side of the lead aircraft and made sure the pilot knew where we wanted to go. Then I was back down and in, and we were off.

How could flying in a noisy, cramped, green coffin, a couple thousand feet in the air, be exhilarating? In some kind of stupid, macho way, I could feel the rising sense of excitement and challenge. Maybe it was like the pumping up a player felt before a football game: the chance to challenge your manhood against the next guy's.

We flew southwest. The hills still lay in shadows. Our timing was good. About five minutes out, the choppers turned to the west. I watched the dark shadows below as we quickly made a turn to the portside and began to descend rapidly. Then again we turned, flying low back toward the east. My muscles tensed, and I readied myself to jump and run like hell. Much too suddenly, we were down, bouncing in the tall grass. Before the birds could stop, we were out ripping through the waist-high weeds in the direction of the first small trees and rocks. Survival instincts dominated all our thoughts: the suicide squad racing down the field after the kickoff.

The patrol, alone now, stopped to regroup in the dim light. Then Alexander moved his point team toward the line of tall trees that marked the beginning of heavy jungle. Like a giant, dark-green barricade, they stared down

on us. We were about a thousand feet up the hillside with
villages below us in the paddies. Running from one clump
of bushes to the next, bent low, we made the jungle and
halted. I knelt in the edge of the heavy bush to make use
of the light of the sun as it began to work its way over
the lip of the South China Sea far out to my right. The
skies were light blue now, and for a moment, I sat watching the sun, magnified by the atmosphere, ascend like a
king in all his power and glory. I couldn't help but recall
Kipling's quote: "An' the dawn comes up like thunder
outer China 'crost the Bay!"

Alexander crawled up and whispered, "Damn pretty
sunrise, but let's get the fuck out of here."

Smiling, I said, "Okay, okay. Let's move to the west
just like we planned. But first, check the map. Down
below, about three miles to the east, are the Nong Son
coal mines. To the north out there about four clicks is
that village of An Bang where we were before. It'll probably take us three days to work our way around these
hills to get there. Stay close to the edge of the jungle.
Let's move for about an hour and set-up and watch this
place. I want to get a feel for what's around."

"Aye, aye, sir," he whispered, and was gone.

For an hour we followed his lead. There were no paths,
and we tried not to make any. Finally, he stopped us and
came back to get me. Then while the others sat in heavy
brush, my corporal led me forward. We crawled to where
the vegetation petered out near a draw that cut its way
down toward the valley.

Nodding in that direction, he quietly said, "Sir, I think
we can move down this dry streambed and get closer to
the paddies. Down there, about halfway, looks like some
good spots to set-up."

We needed to find some places for observation points,
and this looked great. I said, "Get the patrol, and let's
move down."

Within forty-five minutes, we had reached a point only
about five hundred feet above the valley floor. Here the
jungles were nonexistent. Except for some bush and scattered trees in and near the draw, the terrain was filled
with short grass, boulders, and only occasional clumps
of heavier bush. I sat the patrol in the best places I could

to get a panoramic view. Then I reported in to the battalion and finally positioned myself to start watching.

We overlooked a small secluded valley that was somewhat rounded in shape. It was cut off from the rest of the paddies by a fingerlike extension of low hills. There were scattered groups of thatch huts but only a few. One unusual point was that the land was not being cultivated, and it was covered by what appeared to be a tangled mass of vegetation with clumps of trees growing randomly. Clearings appeared here and there, and there was a small hill in the west central part of the valley not quite a mile from our position. We could see at the base of that hill a large pagoda, but it no longer looked used. Watching through my binoculars, I noted that there was a lot of jungle undergrowth and smaller trees growing in and around the building. Monkeys were actively socializing around the place. As we checked the rest of the valley, we spotted other animals, including wild pigs, and once we debated whether an elephant had been seen disappearing in the trees around the edge of the hill. I had yet to see a more natural and wild-looking valley since I had been in 'Nam.

Later, about noon, Alexander pointed out a column of Vietnamese: twelve persons, traversing from our southeast across the low finger into the valley to our front. They were following a trail that would take them behind the hill and toward what the map indicated was a route farther to the west into the mountains. We focused our field glasses on them and counted what appeared to be two people with rifles at the front and back of the column, and ten in the middle, six of whom were carrying large sacks on their backs. We decided the sacks were probably filled with rice, and they were carrying them into the mountains for other units of their army.

I called for the artillery. We plotted a fire mission to hit them on the trail before they could get to the hill. As soon as the battery gave me the report that they were ready, I waited until the column of VC would be walking right into our planned artillery strike, and then gave the command to fire. The first rounds landed near, but just behind the Charlie. The last man fell and didn't get up. The others ran while I adjusted the fire mission and called for a fire-for-effect. The rounds exploded near the VC, who were now obviously trying to make it to the hill for shelter. With the second set of rounds, one more went down, and all dropped their loads of rice. The other ten got to the hill and out of sight before I called an end to the fire mission. I reported to the battalion that two more of Uncle Ho's men had passed on to visit their beloved ancestors.

The next few hours were slow. We stayed put and watched the valleys, but except for occasional Vietnamese passing along trails about a mile away, there was nothing really to watch. The midafternoon sun lay on me like a hundred-pound weight. I propped my back against a large rock and sat squinting through bushes occasionally using my binoculars to look at the old pagoda. The monkeys seemed to be taking it easy in the steaming afternoon shade. I picked at a can of C's and lusted after a piece of sausage sent in a care-package from my parents. I was saving it for later this evening, but it was hard to restrain myself.

Rifle shots suddenly cracked just below me shattering the quiet heat! I spilled the C-rats all over myself as I rolled to the side of the boulder, rifle in hand. I lay in the hot dust with my heart rattling my dog tags.

"Alexander, where the hell are you?" I called out in barely more than a whisper. "What's up?"

There was a moment of silence as the patrol lay still. Then I heard Alexander. "It's okay. It's me. I'm coming in from down here."

I looked down, and there he came crawling up the hill from lower down the draw. He quickly got up to the patrol and moved over beside me. I looked at him and waited.

He said, a little out of breath, "There's one dead Charlie down there. I think we better move our asses somewhere else before all his brothers get up here."

I asked, more than a little concerned, "Man, what the shit happened?"

"Oh, fuck, Lieutenant, I've got this goddamn diarrhea! I have to go out behind some fucking bush every three or four hours. I was down there. Just dropped my trousers and some asshole Charlie jumps up from the other side of the bush and shoots at me! Well, he's a bad shot, and he's laying in my shit back there. We better move. He might have some friends. Maybe they thought we were somewhere around when we blew their friends away earlier with the arty. Sorta scouting-the-fuck around. Now they'll know something."

"Is he dead?" I asked.

"Hell, I don't know. I was trying to pull up my pants on the run!"

"Let's quick-check on our way out," I said, "if he's still living, maybe our G-2 can get some info from him."

Within minutes, the patrol was down in the draw, carefully approaching Alexander's shithole. The quietness was earth-shaking. Then we moved closer. Alexander motioned us to be still. Then I heard it: moaning. He was alive! Quickly we got to him and the patrol positioned itself in the rocks and bush on all sides of the little arroyo. Trying to rush, I remembered the horror stories of the Little Big Horn and wanted to get as far away from this place as fast as I could but felt committed to snatch this VC.

The man lay on his back, his shoulder was a bloody mess, and he tried to move inch by inch to his rifle. His uniform was similar to those we had seen before. I grabbed Red as Alexander picked up the rifle. "Call battalion," I said hurriedly.

Five minutes later, two choppers were out to pick up the wounded Viet Cong, then we hauled ass back uphill to the cover of the jungle.

It took us thirty minutes to make our way back uphill. I think I held my breath all the way. Every Viet Cong within five miles saw those helicopters. I prayed that they figured we had left in them.

Back in the heavy jungle canopy, we took a quick break before shoving off to the west again. I moved over to Alexander and asked, "Now explain to me again what the hell happened back there."

"Sir, it's like this. I can't fart without having to drop my goddamn trousers. The motherfucking icing on the cake is to have Charlie watching your goddamn shithole. The son of a bitch got so excited when he saw my bare ass he couldn't hit the side of a barn if it had been ten

feet in front of him. I think he just about shot his own
foot off. Did ya ever try to turn around in the squatting
position with your damn trousers around your ankles,
pick up your rifle, and shoot some asshole who's trying
to shoot you?''

He paused, looked at me, and finally said, ''You know
what happiness is, Lieutenant? It's a goddamn dry fart.''

I had been leaning against a fifty foot tall tree, one of
the little ones in this jungle, ready to be serious about a
life-threatening situation. Now, I just hung my head trying not to laugh out loud.

The break over, we moved through the heavy jungle
bush to the west for six hours. At times, we crawled, and
at times, walked, but we carefully tried not to leave any
trail. We assumed Charlie would be all over our former
OP like bees on sweet flowers. We damn sure didn't want
them to pick up signs of our trail. Finally, I halted the
patrol with three hours of daylight left. We were about
six hundred feet up the hillside in a little finger of trees
that reached down the mountain from the main jungles.
We had a good view of everything below us, and I told
Alexander that we would spend the night there.

Nothing moved below us. We were still within a mile
of the pagoda but now only two miles from An Bang.
We could see activity in the village, but our artillery this
morning must have made the little valley *verboten* for a
while.

The jungles were always spooky to me, and that night
I lay without sleeping until my first watch at midnight.
Finally, I drifted off sometime after one A.M., only to be
wakened again at 0300 for my last duty. By six, we were
all up grumbling over cold C-rats.

Red moved over saying, ''Lieutenant, the battalion
S-3's on the radio.''

I took the handset from him and listened as our operations officer reported the results so far of the interrogation
of our prisoner. ''We want you to relocate to vicinity
Tango Lima Bravo,'' he said through the static. ''Info
indicates Victor Charlie battalion that area tonight. Info
also indicates Victor Charlie led by a female officer.''

After finishing the short sixty-second conversation, I
sat back and thought, the fucking VC are making a move

on An Hoa and led by a woman! Son of a bitch! Bet she's the one we're supposed to be looking for. I wonder if she looks anything like the one by the lake? Before I could finish thinking though, Corporal Alexander had crawled over. I explained the situation. "We've got to go back. S-3's saying they've got info about Charlie moving on An Hoa." I pointed out the coordinates on the map and said, "We've got to get back here by evening."

"Shit," he replied, "we just came over there. Suppose the fucking VC are still back there checking out the countryside for us."

"Yeah, I know. So let's swing higher up in the hills and double-back using a different route."

We buried our cans and butts and tried to make the place look like nobody had been around. Then, in one short nine-man column, we moved up higher into the jungle, slowly and carefully. The jungle bush slapped our faces, and "just-a-minute" vines grabbed at everything. Even with our slow pace, I hoped to make our destination by midafternoon.

We followed no path but pushed up higher. The jungle was so damn thick that I couldn't see more than two men in front of me. After an hour, I changed the patrol's direction and began to work our way across-slope. We had to cover about three miles, being slowed both by the bush and by caution. Then we were supposed to come down to get a view of the valley and the western approaches to An Hoa.

It was about 1500 hours, midafternoon, when we finally reached our objective. Although we originally were to patrol to the west, we had circled back and were east of our original landing zone.

I estimated our position to be about 800 to 1000 feet above the valley floor. An Hoa was only about four miles away. With field glasses, I could make out the distant movements of Marine Corps vehicles stirring up clouds of dust. About a mile to our east was the Song Thu Bon. It flowed through a relatively narrow valley farther up in the mountains and then past us out into the broad miles of rice paddies. Its route carried it adjacent to our base at An Hoa. From this position, we could watch not only the western approaches to our base but could also cover any movements coming out of the Song Thu Bon valley to the south. At least we could until nightfall.

After reporting in to battalion, we settled into positions from which we could observe the scenery. The An Hoa coal mines lay near the mouth of the Song Thu Bon valley about a mile and a half away. One reinforced Marine platoon had occupied a small hill overlooking the mines. An old French-built rail line snaked its way across the paddies on a raised dike and ended at the mouth of those mines. It was apparently a constant battle to keep the railway open. Sometimes it was down for months due to enemy sabotage. As much as Charlie seemed to control the countryside, I was surprised that it was ever working. Maybe the VC was given a cut in the profits to keep it open?

After two hours of sitting still and watching nothing in particular, I told Alexander that I was going to take the rear team and check out some area farther to our east, closer to the mines. We called our last team "TMT," the Tex-Mex Trio: there was Sanchez from Brownsville, Rodriquez from Laredo, and Garcia from San Antonio. Sanchez carried the spare radio, and he now brought it up on the "net" while I discussed with Alexander where we'd be going. Then the four of us shoved off.

At first we moved at about the same elevation and just inside the jungle line. However, after about thirty minutes, the land began to descend. We followed our noses downward. After another thirty minutes, Rodriquez in the lead halted, and we all knelt in the jungle bush.

I crawled forward down to Rodriquez. He whispered, "Lieutenant, I hear a creek or something. And look at this."

A few feet in front of him was a camp fire. The coals were still warm. It looked like it had been used the night before. Not far in the distance was the sound of water. The jungle overgrowth had thinned out, and I felt like I was back at Marine Corps Schools, Quantico, Virginia.

There was other evidence that people had been around but were no longer there. I whispered to Rodriquez to move on down very slowly, very quietly. I passed the message to each of the others, and we all moved carefully down, about ten feet between each of us. We were low-

crawling and stopped at almost every tree, kneeling and
looking around. The old fires were nothing more than to
heat small meals, probably rice.

In fifteen minutes, we had reached the stream and silently hid on a small bluff overlooking it. Brush had been
cleared on both sides of the water. Footprints, sandal
prints, and boot prints were everywhere. We just sat still,
partly because we were afraid to move. After ten minutes
of silence, I figured, at least I prayed, that all enemy had
vacated the area earlier. I spoke with the team and ad-
vised them that I wanted to check upstream and downstream. Which way were those people going, and how
many were there?

It was about 1830 hours when we stopped again to talk.
We were in agreement: an enemy company had moved
into this area the night before and out again going downhill. They were about eight hours ahead of us somewhere
down this stream. I studied the map. The stream ran down
through the hillside jungle to the paddies and across a
half-mile of rice fields before entering the Song Thu Bon
near the coal mines. It was shielded by trees all the way.

I tried to relate what I was seeing to the information
the S-3 had provided. The evidence in front of us did not
indicate a battalion-size force, but it was possible that
the balance of the battalion was elsewhere. If it was just
a company, it was likely composed of between eighty and
one hundred and twenty people. That few could not take
on the main An Hoa base by itself. However, several
companies could be converging from different directions.

It didn't matter, we had to get back to the main patrol.
There was only about an hour and a half of sunlight left
as Rodriquez led us back at a faster pace than we came
down.

In thirty minutes, we were back with Alexander calling
in to the battalion to report what we had found. I got the
impression that they still felt there was a battalion of
enemy around, and we had found the trail of only one
company. Then the S-3 told us in code to move the patrol
to that creek and on down to the paddies and set up there
tonight and just hide and watch. Then he signed off.

I looked at Alexander and said, "This is going to be
one motherfucking trick. The last time we went down to

the paddies looking for Charlie, I realized a new definition for being scared shitless.''

Alexander answered, ''Yeah, like your anal cavity is puckered so tight you couldn't drive a sixteen-penny nail up it.''

''Well,'' I decided, ''we've got an hour before the fucking sunlight says *sayonara*, and it's going to take all of that to get our asses down to that creek. We better shake a leg. Let's move it.''

With our seventy pounds of packs sucking the strength out of our backs again, we made our way across the jungle. We tried to strike a compromise between caution and speed, and I added a little prayer on the side.

I timed it. Fifty-five minutes, and we were carefully parting the last bushes in front of the paddies. The tree-lined creek continued out across the fields to the river maybe a half-mile away. The main camp at An Hoa was about three miles off to the left, and the coal mines were on the other side of the river about a mile away. A half-mile to our right on this side of the Song Thu Bon, was the hill where one platoon from the 2/5 had dug in. The company we had followed had left their tracks going down the creek toward the river. They were out there somewhere; I assumed they had turned left and were pushing on down to link up with the rest of their battalion and move on An Hoa. I had no desire to be moving at night down in the paddies and was glad the S-3 had said to set-up here.

We positioned ourselves for the night about a hundred feet from the creek. Forget sleeping! Like a long-tailed cat in a room full of rocking chairs, I nervously worried about our semiexposed position. I was more than a little antsy and laid back watching the occasional flares pop in the night skies and drift, harnessed to their toy parachutes, over our heads. The Marines on that hill were nervous, too, and they wouldn't let one flare die before another was sent up. Those flickering nightlights lit up at least a million shadows cast by fucking enemy soldiers. Hell, I knew there was nothing but bushes and trees and rice paddy dikes, but the damned imagination was working overtime. I tried to tell myself that the enemy was down toward An Hoa somewhere.

My first watch began at midnight and went by un-eventfully. At 0100 I woke Red for his turn. Suddenly, a half-dozen explosions thundered in the night a half-mile off. Then more. My God, I thought, what the fuck's happening?

On the platoon position out to our right front, all hell was breaking loose: machine-gun fire, grenades, and a mortar barrage. I heard screams. Then to our left, I saw flashes, explosions, and heard sounds of mortars crashing into the main base at An Hoa.

Alexander was beside me. "What do you think is happening?" he asked. "It looks like Charlie is hitting the platoon by the mines and An Hoa, too."

The screams of battle shook the night less than a half-mile away on that little hill overlooking the mines. Finally, I said, "Shit, hell, damn, fuck, piss! Alexander, we can't sit on our butts. That company we were following didn't go to An Hoa. It's hitting the platoon! They'll overrun the fucking hill. There's about forty Marines up there fighting for their fucking lives. We've got to help."

"That'll make forty-nine Marines," he said. "Sounds like a good number to me." He turned and yelled to the men, "Lock and load you motherfuckers. There's Marines who need our help."

"Alexander, dump our packs here," I said. "Everybody'll take two canteens on their belt and nothing else but all the fucking ammo we can strap around our shoulders."

Then I watched the two hundred-year-old Marine Corps tradition stand tall in the person of my corporal. He had resigned his fate to the hands of his God as he stood bellowing orders, "Listen you assholes, if we gotta fucking die, let's die for other goddamn US Marines. But 'fore you shitheads die, I expect there to be five or six enemy soldiers at each of your goddamn feet. And listen to me! When we get to the top of that motherfucking hill, if you get your back against a wall, make that wall another goddamn Marine. Back to back we'll fight our way through hell, you hear me! God in his heaven got no fucking use for candy-ass Marines."

Then he was silent a moment surveying each of us, and we all waited. Slowly, almost quietly, his voice penetrated our minds, "Marines, lock and load. I'm damn proud to have known you. On your fucking feet."

In sixty seconds, a nine-man recon patrol was running and stumbling in a dark half-mile dash across the paddies to try to relieve the Marines on the hill. People fell, got up, and kept running. I had tuned in to the platoon's radio net, caught the platoon commander's attention, and, on the run, screamed above the battle's noise, "This is Charlie Brown, we're coming in from your northwest. Hang on, we're coming! I say again, this is Charlie Brown, we're crossing the paddies from your northwest. We're coming on the run! Hang on up there! Hang on!"

I heard him scream over the radio, and it went silent. I yelled at my men to push faster, and then I slipped off a paddy dike into muddy water.

It took forever, but finally we were at the foot of the hill. There seemed to be a volcano erupting at the top. We were coming up behind the Marines, or whatever was left of them. Then I heard Rodriquez start shouting as we tried to run, stumbling up the hill. The noise was so loud, I didn't understand. Then I did. He was trying to sing! The little shit was belting out, "From the Halls of Montezuma, to the shores of Tripoli . . ." We all started screaming the Marine Corps Hymn. Chills of fear that had begun to grip my guts were, in a second, driven from my body by countless decades of pride. This was not a little Vietnamese hill, this was Mount Suribachi!

Then I heard shouts from our buddies at the top, and we were with them. A crazy, bloody, screaming confusion suddenly hammered my face. A mortar blast knocked me off my feet, and bullets ripped the air and the ground around. The Marines hung on to the back edge of the hilltop. Enemy soldiers held the higher side. I could see them like eerie shadows under the sporadic light of flares floating away from us. A quick glance told me there were only about twenty Marines left. At least three times that many communists faced us. We were slightly downhill from them, as they had overrun our best positions first. The platoon had lost its radio and platoon commander. I looked for Red and saw him crawling for me on his stomach. His leg was a bloody mess, and I reached out to pull him into the hole I had found. My feet straddled a dead Marine. Reaching the radio, bullets tearing the air around me, I quickly called for artillery, but it would take them precious minutes to start pounding us. Red was firing his rifle beside me. I lowered my head and didn't want to raise up knowing that waves of bullets flowed to and fro in both directions, but I had to. Fighting back fear, I rose and quickly leveled my rifle.

Suddenly, Marines started cheering. The enemy was being hit from behind. I aimed my rifle on top of a sandbag and saw the unbelievable. A Marine the VC had passed over for dead had risen behind them. He stood in full view with an M-60 in his bloody hands firing torrents of lead into the backside of the enemy. With renewed vigor, my Marines increased the crossfire on the enemy. To my right, I saw Alexander throw a grenade. Then he was knocked over backward, his skull crushed open by an enemy bullet. A sick anger struck my soul.

Out of the corner of my eye, I saw an enemy soldier kick the grenade into a hole. It exploded harmlessly. In the same second, I took aim on the soldier who was himself standing without fear in the face of withering Marine fire. He was organizing and leading an attack with a small number of his troops back toward the Marine who, with his machine gun, fought like a wild nightmare behind them.

The enemy leader was in my sights, not a hundred feet away, when under the light of a newly exploding flare, his hair fell down to his waist. I hesitated. Son of a bitch, it's the woman! Then she was out of my sight.

We fought like crazy, cornered animals—Mad dogs all! A grenade landed in front of me. I dropped into the hole. Red was screaming, "Rodriquez!" There was a muffled explosion, and I was up.

"Damn you stupid Tex-Mex son of a bitch." Red was yelling and pulling at Rodriquez. He rolled him over in front of us while I fired my M-14. Then it sunk into my dumb cranium that Rodriquez had jumped on the grenade to protect Red and myself. Rodriquez's body rolled over and his guts rolled out. I bent over and threw up in the hole where I stood. But there was no time, I had to keep fighting to live. As I did, Red held Rodriquez in his arms and cried.

Then, sounds of whistling trucks came tearing through the air. Before I ducked away from the incoming artillery, I saw the battlefield in front of me. They had killed the Marine behind them and were trying to reorganize. In that brief second I saw her again. The breeze blew her long hair as she stood shouting commands. It was her; I knew it was. I couldn't forget that face, even under these flares. The naked, brown-skinned woman by the lake with a rifle pointed at my face was now fighting for this hilltop leading a company of Viet Cong.

Down into the hole I dropped. I hardly realized that I lay in my own vomit as the 105s began to blow the hill apart. Groveling in the dirt, I called for a fire-for-effect. Red lay beside me with the radio. He had dragged Rodriquez's dead body in beside him. I closed my eyes. We then began to be slammed into the sides of our holes, and I thought we would be killed by our own artillery.

But in five minutes, the shelling stopped. I was still alive. Carefully I raised my head. The smoky silence was spooky. Except for the ringing in my ears, there was no sound. A flare popped in the night above. The battlefield glared back at me eerily. They were gone. Then a couple of bodies moved. I heard a groan.

Slowly a remnant of Marines raised themselves out of their holes. Twelve of us then cautiously moved across the dark hilltop lit only by shaky flares floating high above us. We found only sixteen enemy bodies; they must have carried off the rest. We had to have killed more than that! I walked back to my hole and sat down. Unconsciously, holding my rifle, I stared off into the night. I was dazed. All the confusion and the smell of death. And the woman.

Who was she? Why hadn't I blown her to hell when I had the chance? What hell was happening to me? I sat there stupidly thinking while the dead lay all around, lit up by the pale, flickering flares. Then somewhere near my feet, a thousand miles away, I heard Red still crying.

CHAPTER 5

Blood and bones of young and old;
Mothers weep till their tears are dry . . .
A country's beauty torn apart . . .
Brother's killing each other . . .

—Thich Nhat Hanh

*F*ields of blossoming rice being raped by the boots of the invading armies twisted my heart with hatred for the Americans. I had seen them, arms bared, guns ready, patrol through villages eyeing the young woman with domineering, lusty stares. Tonight it was my turn.

It was almost midnight. There was no moon, and I lay quietly in the grass on the bottom slopes of a small hill overlooking the Nong Son coal mine near An Hoa. The wind whistled softly through the grass, and we remained as silent as our ancestors lying beneath the earth. The enemy had placed one infantry platoon with an attachment of their heavy 4.2 inch mortars and the lighter 81-millimeter mortars on the hill above us. They were dug in with trenches and bunkers and had one three-man listening post between us and their perimeter. Eleven years of war, ever since I escaped from the colonel's whorehouse, had given me the experience that I needed, and now I prepared to whisper the command to attack.

Crawling, slowly and silently, we began our quiet move up the hill. Like one hundred jungle vipers, we pushed inch by inch toward the kill. Three long lines, one behind the other, my platoons carefully, slowly slid through

the grass toward the enemy. Only the breeze could be
heard gently whistling through the weeds.

Then we were there. I could make out the outline of
the enemy Marines in the listening post not more than
thirty feet in front of me. One man appeared to be awake.
I quickly signalled the attack and called for our fire support.

A thunderstorm of rifle shots and war cries burst out
all around, and I heard the sounds of our mortars slamming into the Marine perimeter ahead of me. We took
the listening post in stride leaving three enemy dead behind us. I threw the center of our force at the highest
portion of the hilltop. Our supporting mortars, perfectly
on the mark, rolled barrage after barrage across the hill,
staying just in front of us. The infantry and sapper teams
followed in its wake. The noise of battle was like a violent typhoon, and the dust, flames, and mortar fragments
marched across the hilltop leading the way. In the darkness, lit only by our exploding mortar rounds, the sappers threw demolition charges into the bunkers where
awakening Marines were eliminated. Not all, however,
were caught off-guard.

Two Marine positions, each manned by several enemy,
lay directly in our path on the edge of the hill. The one
on the right gave a brief fight before being overrun. On
the left, however, four Marines put up a savage fight. I
threw myself in a bombed-out bunker and lay flat shouting instructions as bullets flew like a rainstorm. It took
four attacks to eliminate the enemy position on the left.
One lone American machine-gunner, after the others
were dead, had refused to stop fighting although
wounded. His gunnery had cost us time and men, but we
were past him now as he joined his dead friends.

Our men fiercely battled to the center of the hill. The
fighting was close and terrible. Face to face, rifle to rifle,
and bloody scream to bloody scream the fight raged. We
had blown several bunkers and more than half the hill
was in our possession. The night was lit by explosions,
and the enemy launched illumination flares which slowly
parachuted out of the night sky floating in the breeze.
Under that flickering, erratic light, shaking like a cowardly ghost drifting over our heads, both the Marines and

my men closed with each other battling for every foot of ground.

With my first two lines fiercely closed with the Americans, I now committed my last platoon in a swift charge on their right flank. In fifteen more minutes, we had their heavy mortars. The sappers blew them in their pits. I had lost twenty men but knew that the enemy was down to only that many left. They would fight to the death. They were now like a cornered, frightened, and insane rat ready to die in its corner. One more bunker and we would have the 81-millimeter mortars.

I was with my platoon leaders. More casualties had been taken than I expected, but we now regrouped and were ready to make the last assaults across the lower portion of the hilltop. We could count the fire from one remaining machine gun plus maybe eighteen to twenty rifles. We held the superiority in numbers and the higher ground. I felt that in a few minutes we would have the hilltop, and all the enemy would be put out of action. However, we had to hurry as their reinforcements could be on the way. Heavy enemy fire kicked up dust all around and occasionally found its mark on one of my men. I knelt shouting commands.

At that moment a searing pain sliced across my left leg, and the lieutenant beside me plunged face forward as if a tiger had crushed him from the back. The firing was coming from behind! Sudden rushes of anger and fear engulfed me as I spun around, leaped forward, and returned fire at a marine in a position that we had just overrun. It was that machine-gunner that had caused us so much trouble in the first place!

I cursed in anger as I realized that some of my soldiers had been in too much of a rush to make sure everyone was dead behind us. Quickly, I counted ten more of my men who had been shot from behind by this one enemy. He stood with a machine gun in his arms firing continuous waves of bullets at us. He screamed above the din like a man crazed. Now, although we outnumbered our enemy, we were caught in between their guns. We had to kill him quickly.

I jumped to my feet and called for a team to lay down a steady fire on this lone enemy's position and screamed for my 2nd Platoon commander to lead a team after me to take the enemy. A grenade landed at my feet. In anger, I kicked it away, and it exploded in an empty fighting hole.

My hat was shot away, and I felt my hair fall. Suddenly, a pain burned across my side, but we now were attacking to the rear. We ran, rolled, got up, and ran forward again. The team to my right poured out a steady stream of covering fire, and we shot as we ran. That lone American faced our fire and returned the same. Brave fought the brave. Then under the glimmering light of the flares floating out of the darkness, I saw him go down. We dashed forward, and one of my men drove a bayonet through the dead man's chest.

I knelt beside his dirty and bloody face for just one second before we dashed across the battlefield back to the company. I had lost two more men and precious minutes.

We ran back. At least thirty of my men were now dead, and I had to regroup the company. The enemy by now had been reinforced. We heard them shouting. I grit my teeth hating the choice I had to make. Another Marine unit had managed to come up from below. They must have run all the way! Then I heard their artillery thundering through the night. I knew the battle was over. I had to get my men out of there before the artillery ripped us apart.

Years of jungle warfare had trained us well in the tactics of hitting hard and then slipping away, and in five minutes, we were back down on the river sheltered by the trees. Their flares still eerily lit the dark skies, and their artillery searched for us like crazy demons. Carrying our dead and wounded, we moved quickly away toward the jungles, counting our casualties and estimating theirs.

We had lost thirty-five, just over one-third of the company. Quickly, we regrouped. We thought that thirty to forty enemy had been either killed or wounded. Their heavy mortars were destroyed, and, although we were not able to completely take the hill, we had put out of action one reinforced enemy platoon. As we moved away into the mountains, I thought, if it just hadn't been for that one wounded American who had come back from the dead behind us! For just a moment, I had to admire his courage. But I shook the thought out of my mind. They were the enemy! Then, for a short-lived moment, I saw the blond-haired one from my past. I had seen him in the helicopter. Suddenly, one of my platoon commanders drove the thought of him from my mind. He stood in front of me reporting the status of his wounded. I placed my hand on his arm and pointed, giving orders. As he left, I felt my hand wet with what I knew was blood from his arm.

When we returned to our base camp, I felt the frustration of having to report that we had failed to fully accomplish our mission. My brother, Ba Can, commanded our battalion and was waiting. We hugged each other, but it had been a long time since I felt that I could touch my brother in love. Over the years, he had slowly grown angry and distant. Hatred and a driving determination to kill the enemy had taken possession of his soul. I was his only family left, but his god had become this war. Even my desire to seek revenge on the enemy seemed insignificant next to his.

A smile briefly flickered across his lips as we stood under the jungle canopy. He noticed the blood on my pants and shirt and said, "Take care of those. Small wounds can get infected. Then come to the command center."

I did. Two other officers from our battalion, along with a liaison from the 2nd Division greeted me. They all remained silent as I spoke for about ten minutes explaining the details of the battle. I apologized for not completely destroying the enemy on the hill.

Ba Can said, "You did well. It is easy to ambush the Americans, but to drive them off a fortified position with their supporting artillery is much more difficult."

We spent another hour going over the battle. Our comrade from the north was particularly interested in my accounts. But finally, I was allowed to clean both myself and my weapon, with the instructions that tomorrow would be spent preparing for our next battles.

I knew that the next plans had two separate missions. Both actions were designed to take place on the same night. I knew the general nature of the attacks and felt elated that it was my command which was to lead one.

Ba Can had said that he also intended to be with me. That attack was going to hit the prison at Hoi An. The same place that had held my mother. I could see the blood lust in Ba Can's eyes.

That night I lay in bed and thought only about the experiences I had as a fourteen-year-old girl. I trembled thinking of how filthy I had been made to feel by those crude government soldiers. For eleven years my mother had been missing. They had taken her into that pit, and then to hell. We never saw her again.

Momentarily, I drifted in my thoughts. I despised the Vietnamese traitors and tyrants, and I couldn't wait to destroy their prison and free my people. I felt the hatred rising within me again. Sometimes, though, my loathing of our enemies gripped my soul so terribly, that the need for revenge I felt made me feel sick.

I tried to think of other thoughts. I forced myself to remember Mother. I pictured the two of us together. I was dreaming myself back home. Mother was there, and I with her. We walked, talked, and held hands. I closed my eyes and willed myself more deeply into the world of that time. I walked by the beach again. A fleeting sense of peace touched me.

But despite my need for happiness, my thoughts wandered into the shadowy sides. I saw a friend crying, her face swollen by the soldiers fists. She handed us a notice that they had thrown in her bloodied face after they had taken four of our most trusted workers. I read the note. It announced the initiation of the *To Cong* campaign. It was easy to see that they meant to murder all members of the Viet Minh and their sympathizers or force them to repent, denounce, and reject communism at public ceremonies. I remembered being confused. The war was supposed to be over! There was a peace treaty, and elections were to be held the following year. The Americans and their Vietnamese puppet, Diem, were repudiating the agreements.

It was again 1955, and a sense of awful foreboding swept over me. I felt myself holding Mother's hand. I saw her face as tears began to gather. Her gaze settled on me, and she sensed what I was feeling. Smiling, she said everything would work out and told me to help our friend home.

We cleansed her wounds and tried to comfort her, but it was hard with her husband and the others taken by the military police. Then Mother asked me if I felt that I could go to the jail and try to find out what had happened. They didn't know me and the plan would be for me to ask for work and watch out for any evidence of our friends. She said, "They should not harm a young girl who has no history of revolutionary work. If you think you can do it, we need to find out about our men."

I dug deeply for courage and asked, "When do I go?" She smiled and then dressed me as a young girl.

The jail was in Hoi An, and it was a nervous forty-five minute journey. It was midafternoon when I finally got to the town. I anxiously made my way along the streets past the market and a large pagoda and finally found myself in front of the military building. To me the building was huge. It had been built by the French using Vietnamese labor.

I was very nervous but determined. I walked up to the door, took a breath, and managed to knock on it. A soldier came to the door and looked down at me. With an irritated voice, he demanded to know what I wanted. I nervously asked, "May I please speak to the person in charge?" I didn't understand why he did not slam the door in my face, but he instead laughed and asked the corporal of the guard if he had sent for any girl, "as a cute young one is here to see you."

A shiver traveled the entire length of my body as I heard the corporal yell to send me in for him to look over. Rudely, I was ushered in. The man sat behind a desk wearing small round glasses. He slowly took them off revealing equally small eyes. His cheeks were plump as was his body. He just watched me, waiting.

Trying to be apologetic, I asked the corporal, "Are you the person that I should see about applying for work?" I was shocked as his round face split by a venomous smile as he gave a great laugh and spat on the floor. Then he gave me a rag to clean up his spit and told me that this was a test. I took the rag and on my hands and knees cleaned the spot on the floor of his spittle. Then I felt a hand slap my bottom, and startled, I jumped to my feet. The two men in the room were laughing, and the corporal was barely able to control his amusement. He said I needed some fattening—"a little too skinny" was his comment.

Then he rose to his feet. His short round body was only a slight bit taller than mine. He grabbed me by the hair, jerked my head back, and glared into my face, his breath reeking with the odor of wine. His strength was frightening. My heart pounded with fear, and I tried to find courage.

He threateningly growled in a low and coarse voice, "Are you a communist?"

I choked and said, "No."

Then pulling me by the hair he threw open a door and half dragged me down a row of cells to one rear room with a closed door. There was a window in it, and he forced my face into it as he peered over my shoulder.

In horror, I saw four men tied to the ceiling by their wrists, naked. Their arms were held above their heads by ropes, and their toes barely touched the floor. Blood oozed from their mouths, heads, and feet. Government soldiers had large sticks and were viciously beating them, screaming at them to denounce communism. The corporal kept my face forced to the window and crudely whispered, "I can't wait until I can get a woman in prison here." Although fear made me speechless, and although I was repelled and sickened by this animal holding my hair, I was shocked even more when I saw that these tortured prisoners were our four friends from the village. At first, I hadn't recognized them with their faces so bloodied.

I gritted my teeth as fear was swallowed by anger, but I told myself not to betray the job Mother had given me. The corporal then slammed me into the wall and pressed his body close to mine. Pain shot through my body as the side of my head rocked off the brick. He talked in a low vulgar voice, saying, "When the communists were here, did you lose your virginity, girl? Or are you saving it for me?" Then he laughed.

I began to tremble but forced myself to remain calm. Stammering I said, "Sir, I am a poor farm girl, and my family needs money. I do not care about the communists; I only care about our next meal.'' I kept reminding myself of the job Mother had given me.

He looked closely at me and took me back to the front room. He said that he would talk to his sergeant, and then he grinned evilly, saying, ''Come back tomorrow if you want to work.''

I left the guard house and walked slowly until I was out of sight, across the river, and then sickened and angry, I ran all three miles back home. I felt nauseated by everything that I had just experienced. Purposefully, I walked into the sea fully clothed before I went home. I wanted to wash the sickness from me. I went to the ocean and dove into waist-deep water and swam for a short distance. Then slowly, I walked out and along the beach.

As I came up to my house, I found Mother and Grandmother anxiously waiting for me. They hugged me and, fearfully, asked what had happened. I still felt sick, dazed, and tired. Then the nausea welled up within me. I pulled away from them and ran to the back of the house and vomited all I had eaten. Ashamed and sick, I collapsed into Mother's arms and cried. She tenderly picked me up and carried me to my hammock and lay me down. Both Mother and Grandmother worriedly watched over me, and I saw tears in their eyes.

When I was finally able to speak, I told them all that had happened. Grandmother knelt beside me and held one hand. Mother held the other, and I saw angry tears roll down her face. She threw her head back and looked at the roof a moment with clenched teeth. Watching her, I quietly realized that she was refusing to allow herself to cry. With her free hand, she wiped her eyes and looked back at me.

She kissed me and said, ''Kim Lan, please forgive me for sending you. I should have known. You shall never have to go through that again. Stay with Grandmother and just rest. I need to go find your Grandfather and Ba Can.''

Later that night, the rest of our committee came together, and I told the assembled group of Grandfather, Bich, Ba Can, and Mother of all that had happened. Grandmother stood behind me and asked Mother, ''Did not this peace treaty you were talking about give all of us, men and women, the chance to vote, to be elected to office, and to campaign for others to be elected? What has happened?''

Mother replied, ''That's true, but these people are evil. I do not understand what they are doing! They dare not spit into the face of Uncle Ho and his army, not unless they have gotten support to do so from others.''

Grandfather looked at her and said, ''Who? Do you think America is the one?''

Mother said, ''We have beaten the French; they are the only ones left.'' She added, with sadness in her voice, ''It must be so, but I pray that we shall not have to fight again.''

Ba Can then firmly, but respectfully, said, ''If we had left last night as we discussed, our four friends would still be alive. They now are probably dead. I know several others who would go with us.'' He then looked around the room and asked, ''Will anyone go with me to the mountains while there is still time?''

Bich then said, ''I believe the only reason I am still here and alive is because I was in my boat shrimping all day until late. My wife told me that a soldier came by today and checked around the house. But how can I leave her?''

Ba Can said, ''If they take you tomorrow, will she be any better off then if you are in the mountains?''

Grandfather then said, ''Ba Can, find your friends tonight and go.''

He looked at Bich saying, ''If you wish to go with him, we will look after your wife. You still need friends in the villages, and we shall be that for you here. And my daughter, what about you?''

I held Mother's hand tightly and knew that where she would go, so also would I. She replied, ''I must remain, at least for a while longer. Safe homes have to be set up. Signals need to be agreed upon and some way to communicate. Then maybe I can join Ba Can and Bich.'' I spoke, and said that I would help Mother.

Before daybreak, a dozen men from the village, including Ba Can and Bich, disappeared. They would stop and get weapons from a small cache of rifles and ammunition that had been hidden after the peace treaty was signed. I had cried and hugged my older brother and said, "I will see you again, and we shall always have food ready whenever you might come."

Later that morning, Grandfather and I had work to do in the fields in preparation of the next planting season, while Grandmother took fish to the market in Hoi An. Mother left to see Hanh, Bich's wife, with the intent that they would go to comfort the wives of our men who had been taken to jail. It was hard to go to work with so many nightmarish things happening.

As Grandfather and I came to the large irrigation ditch outside our village, we noticed several people excitedly trying to get something out of the ditch next to the small bridge. Grandfather and I walked over and realized in shock that there were men's bodies floating in the brown water. As the naked bodies were pulled up on the land, Grandfather cried in rage as he recognized the swollen and battered corpses of our friends who had been taken to jail. There were three other men with us at this early hour, and all looked to Grandfather and angrily promised to help him in whatever ways they could. Grandfather was the secretary of our little village's Party, but I could only helplessly watch his bitterness and frustration. We had been a part of these men's lives and had known their fight for liberty and justice. The deep cuts and bruises bore testimony on their dead bodies of the justice that existed at the hands of the tyrants, who had risen again to rule over us.

By evening Grandfather had organized a large ceremony. Almost all the village responded and in a long burial train, paraded past the hated landlord's villa on the way to the graveyard. Little tom-toms sounded and bells chimed amid the fragrance of burned incense. There was much crying by the time we arrived at the site of the graves. Our friends were buried in graves mounded and shaped like sacred tortoises. Men and women knelt and bowed to the ground while the incense perfumed the air. I was greatly moved in pity and love for my people. Never had a burial ceremony meant more to me. I felt even more compelled to help fight the monsters who had returned.

The next day I went with Mother to see Bich's wife, Hanh. We intended to speak to her about what we should be doing to safely provide food and shelter for her husband, my brother, and the others who had gone to the mountains. When we arrived, neighbors had gathered and were angrily talking. They rushed to Mother and told us that Hanh had been taken away by a special police force. The people said that they had worn different uniforms than the soldiers and had taken Hanh toward Hoi An. Fearful that she may also be killed, Mother told me to take this information back to Grandfather and Grandmother and to wait for her to come back. She said she was going to Hoi An to find out what was happening, but that she did not want me there because of what had just happened to me. I argued with her. I cried, "You cannot go! They will realize that you were with the Viet Minh! They may even now be searching for you!" However, she insisted, and I had to obey.

I returned and finally found Grandmother and told her what had occurred. Grandfather had gone with a neighbor to help net shrimp, and we waited uneasily. When he returned at dark, Mother had not yet come back. It was too dangerous to travel at night with these soldiers and police suspecting anything that moved outside the villages in the dark. So we anxiously and sleeplessly waited, only occasionally dozing off. She did not return.

The next day all three of us went to Hoi An. We passed anxiously along the narrow streets past the rows of thatch and tin houses. When we came to the military post, I was told to wait at the pagoda a short distance away, while my grandparents went in. I wanted to go, but they insisted that I stay away.

They were gone for only a short time, yet it seemed forever. When I finally saw them coming down the street, making their way past people going to the market and street vendors, the looks on their faces spoke the worst. Fear, anxiety, and anger raced through every part of my body as Grandmother, trembling with tears running down her face, almost collapsed on the steps of the pagoda. Grandfather stood shaking with fists clenched, and I was almost frozen in fear when I saw a look of distant, dark hatred on his face that I had never seen before. He stood silently, threateningly looking off toward the end of the world. I held Grandmother and looked into her eyes and apprehensively asked her what had happened.

Her body convulsed in sobs as she told me that Hanh was still in jail, but that Mother had been taken by military vehicle to Da Nang, from where she was to be sent by ship to Con Son Prison Island. I shivered in disbelief. My body was ready to explode. Grandfather stood beside us waging a silent, fierce war within himself. His daughter, my mother, was now ripped from our lives again and taken away into the hands of torturers. Then anger and fear began to eat away at my sanity.

I couldn't move as I felt an uncontrollable grief quickly overwhelm my entire being. This was not possible! We had won the war, and Mother was home with me to stay. I felt tears flooding down my face. Then, as if in a numb, raging nightmare, I was running down the street. I felt nothing but an all-powerful need to strike out at the uniform of our enemy. Vaguely, on the edge of my vision, I sensed myself bumping into, running over, or past people, but that was another world and had no meaning. My whole being was focused on the military post by a force I didn't understand, nor did I care.

Like a wild animal, I threw myself hitting, clawing, and kicking into the face of the first policeman coming out of the door. I saw blood on his face, and I felt a heavy blow, but no pain. I was picking myself out of the dust and attacking again. I heard no sounds and felt nothing. Then I knew only a moment of blackness.

On the outer edge of my madness, I heard Grandfather yelling and felt Grandmother's arms and hands. In a blurred vision, I saw a rifle butt double Grandfather over. I tried to get up, but my body would not respond to the urgings of my mind. Somewhere from another world I heard a voice condemning us. I heard words, ''Rabble! Communists! Go to your homes; we have plans for you later.''

When I woke, the pain in my head throbbed. I saw Grandmother's concerned face. Glancing around, I realized that I was home, and I started to sit up. Quickly though, I eased myself back down as pain ripped through my head. For the next three days, Grandmother nursed me slowly back to health. I had a deep bruise on the side

of my head from a pistol butt. Grandfather was suffering
from broken ribs. I no longer was in the misty, vague
world of madness, totally absorbed by an insane desire
to kill that blocked out all other senses. I could think
again, and I could begin to calculate and plan.

One week later, we buried Hanh beside the others.
The horribly bloody and battered body of what was once
a beautiful young woman was dumped on our street.
There was a notice pinned to her naked breast stating
that those who did not renounce communism would die.
A sympathizer inside the police compound had told us
how she died. Arms bound behind her, she had been tied
by her hair to the ceiling so that she could barely stand
on her toes. Her clothes were ripped off, and she was
repeatedly beaten and raped with wine bottles time after
time. Her toes rested in a deep pool of her own blood
when she finally hung limp, dead.

Suddenly, I jumped to my feet, muffling a scream.
Cold sweat streamed down my forehead. I looked around
in the dark, and then slowly sat back down on the cot. I
was back in our mountain camp. It was 1966, but the
nightmare of my past continued to haunt me, and this
time I had willed it. I hadn't seen my mother for eleven
years, and I welcomed my hate of the enemy. Sometimes, however, the horror of the past was too much. I
spoke out loud to no one but myself. "I am alive, and I
now have a husband to live for, but soon I will also have
a chance to burn to the ground the jail that haunts me.
Maybe then there will be one less nightmare."

Yet, I couldn't sleep. So I walked around the camp
high in the mountains. I noticed Ba Can's lamplight
faintly burning through the narrow openings of his hut.
My brother was still awake going over plans. Sometimes,
I thought he had more than human strength.

I walked to a small clearing on the edge of the jungle
and looked out over miles of valleys below to see in the
distance the dark nighttime shapes of the Dai Loc Mountains where my husband was. I sat on the grass and
stared. "Van Thi, my husband," I said. "Why aren't

you here when I need you? Is our life to be such that we will only see each other for a week every six months? Why, why must it be so?''

CHAPTER 6

The enemy's hopes are bankrupt, we have reached an
important point when the end begins to come into view.
—General William Westmoreland (1968)

*T*he dead had body-bagged it to Da Nang. Me? I just
sat outside my An Hoa tent, drinking a not-so-cold beer,
and watching the hills fade in and out between clouds of
dust. Marines were dead, Marines were hurt, but that
dark-eyed tigress was out there roaming the mountains
somewhere. I could see her still: long hair flying around
her body as she shouted commands and challenged our
weapons to take her out. I didn't like how she seemed to
be carving a niche for herself in my mind. I didn't understand it. There was a deeper meaning, and I didn't
know what the hell it was.

From opposite corner of my mind, I heard Red crying
again. He had held Rodriquez's body, intestines lying in
his lap. My radio operator's right leg had been shattered,
but he hadn't seemed to notice. Red had determined to
go back in the body-bag bird. He would never leave his
buddy. Alexander had also been taken out on the same
bird. He left part of his brain on "No-Name Hill," and
I knew part of my soul would be forever planted there.
A certain fatalism settled around me like a fog as I continued to stare off into the high mountains. It was like

preordained fact: someday I would be going up there, far above the battlegrounds.

Lance Corporal Williams came around the side of my tent and squatted beside my chair. I could feel his eyes on me, and then he quietly looked off at the hills. Finally, he said, ''What's gonna happen, Lieutenant? We're down to six people counting you and me. We going back out there?''

I drank the last swallow of my beer, crushed the can without much thinking, and looked around at him. If there was anyone who could have been a tiger hunter, it was this one. For a long second, I looked at him trying to get my mouth in gear with my brain.

Then finally, I managed, ''Williams, I've never said to your face that you're the best point man I've ever seen, but I'm saying it now. I shoulda told Alexander and Rodriquez and Red how much I thought of 'em. They were good people. I'm gonna get you made a corporal, and you're my squad leader as of now. Battalion's sending us three new people, and it sounds like maybe in a couple of days we'll be going back out there some-fucking-where.

''Shit, Williams, everybody's minds have got to be scrambled more than they're showing. How they really doing?''

He drew a bunch of nothing on the ground with a stick while he talked and just kinda stared through the earth. ''Everybody's shook. Sanchez and Garcia were real tight with Rodriquez. They're taking it pretty hard. Peterson just talks about Alexander. He saw the brains blown out of his head. And Doc, well, he's the saltiest. He seen shit with the grunts before he came to Recon. He's okay.''

''How 'bout you?'' I asked.

Slowly, a grin spread over his light brown face as he continued to casually watch his scribbling in the dirt. His curly black hair was kept cut so short that it was almost shaved. He was still squatting as he turned his coal black eyes up to mine and said, ''Williams? That son of a bitch is okay. You don't run point for as long as I have and not get a tough hide.''

His smile didn't leave his face as he continued. ''I was looking over the top of that fucking hill before the choppers came in this morning. I found this stuff on one of the gook bodies: this picture and letter. A Kit Carson scout translated it for me when we got back here. The picture is the gook's family back in his home. The scout wrote down a translation. I'll read it:

> "Dear Mother and Father,
>   I am often homesick and have worried for you when I heard of the American bombing of our home. Do not worry about me though. I am fine. We even make nougat in a pan over our camp fire. In fact, we always argue when to take the pan off the fire. The syrup is brown and hardens around the peanuts and is delicious. Then we make coffee while the nougat cools. I feel very close to my friends, and I am proud to be a soldier. Tomorrow I will finish this letter. We must go now. I love you."

Williams handed the picture and letter to me. Then his smile evaporated and he said, "Lieutenant, I don't want this shit. Could you give it to the S-2 or something? Maybe they can get something out of it. I just can't carry this around."

He stood up, handed it to me, and walked away. I watched him head back toward the men and then looked at the picture. It was a family photo. A fucking family photo of our enemies! There was the mother and father, two boys and one girl. The smallest boy looked a lot like a brother of an old girlfriend. Williams, I thought, if there was anything I needed right now, it wasn't this.

Taking some matches, I made a tiny funeral pyre out of the paper with the photo on top. Then I burned it, and thought to myself, Fuck the S-2; let the kid rest in peace.

I thought about her again. I saw her naked by the pond ready to blow the shit out of the chopper and me but not doing it. I saw her in the middle of her troops leading their charge against "No-Name Hill." I looked into the mountains and asked out loud, "Hey, lady, who are you? Why aren't you back with your family? What were you doing naked with a rifle to your shoulder?" Then I paused before adding, "Someday, let's you and me talk, okay?"

I got up from my chair and walked toward the tent housing the battalion beer parlor mumbling, "If we see each other again, I hope you don't shoot my ass off, lady."

The next morning found me in the S-3 shop. The ops officer, a Major Whitehouse, discussed with me the possibilities of a patrol up that narrow valley past the Nong Son coal mines. It wasn't but a couple miles wide and hemmed in by four- to five-thousand-foot mountains. Right down the middle ran the Thu Bon river. Whitehouse was new in-country. He stood about three inches taller than me and was Marine Corps green through and through. He talked tough and businesslike. He proudly said, "Lieutenant, I bet we get a couple of Medals of Honor out of that last battle. I'm damn proud of our troops. But we gotta keep pushing Charlie. I wanta send you up the valley past the coal mines. The COs interested in checking out the villages farther out there."

He wanted me to go down into the fucking valley. No fucking way, man! After a not-so-short argument, I finally won a compromise by agreeing to get as close as I could to them while remaining in the lower foothills. We would be quickly stirred-and-fried on the valley floor with all of its villages and unfriendly faces.

That afternoon, my three replacements arrived. One would go into each of the three teams. My new radio operator was named Rivers. A PFC Hatch would move into the point team with Williams and Peterson. Lance Corporal Trevino would replace Rodriquez. At least our TMT could be reconstituted. Peterson would now take point while Williams took command of that team.

Late in the afternoon, Williams and I went for a helicopter recon of the valley. We christened the place "Antenna Valley" for its long, rodlike appearance from the air as it pointed from An Hoa toward the jungles of Laos. The valley seemed to be a quiet, peaceful place with Vietnamese farming their paddies. But we knew they gave a portion of their rice to the VC.

We checked out every fucking nook and cranny around the lower hills and found shit for landing zones. There was one little dead-end cup of land stuck up a draw and covered with elephant grass that we finally opted for. It was pretty far out. I was not enthusiastic about the proposition, but there weren't any real choices.

We could see from a distance the upper reaches of the valley and flew in that direction which would bring us very near the jungle-covered Laotian border. I wanted to see the "free-fire zone" I had heard about. As we came near, and before we circled to return down the valley, I saw a pockmarked landscape. It looked like a disease had chewed up the land: an earth-pox.

Williams cupped his hands around his mouth and yelled above the chopper noise, "What the hell happened down there?"

Yelling back, I answered, "That's what you call a free-fire zone. Any aircraft wanting to dump its load of bombs can do so in that area without clearance."

"Man," he said, "I bet we got lotsa amigos out here!"

As we flew back, I estimated that there were probably five to six thousand people living in scattered hamlets up and down this long, skinny valley, maybe more.

The next day Williams and I went over the patrol route with the squad. Everyone was showing some anxiety about it, and Williams summed things up when he said, "Those little motherfuckers out there have been living with the VC for twenty years, and they got a hard-on for us. Best everybody keep their goddamn brain-housing group squared away." Regardless of the nervousness, no one bitched, and they all prepared like the professionals they were.

The following morning was still dark in the west and turning orange behind us as we rode our green birds up the narrow Antenna Valley. Despite the early hour, the temperature hovered in the mid-eighties and the humidity was higher yet.

We all looked like bad fucking news: painted faces, bush hats pulled low, and rifles at the ready. I was beginning to get my confidence up and thought of that famous old Bible quote: Yea, though I walk through the Valley of the Shadow of Death, I shall fear no evil, 'cause I'm the meanest motherfucker in the Valley.

But try as I may, a few butterflies still fluttered around my stomach. I worried about the LZ we had picked. It had looked bad, but we wouldn't know how bad until we jumped out of our birds.

Then I saw it coming up around the corner of a hill, and we were going in low. In seconds we were close to the ground and jumped. It always amazed me how those pilots could get themselves away so damn fast and leave us so fucking alone. And we were!

Now I knew we were in dangerous shit. Williams had the point team moving uphill through head-high elephant grass that sliced through our gloves like razors. It was like we were trying to push our way through mother-fucking pampas grass. Rivers was behind me, desperately trying to contact the battalion over his backpacked PRC-25. It was useless. Our LZ was a dead pocket. The nine of us pushed as fast as we safely could to get to higher ground. We were in a bowl that trapped the heat and humidity and blocked all radio transmissions.

Shit, Lord, I thought, don't let any Charlie see us now. I felt like that fat rat, surrounded by four-hundred-pound cats.

By midmorning, we got up to a saddle in the hill. Behind us to our northeast where we had just come from, about eight miles down the valley, was An Hoa. Mountains rose up immediately in front of our noses to our left and dared us to come any farther. Our mission wouldn't let us go up there, but we had to get more distance between us and our LZ—and get radio contact with some friendly ears.

Finally, we moved to our right getting out of the miserable sea of six-foot grass and into the jungle going up the last little hill that overlooked the valley floor. Sweat had washed our camouflage greasepaint down our faces in dirty streaks, and we still had no radio contact. Worried that we could run into VC without any communication with the battalion, I pushed the patrol on, working up the hill. There were no trails, which meant that we might be by ourselves. At least we might have some breathing room.

The jungle undergrowth was thick, and the trees towered high over our heads. We were trying to move as quickly, but as silently, as we could. Williams ran the point team, and I continued to gain respect for this Marine; no one could match him. He was 6 feet 2 inches tall, lean but muscular, with a smooth light cocoa skin. His ever-present, almost shy smile did not reveal the adeptness he had in silently moving like death through the jungles.

About halfway up the hill, we all froze; the hair on my neck went stiff. Something, or someone, was approaching through the jungles to our rear, making a loud ruckus. We dropped to the ground, slithering into the leaves and rotting wood lower than the leeches. Then racing through the midtree level above us, about fifty feet up, we saw a wild, crazy troop of monkeys. It looked as if they had silver heads, hands, and feet, with black hair on the rest of their bodies. I felt a little foolish and signalled the patrol to continue.

Finally, about six hours after landing, we made radio contact with our home base, and set-up on the jungle hilltop. We weren't but about three hundred feet off the valley floor, still in thick jungle under towering trees, but we would be able to patrol close to the paddies and climb some trees to watch the villages from around our little base camp.

Once I was assured that the patrol was well positioned, I was about ready to collapse when I heard Peterson not-so-silently cursing. Going over, I found him with a cigarette in one hand and his prick in the other. He was torching a bloated leech off the head of that very sensitive organ which was already turning purple. Although the leech had a strong mouth-lock hold, it quickly loosened its grip and fell to the earth suffering tail burns from the cigarette. As Peterson squashed it into a bloody mess under his boot, he looked at me and said, "I wish the little cocksucker woulda had a bigger mouth."

I returned to my team almost laughing but at the same time a little nauseous and decided to check myself thoroughly. There was nothing so obnoxious as finding a half-dozen leeches, bloated with your blood, hanging off your body, and I found them. At least I could be thankful that none had gotten quite as adventurous as the one on Peterson.

For two days, we patrolled from that hill in various directions toward the valley, often having to climb trees to get better views. But the hill served as our base, as there was nowhere else that we were able to establish radio communication with our battalion.

There were a lot of signs of human activity in the valley, but we observed no VC military units. Apparently, the openness of the valley was too much for them during the day. There was no doubt, though, that they had free access through it and used it for a source of supplies. We knew they had to be around, and the patrol remained very damn cautious and painfully quiet.

After three days, nothing had been seen. It was like we were in the halls of Congress and everybody was on vacation. It would have been easier on our nerves had we seen some bad guys. This not being able to find anything was wearing on us—there had to be some shit around.

We were due to be extracted on the evening of the fourth day, and that morning, I decided to take a four-man patrol a little higher into the mountains. I knew the battalion S-3 would want more than "we didn't see a thing," when everybody knew Charlie ran the countryside out here.

So, I grabbed TMT, and we shoved off. We worked back toward the mountains—down to the saddle and then through the tall grass and boulders to the jungles on the other side. Then, cautiously, we began our upward climb. There still were no trails.

After about three hours of slow moving, Garcia signalled quietly for me to come up. He was overlooking a stream. It was just below us a hundred feet, and there looked like a wide trail running along beside it. Jungle canopy blocked all sunlight, and the undergrowth was still thick. We knelt on the damp dirt, peering through the vines and leaves of about ten million jungle plants of various shades of green. But we managed to position ourselves to watch that trail, and decided to stay still for a while.

Not fifteen minutes went by before an enemy patrol of ten men was spotted moving up the trail. Every one of them carried a rifle but walked rather casually. They continued on until disappearing not too far away. I talked to the team and decided to carefully move farther up the mountainside staying a little higher than the trail to see if we could find anything.

No one walked tall. We were either bent over or crawling, but we quietly managed to move around, under, or through the bush and used up about thirty minutes doing it. There wasn't much time to go farther and hope to get back to our base on time. We saw no more enemy on the trail below us. Finally, I decided we had gone far enough by about noon, and we set-up just to gulp down a Hershey bar. Not wanting to make any noise opening cans of C-rations or to take too much time, I had told everybody to bring candy, and that's what we ate while we sat covered by the umbrellalike plants. So we sat, each facing a different direction, and quietly ate our chocolate.

After ten minutes, I was about ready to give the signal to backtrack when my blood went cold. Voices. Vietnamese voices were drifting down from above us.

A loud *crack* snapped near me. I quickly glanced around. Sanchez grimaced. He must have broken a fucking branch. Shit! They had to have heard. I listened; we all listened. The voices had stopped, but they continued walking. We heard footsteps go past us maybe thirty feet away. Vaguely, I could catch sporadic glimpses of uniforms through the bush. There must have been six or seven of 'em.

We didn't intend to ambush anyone. Our mission was to gather information and to leave without Charlie knowing we had been around. I prayed they hadn't heard us. There had to be a trail just ahead that we hadn't known was there. I wished we had gone the extra thirty feet and found it. Surprises scared the shit out of me.

Then they were gone. The jungle was so fucking quiet. I thought to myself, Collins, get the fuck outta there.

Slowly we followed our path back, crawling at first. We watched the trail below but saw not a soul. It didn't feel right. I heard myself mumbling, ''Shit, hell, damn, fuck, piss.''

Over the next three hours, as fast as we could move quietly, the patrol pushed through the bush. Finally, we made it back to the saddle near our base camp. We radioed Williams we were coming in.

Once back, we regrouped ourselves with the other five,

and I explained what we found to my squad leader. The choppers were due in about sixty minutes, and we decided to move down to watch the boulder and grass covered saddle that was to be our LZ. I couldn't shake the feeling that they might have heard us and found our trail. It took about fifteen minutes to get packed and organized.

I was suddenly shocked by bursts of gunshots and the impact of bullets smashing into the ground around me. Scrambling with my rifle, lying flat, I looked first toward the jungle and then up into the pale face of my radio operator, Rivers. He stood beside me with his rifle hot in his hands and pointed into the brush about thirty feet away. I saw a body draped over a log. Quickly, we checked the area. There was just one. He wore a uniform with a soft bush hat and carried an AK-47 rifle. He was dead.

Rivers said, "He was just standing there. I thought he was one of us out to take a leak. Then he opened up with his AK. Scared the piss out of me."

The Viet Cong, or North Vietnamese, whoever he was, shot very poorly that day, but I figured that he had to have come up the same way we had to go down.

Williams said, "He found our trail, and there's probably others behind down there where we gotta go."

We didn't have any option. Before moving out, I reported by radio that we had made contact with VC and were moving to the landing zone. Quietly, we threw on our packs and cautiously moved down the hillside. Snaking our way from tree to bush to tree, we moved off the top and lost all radio contact with our battalion. We could not have it again until the choppers came overhead. We all were alert. VC could be anywhere in front of us, coming in our direction, as we were going in theirs.

Finally we reached the edge of the tree line and very carefully peered through the last barrier of jungle to check out our LZ. We had crossed this hundred-yard stretch of boulders and grass not but an hour before. Where the dry razor grass ended, the jungles abruptly began again, rising upward with the mountain slopes. This had been the path for my little patrol. We now had the hilltop behind us, those mountains across the saddle to our front, and steep slopes down to the valley draws on either side.

Rivers suddenly grabbed my arm and pointed to a clump of boulders by the edge of the jungle on the far side of the saddle. There were three VC with rifles just disappearing around the rocks and moving into the trees away from us.

We lay silently on our side, just within the jungle's edge. In the heat, the insects buzzed around us, but no one moved. No one spoke. We were set-up as best as we could be in that hole. The rear team was about thirty meters behind us, a little farther up the hill, covering our backside. The point team and mine lay quietly behind trees. I listened to the silence—like a hot, dusty weight it rested uneasily on my shoulders.

Stoically, I watched an ant crawl across my hand and was bitten by other insects while we waited for our birds. Finally, Rivers leaned over to whisper that he was in radio contact with the choppers. The radio was turned down low. I took the receiver and placed myself behind a tree and whispered to them. Then I saw 'em clearly. There were two CH-46s, each big enough to carry the entire team. I told the lead pilot about our previous enemy contact, but that there was no firing at this time.

I spoke quietly into the radio. "Why don't you fly over the LZ, but at a thousand feet, and see if you draw any fire?" They agreed.

As the birds came over, a hailstorm of automatic weapons fire burst out of the jungles across our LZ in front of us and from the lower ground on both sides. "Shit," Rivers said, "the assholes are all over!" I spoke with the pilot and reported what had happened.

He said, "We're low on fuel. Returning to our base to refuel."

"Like hell!" I almost screamed. "We don't have radio contact with anyone but you. Get somebody else out here before you leave." Within a few minutes a light observation plane was overhead talking to us, the choppers were gone, and I was very damn nervous and pissed—out of fucking fuel, shit!

For the next twenty to thirty minutes that pilot called in one of the best air shows I had ever seen. Artillery was useless out here, but a pair each of F-4s, F-8s and A-4s screamed down the hillside behind us and abruptly up the mountain in front, almost touching the hundred-foot tall trees. The boulders and jungle-front facing us were cremated with rockets and napalm. The valley draws were also hit. The Fourth of July couldn't have been better!

As the jets were finishing, our 46s were back on station and coming in. I spoke with the pilot and said, "I'd recommend that you come with one bird, and the whole patrol get on it, and let's not do two trips in and out with both your choppers. If any VC recover from the bombing runs, they'd probably get the second chopper, but the first might slip in and out." He agreed.

As he came quickly down with his thundering *wop-wop-wop*, it was obvious that the huge machine would not be able to sit down on the narrow ridgeline strewn with boulders and tall grass. He hovered with both the side and rear hatches open. The patrol jumped, stumbled, clambered, and were pulled aboard as the chopper, like a nervous wild stallion, hung and bounced about three to four feet off the ground. Then we were off. I held my breath till we cleared the valley.

Williams looked at me, grinned, his snow-white teeth gleaming through his fading facepaint, and said, "Like I said, there's a pisspot of bad motherfuckers out here, all with a hard-on for us."

We were scheduled to be back in camp for three days, and this had been Doc's last patrol. He was rotating home; back to the World. I took twenty-four hours off and went with him back to Camp Reasoner at Da Nang. I needed to check in with the Third Recon Battalion, but that was mainly an excuse to catch a John Meyers's night on the town.

We got back in the early afternoon, but Meyers was gone to China Beach for an afternoon of R&R. So I checked in to the S-3 and then to the company.

By supper, Meyers had brought his big hulk back complaining about a sunburn, but in between he said, "Talk to me about An Hoa. Course the only way to talk is with brew in your hands—so let's go get one or seven or so."

We walked over to our mess hall/club, which was nothing more than a giant, strong-backed tent. As we sat down, he said, "I hear you been chasing a woman around the hills down there. You gonna explain?"

"I don't know how to, John. I think she's got under my skin. Like some kinda mystery that's sucked me in as a player, and I didn't even ask to be in the game. Only in this ballpark, a body can die."

"Have you seen her? I mean like close enough to recognize her if you saw her again? What's she like?"

I stared into my beer, talking to the can. "The first time I saw her, no one else did, just me. She was standing naked, long black hair flowing around her. There was a lake next to us. We were in a clearing in the middle of the jungle and were running like crazy from a whole pisspot full of Charlie. She had a rifle to her shoulder, and was ready to blast holes in our chopper as we were leaving. But she didn't. Just lowered her rifle and watched us. That scene has chiselled itself into my memory. It's almost hypnotizing to think about. You're the only person I've told that to."

"My God!" he replied. "Son of a fucking bitch! What a scene! It oughta be in a movie!"

I smiled weakly and continued, "Then we ran into her on that hill over the coal mines. She commanded that VC company like Chesty Puller and stood in the face of our fire giving orders like she was in control of the whole situation. Shit, Alexander threw a grenade at her feet before he took it through the running lights, but she just kicked it into a hole before it blew up."

"My God, I bet she'd be a good fuck," John mumbled looking into his beer.

"A good fuck!" I answered. "Shit, Meyers, is that all you can think about? Man, that woman would cut your balls off just as soon as look at you. Anyway, I must wake up every other night dreaming about her."

"With a hard-on I bet."

"Stuff it, you asshole. Let's go downtown or somewhere that's got more fucking atmosphere than this tent."

"Sure, sounds good, but let me check with my sergeant and make sure he covers for me."

Long evening shadows were creeping across the camp

as we walked toward the motor transport pool. One of his corporals was in the office, but he couldn't find the sergeant. Finally, after a lot of hemming and hawing, John got out of him that the sergeant was in downtown Da Nang at his "girlfriend's."

"Shit," John exclaimed, "this broad he calls his girlfriend screws every swinging dick she can find, and there's a thousand miles of it around here. He's gonna get 'black syphilis' one of these days."

"Is this the pot calling the kettle black?" I asked.

"Fuck you, Collins. Let's go down there. I know he's been there for hours. He's had time to get his rocks off two or three times. Time he came back, and I know where she lives."

By the time Meyers and I had left and found our way along the narrow streets of Da Nang, it was dark. The streetscape was dimly lit by only a very few lights, mainly those lamps shining from within buildings. A few trees grew between the uncoordinated and motley mass of shacks, buildings, and open sewage ditches. People milled about while street vendors walked around and sold their wares.

Finally Meyers stopped in front of one building and said, "He's in here. There's the jeep. I'll get him, and you can watch the wheels."

I looked at Meyers go up the stairs and thought to myself, the son of a bitch sure knows his way down these backstreets right up to this door. However, it wasn't a minute before I was surrounded by about a dozen Vietnamese.

I never felt comfortable when Vietnamese gathered around, and I gripped my pistol even though I left it holstered. Each one of them was trying to tell me something from candy to a virgin sister. I turned in my seat being very watchful, trying to keep one eye on the people in the light around the jeep, and the other on the shadows a little distance away. Still, I tried to be friendly. I didn't really want to buy anything; I didn't trust them or their products.

Shortly, I heard a strange cry from a street vendor coming around the corner. He came up to me and explained in broken English that he was selling *hot vit lon*,

half-hatched duck eggs. He was very proud of this delicacy and thought that I should buy one or more at a dollar
each and love to eat them. This was the first time I had
ever heard of *hot vit lon*. Then I realized what he was
describing to me. Good Lord! There was no way that I
was going to eat a whole and almost raw baby duck with
little feathers that had its life stopped in the shell just
short of hatching. The man, however, pushed the subject
and showed me how he kept these "hard-boiled eggs"
warm in a basket of rice husk. He even offered me a shot
of rice wine with which to wash it down, along with salt
and pepper for seasoning.

In order to try to win friends and not insult anyone, I
compromised and told him that I would buy an egg for
each of the dozen people around the jeep at a reduced
price. He agreed to three for a dollar, although I felt that
I was still being taken. Then I watched in amazement at
how the people ate these things with such relish! I almost
gagged watching 'em.

Then Meyers was coming out of the house. He walked
up to the driver's seat, got in and said, "I found him
sitting in there eating some Vietnamese shit-food. He's
going back now, so let's you and me go to the White
Elephant. Speaking of shit-food, how about them baby
ducks. Man, you talk about sick! I'd rather have a dripping prick than eat half-roasted baby ducks still in the
shell. Crap! Makes me gag."

As we pulled away, I was still trying to be friendly and
waved good-bye, smiling to everybody. Halfway to the
club, I checked the time. "Shit," I bellowed, "those
little assholes lifted my fucking watch. I buy 'em baby
ducks to eat, and they steal my fucking watch!"

At that moment, thunder rolled along the ground some
distance behind us. We stopped and turned in our seats.
Balls of fire were now ascending into the night sky from
the airbase.

"That's the goddamn airstrip," John said.

"Jesus, Mary, and Joseph," I added, "Charlie's on
the fucking landing strip! But maybe it's just rockets.
Maybe they're not there in person."

We watched from about three miles. It was a very
strange and sobering experience. All hell was blowing

up, and we were spectators. We decided to return to
Camp Reasoner.

Passing within a half-mile of the base perimeter, it was
obvious that it was only a rocket attack, but Christ-
almighty, it looked like they hit everything. Jets were
burning. Buildings were burning. A lot of fucking money
was burning up. I wondered if any barracks were hit,
and then I remembered Doc. I hoped he had gotten out
earlier and wasn't in the middle of that shit. What a miserable deal of the cards—to be waiting for a plane out of
'Nam, and have Charlie blow the plane and air terminal
to hell right down around your ears!

CHAPTER 7

> I swear to fight to my last breath,
> To erase from the land of the South,
> Even the shadow of a foreign soldier,
> To bring bread, peace, liberty over
> . . . my sacred Motherland.
>   —Lien Nam, *I Am a Fighter of the Liberation Army*

It was useless to try to sleep. Slowly, I walked under the half-moon, near the edge of the jungle and looked out over the valleys far beneath. The grass was soft, and I sat leaning against a rock that was as large as I was. Alone in the moonlight, my dreams reached out to capture my husband. Aching for him, I imagined his arms around me and drifted in thoughts of our wedding day.

The presence of the war, however, could never be escaped. Explosions in the darkness from an enemy bombing attack erupted miles below in the valley. Then a few people passed by like specters, quietly moving through the shadows and trees, bringing information and supplies under the cover of the friendly night. I followed them back into the camp. Standing within the dark shadows of the jungle's giant umbrella, I glanced around the camp. Dim light shone furtively here and there between cracks in doorways that momentarily opened and then quickly closed. As a soft breeze gently stirred the trees, I gradually made my way back to bed and lay down. Closing my eyes, my thoughts floated on the currents of the wind that were stirring around my hut.

The next morning the songs of birds high above in the

trees awakened me, and I was quickly up. Looking out, I could see the long, slim shafts of sunlight slicing through trees that towered into the heavens. I made myself ready and walked over to Ba Can's command center. I glanced at the men in the building and wished that another woman was in the command group. Except for me, Ba Can had the women working only with support units in his battalion. I picked up a metal cup, filled it with hot tea, and sat down to listen as my brother talked excitedly with subordinates.

Ba Can reported that last evening one of our rocket platoons had taken the newly arrived 122mm rockets into a valley near the Dai Loc Mountains. Ba Can exclaimed, "The Americans and their puppets did not know we had these, but they do now!" He laughed and described in detail the attack. Our men had fired fifty rockets into the main Da Nang airbase. Intelligence teams had received copies of the American "after-action" reports which showed that the rockets had destroyed ten aircraft, damaged forty, destroyed thirteen barracks, an ammo supply point, and killed or wounded one hundred and eighty-four Americans. Our unit that had launched the rockets had slipped away without receiving one casualty.

"We are showing our people that we can do battle with the Americans," Ba Can said with satisfaction. "Wait until they see us destroy the hated prison in Hoi An. We shall take revenge, and the enemy will choke on his own blood."

I watched my brother. His eyes flashed. It was contagious, and I again felt the excitement and anticipation of impending battle. Ba Can had given me the responsibility of commanding the raid but had also informed me of his intent to be there.

"I have business that is unfinished in Hoi An," he said. The dark look of eager hatred on his face was enough to cause anyone to back away and shudder.

For the next seven days, we laid plans, debriefed scouts, and rehearsed our men. There were twelve hundred prisoners that we meant to free. Our information was that none had committed crimes against the people, but all had been thrown in jail for the political purposes of the puppet Saigon government. We had captured uniforms of the lackey ARVN soldiers, and our plan was to infiltrate my two remaining platoons into the city dressed as enemy. At the designated time, we would attack while a platoon of our mortars pounded the quarters of the soldiers and their American advisors.

After a week of preparation, we moved out of the mountains. Carefully, we infiltrated the countryside near Hoi An. Many of my men had come from this area, and I made sure that each team had at least one person who was familiar with the city. By teams we eased into the outskirts of the town. Safe homes had been established, and each team was to enter a home in the early evening hours to remain there hidden in underground shelters until two hours before midnight. Then we were to move to our assembly point at the pagoda from our various positions around the city. I anxiously moved through the town and set myself in a friend's home across from the pagoda.

I watched the old temple thinking of its many memories. But soon had to put the old behind me and concentrate on the business at hand. At the appointed time Ba Can arrived, and the teams reported in. I personally set them in attack positions. Occasionally, I looked at Ba Can. His face was almost contorted in a picture of quiet, calculating hatred. He had become a dominating figure in the revolution, and to look at the coldness in his eyes made me think I no longer knew him. My brother had been transformed by years of warfare, and for a brief moment I wondered about myself.

It took almost an hour for all the teams to come together and regroup into the two platoons. It was time. At one hour prior to midnight, we heard the dull whistles of our incoming mortars. At the moment of the first explosion, we were running. My first platoon crashed through the doors of the prison, having first blown them with satchel charges. Quickly and efficiently, the second platoon set up outside the barracks to ambush those soldiers who fled the exploding mortars. In minutes the prison area was in chaos. Prisoners were running in streams out of the jail, at least those who could run. Many seemed to be crippled or too weak. We helped those and gave directions. Squads began to organize our released friends and lead them away, and others laid down a covering fire.

Things were happening so fast that I couldn't be aware of everything, and I hoped that our training and preparation were working and would carry us through. Everything was total confusion around me, and all too soon it was time to quickly and carefully move along our preplanned routes out of the city. As we began to backtrack, I made sure that fires had been started in the prison.

I stood near the door of the burning building and fired my rifle at any soldier who tried to come out. I felt my teeth clench in anger as years of hatred burst through the barrel of my AK-47. I wanted no part of this building to remain standing. I wanted to kill all of those who had killed my family, and my anger fueled the fires that were growing inside the place. The night skies were now becoming bright from the flames of the torture cells of the Saigon government.

Standing for a moment in the center of the main street holding my rifle at my waist, I felt a surge of strength and satisfaction at some measure of revenge that I had been able to pour out on the murderers of my mother and family. I watched in pleasure as the hated prison vomited flames. The teams laying down the covering fire began now to withdraw, and I pulled back with them. But I occasionally glanced back at the burning of old nightmares.

At the river, the prisoners were already being ferried across. My platoon commanders were doing their jobs. I looked for Ba Can but did not find him. Questioning my soldiers, I could find no one who had seen him since the fighting. I became increasingly worried and grabbed one team and told them to follow me back into town.

We moved quickly through the shadows, the burning prison serving as a beacon. Still uniformed as ARVN soldiers, we encountered little difficulty. The townspeople were nervous but remained in their homes. However, soldiers and government officials were now cautiously moving around. They looked like leaderless fools.

Now we were near the pagoda. The barracks and prison were not far away. As I rounded a corner of the old temple, I noticed a person in the flickering shadows only about twenty feet away. Cautioning my men to remain still, I moved closer.

It was Ba Can. He stood over a man who cowered in fear on the floor. I looked more closely and saw that the man was wounded, and I watched morbidly spellbound. Ba Can was laughing and the man pleading.

I heard the man cry, saying, "No, I do not know you or your family!"

Ba Can laughed again and said, "You lie. You have been here for years. I've seen you, you fat pig. Your face is etched into my mind like the face of Buddha on these statues. I know you, and I've waited for years to cut your fat body. The rings on your fingers speak of the wealth you have taken from our people."

The man started to cry again, but Ba Can crushed his mouth with the butt of his rifle. The blow was so forceful that it stunned me. At first I thought that the rifle had splintered, but then realized that it had been the sound of bone and teeth cracking. I stood still in the shadows.

Then Ba Can cut through the man's pants. With one hand he grabbed the man's penis, and with his knife in the other, he quickly cut it off. I stood dazed at the level of hate that poured out of my brother. He then jammed the small bloody stump into the man's crushed mouth, and then with his knife slit the poor, slobbering fool's throat. I stood dazed by the flood of hatred.

At that moment, immediately behind me, rifles began to sharply snap the eerie stillness. Instantly, I wheeled about and dropped to one knee, rifle at the ready. My men shouted, "Government soldiers! We must leave."

Three government soldiers lay dead not thirty feet away, and I shouted, "Ba Can, come this way." I jumped down from the pagoda and landed running, yelling for them to move to a side street across from the temple building. I turned to look for my brother.

Flying out of the shadows of the pagoda he came laughing. He leaped high and far, landing in the street, and ran past me shouting, "Come little sister, our mother, father, and grandparents are at least partially avenged." There was not time to think as we ran down dark, narrow, dirt streets past rows of thatch or tin huts. The people stayed inside.

We got to the river as the last ferry was leaving. Jumping on, we set up men with rifles at the rear of the boat to watch for any enemy. It took ten minutes to get across, and there was no time to relax. It was only midnight, but we had to organize the people who had escaped and begin to move toward the mountains. Speed was essential, but not easy with close to a thousand escapees on our hands.

By dawn, we had reached the foothills. We knew the enemy would have observation planes up during the day, so we placed everyone in the tree-covered valleys and ravines. Little streams and pools of water provided some relief to the dirty, thirsty group of former prisoners. We had enough of a rice cache in the area for a little food. We intended to spend the daylight hours here, out of sight, and then to move into the mountains after dark.

We had nine hundred and six men, and fifty-two women. Many were sick or suffered from wounds inflicted on them in prison. Almost two hundred and fifty prisoners were not accounted for, and I presumed that they had either been recaptured or had escaped on their own. We were missing five men from our original force of sixty-five.

That evening, about half of our escapees elected to try to return to their villages, while the remaining wanted to go into the mountains with us. About one-third had actively supported the revolution in the past, but the balance had been ordinary villagers whom the puppet government had thrown into jail. The government feared these people were giving support to us. Now our main problem would be to provide food, clothing, weapons, and training for these new recruits.

However, while we waited and organized, I sensed a growing restlessness within myself. It was like ants had gotten under my skin and were crawling around within me. Before we started out that evening, I lay back and began to try to understand whatever it was that made me so uneasy. Then slowly as I thought about the previous night, I began to see myself shooting and killing and gaining pleasure in it. I heard again Grandfather's warning not to allow hatred to control my life. Suddenly I felt revulsion at myself. I knew that I had allowed to happen what he had cautioned me to guard against. It was as if an evil, hateful spirit had begun to use my mind and body. I had seen the sickness it caused to others, and my stomach felt slimy inside me.

As the sunlight began to paint new colors on the western sky, I sat alone. I held my head and tried to think through my confusion. At times, I had grown weary of year after year of war, destruction, and barely escaping capture, torture, and death. I wanted it to end. I remembered clearly the death of my grandmother, and Grandfather's final words. It was at a time when I had naively attempted to gain support for the revolution from my aunt and her family in Da Nang. It was the last time I had visited that large seaport.

I drifted in my thoughts, and I could almost feel the sights, sounds, and smells of the big city. I was still young then and had been excited about the thought of sharing our revolution with my extended family. Now again, I could feel myself walking the nighttime streets of Da Nang. I was there, and I could sense the certain thrill to be in the presence of danger.

I could see vividly a big warehouse with American words painted on it. From a distance, I saw the puppet military police. In the darkness, the shadows and alleys became my pathways. I watched vendors sell their goods walking in the early night up and down the streets. Lights from homes and an occasional streetlight lit up little plots of ground here and there, and once in a while a military jeep would pass by with its headlights probing the dark.

Making my way as inconspicuously as I could, I soon arrived in front of the house owned by my uncle. At the last minute, I began to have doubts. Remembering that he worked as an administrator in the government and looking at this fine, stuccoed house of French design, I thought that they may have allied themselves with our enemies. But I could hardly believe that my mother's sister would become involved in such things. To be careful though, I thought I'd not reveal my true mission until I knew their attitudes better.

Building up my enthusiasm again, I walked up their sidewalk and knocked on the door. After a moment, a woman answered. I did not recognize her, but asked, "Is this the Thi residence?"

"Yes, but it is late. Who are you?"

I guessed by the way that she acted that this woman must be a servant. However, it was not too late that I would be disturbing people from their beds. So I said, "My name is Nguyen Kim Lan, and I am the daughter of Mrs. Thi's sister. Could you tell her that I am here?"

She disappeared inside. I heard some voices and then footsteps, and the door opened. There stood my aunt. She cried, "Kim Lan, I hardly recognize you. It's been so long. Please, please come in."

I smiled and bowed slightly saying, "Aunt, it is so good to see you again." I stepped in, and we politely hugged each other. I quickly noticed the presence of my four cousins. At least I felt they were my cousins. It had been so long, and they had all grown. We kissed and hugged, and they seemed sincerely surprised and happy to see me. I began to feel a little more relaxed.

My aunt then said, "Your uncle, I'm sorry, is out of town. You know he has an important job with the government. He is attending a meeting in Saigon. He flew down two days ago and should be back in another two. Maybe you will be able to stay until he returns?"

I smiled politely and said, "I'm not sure. Maybe I will be able to do so."

She then asked, "Please tell me about your grandparents." Before I could answer, however, she continued, "I haven't heard from them in a very long time. It's so nice that you should just now arrive. Only this afternoon I was reminiscing about Father and Mother, and my sister and I when we were young. I can remember so many happy times. We swam together in the ocean and enjoyed the beach so much. Of course, I never could stand bending over all day long in the rice fields, but the country was beautiful. Sometimes I think it's so crowded here. There are so many refugees from the fighting coming into town. I think half of them are criminals. I worry more about going out of the house than I ever have, but I love the beach when we can get there. Kim Lan, you're sitting there so quietly, please feel free to speak. Have you come to escape the fighting?"

She talked rapidly through a stream of words that seemed not to have much thought behind them. My four cousins sat silently near us and watched me with curiosity. I hadn't seen them in six years, and their ages now were nine, thirteen, fifteen, and sixteen. As I glanced at them and before I could answer my aunt, she added, almost as an afterthought, "It is terrible what the communists are doing!"

I looked back at her, and as I was beginning to open my mouth, the nine year old said, "We heard your mother was a communist and was sent to jail. Communists hate Jesus and God. Have you come away from the fighting to live with us? Do you want to become a Catholic and learn about Jesus and fight the communists?"

My aunt scolded her son, but confusion was beginning to overtake me. I glanced at the walls of their home and saw hanging from them symbols of the Christian religion of the French and was reminded of the fact that my aunt had become a Christian when she had married her husband. He had been raised one, and now so also were their children. She apologized to me as I tried to smile at my smallest cousin. I did not know how to deal with their religion, and so I concentrated on my aunt's question about my grandparents. I explained how they were doing, and that, other than getting old, they were in good health.

We changed the subject, and I began to reacquaint myself with the four cousins. Before going to bed that night, we made plans to visit the city the next day.

That night, I lay in a soft bed and realized for the first time that although these people were a part of my family, they lived in a different world and spoke another language. However, I decided to talk to them tomorrow, to see whether their comments about the "communists" were only a thin front which I could change if I were able to find a way to tell them the truth of what was happening in the country, outside this one home in Da Nang.

The next morning, I was awakened by the aroma of cooking food. Getting out of bed, I made my way to the kitchen. No one was moving about the house yet, except the servant woman who was in the process of preparing breakfast. I began to feel guilty that a part of my family

lived so well, while so many of our countrymen elsewhere lived and died under the hard hand of this Diem
dictator.

In a few minutes, my aunt walked in and said, "Ah,
Kim Lan, you're up early. I guess it's from living with
the roosters. You know you should consider moving to
Da Nang. There are many more opportunities here. I
know that a year would not go by before you would catch
yourself a husband. You are attractive and eligible. Learn
from me. Look for a man with a good job, and one that
is in the government. If not France, then it will be American assistance that will always be here. Know where the
advantages are. What else can a woman do? I wish I
could get my parents here, but they'd as soon die as to
leave their rice fields. But you, Kim Lan, think about it
as we tour the city today." I smiled and was polite.

Later, after breakfast, we walked the short distance
from their house to the main boulevard by the Han River,
although I noticed my cousins using the French name for
it, the Tourane. Many old French buildings lined the opposite side of the boulevard. The river emptied into the
bay on the north end. Flowing northward through the
city, it was filled with many sampans and all kinds of
different boats and ships. I walked and stared at everything.

At midday, we ate along the docks at a restaurant built
over the river and watched, listened to, and smelled the
sights, sounds, and odors of a large shipping port. Just
up the river, many homes, like this restaurant, were built
on stilts over the water. Many of the small boats had
covered living areas, and whole families lived, slept, ate,
and worked off these riverboat-homes.

My cousins eagerly talked to me about their education
and the fact that they were learning both French and English in school. The oldest was nearing the time when
his schooling would be complete, but all he could talk
about was going either to France or America to study.

Finally, I asked, "What about the revolution that's going on?"

He answered, "The communists! Ha! They don't
amount to much. Our government and army are in full
control. See, look around you. We are completely free

to walk our streets, to eat where we want, and to enjoy our life. The communists may have some outlaw bands, but that's all.''

I felt my anger rising and spoke before I had planned, ''I love my mother very much, and she fought for the revolution. She was living by the dictates of the Peace Treaty of 1954, when she was carried off by the police.'' Silence settled over the table. You could hear the water washing against the docks below us.

But I felt I had to continue. I went on with my voice rising. ''My mother was a good and wonderful person. She never even thought of fighting, but the French and their cowards from our country lied to her, beat her, raped her, and forced her into the hills. She fought and came back after the war and wanted to live in peace and help bring about free elections. But she was taken away and is now likely dead. The police took her. Then elections weren't allowed because they knew that the people would vote for Uncle Ho.'' I felt tears begin to well up in my eyes, and I noticed a few people at other tables looking at us.

I looked at my aunt and cousins who were watching me with a strange silence. Continuing, I said, ''Please know that most of the country, and I expect many who live here in Da Nang, feel the same as my mother and I and my grandparents. Listen, please, you are good people, but you just do not understand what's happening in your own country. The people are rising up, and the day is not that far off that Diem and the Americans will be here no longer.''

My aunt looked pale and horrified. She nervously glanced at the nearby tables, before saying to me, ''I'm afraid, Kim Lan, that you cannot stay here. You must leave now. You will come to no good end, and you place both myself and my children in danger by saying these things and being here with us. Do you not know that it is against the law? Do you not know that you can be put to death for even speaking like this? Do you not know that our honorable president has resurrected the use of the guillotine to sever the heads of insurrectionists and strike fear into the hearts of our enemies? I can see in your eyes that you have been misled into believing these things that you have just said. I shall talk to our priest and say prayers to the Blessed Virgin for you. If you will change and help our democratic government, you are welcome to return. Otherwise, you must never see us again. Please, leave now before your outspoken and scandalous thoughts cause us all to be stripped of our positions and lost forever in prison."

I had been leaning forward but now sat up straight, shocked. My aunt, turning red-faced, looked down at the table. My cousins alternatingly glanced at their food and then at me. I tried to smile at them as I got up to leave. The other people in the restaurant looked at me as I walked out, and I noticed that the man who had seemed to be the owner of the place was now on the telephone casting hurried glances in my direction. Walking through the doorway into the noontime sun, I began to realize that I had allowed my emotions to overcome reason, and that it would be better for me to leave this area immediately. I felt a tear on my cheek, and as I ran across the boulevard, I wiped it away and then lost myself as quickly as I could in the crowds of people.

Daring not to return to their home to pick up the second set of clothes that I had brought with me, I made my way south by way of side streets. I hardly had time to think about the situation with my aunt and cousins before it seemed that police and military uniforms were everywhere. Fortunately, the clothes I wore were much the same as many others, and I blended in with the citizens of the city as I made my way toward the open country and villages. Once there I knew of safe homes in which to hide on my way back to our forces.

I still, however, had to get out of Da Nang. The streets were crowded with people. Some were selling, some buying, and some, like me, were just rushing through. Bicycles, motorcycles, and military trucks were everywhere, and everything and everybody competed with each other for space. Walking quickly, but trying to keep myself from running, I rounded the corner of an old French building. Suddenly, a small dog, chased closely by a larger one darted past me, low growls and shrieks of fear coming from their throats. Instinctively, I leaped aside to avoid the rushing animals. As I did, in the same moment, someone crashed into me sending the two of us sprawling into the street.

Urgently, I struggled to regain my feet and avoid the many vehicles. Out of the corner of my eye, I saw the dogs disappearing down the street. Then my ankle gave way, and I was thrown off-balance, hobbling on one leg. I felt a hand on my arm. For the first time I looked at the person into whom I had crashed. An army uniform was the first thing that I saw. His hand held my arm, and a horribly cold feeling stilled my body. I stared at him speechless. His uniform was that of the South Vietnamese Army.

Then he smiled and said, "There are too many crazy dogs." He glanced toward where the dogs disappeared and then back at me. I still couldn't get my thoughts sufficiently together to talk, but he tried. "Are you hurt? I think your leg may be. Can I help you?"

I shook my head, finally able to speak, "No, thank you, sir. You are very kind. It was my fault, and I'm so sorry. Are you hurt?" My breath had almost stopped in fear. But there was something very young and innocent about this soldier. He looked as if he was recently off the farm. Regardless, I needed to leave at once. This whole situation would attract the police.

He said, "I am fine, but let me help you."

"No, no, I am late," I almost too hastily replied. "My parents will be angry. But I thank you for your concern."

I limped away, turning once to smile and see what he was doing. He was gone, and my heart pounded in my ears. I moved more quickly in the direction of the countryside. I prayed and never saw him again.

It took me three days to travel the twenty miles to Chien Son and to Grandfather and Grandmother. The Vinh Dien River was my easiest route. It gave my ankle time to heal as friends ferried me from village to village. I made my way upriver, hiding with whomever I could trust. Police were everywhere. I had friends who had disappeared as my mother had, but I was determined to make it safely. I lived in holes in the floors of friendly homes. On one occasion, I had to spend most of the night in a muddy rice field with suspicious police encamped in the village. Ever since I had escaped from the colonel's whorehouse, I no longer had an identification card. In-

stant beatings, torture, and imprisonment awaited me
without it.

Finally, on the evening of the third day, I approached
Chien Son and home. It had been three months since my
last visit to my grandparents, and I eagerly walked down
the tree-lined paths to see them. It was early in the evening when I got there, and as I entered the open doorway,
Grandfather was walking into the living room with
Grandmother working behind him in the kitchen. He
smiled and opened his arms to me.

As a wonderful warm feeling swept over me, I smiled
and wordlessly walked forward into his arms. I looked
at his face which had, in the last few years, begun to
show the signs of his advanced years. He seemed more
tired than I had ever seen him. As I hugged him, I saw
his eyes become misty and a lonely tear make its way
down one cheek.

Then Grandmother turned and almost jumped when
she saw me. She said, "Kim Lan, my child, my child,
why do you so quietly sneak up on your old grandmother? Some day you will startle my heart into silence."

We held each other, and I said, "It is so good to see
you. Just being home and touching you makes me feel
good again. The fears and problems take leave, and I'm
left with only love and fond memories."

"Sit down, sit down, and tell us of your travels and
adventures," she said. We sat on mats on the earthen floor,
and Grandmother brought out some rice cakes, saying,
"I've just finished them, and I'd guess you are hungry."

As I took a bite, I had to fight back the tears. This was
truly home. My parents, grandparents, and generations
past had all been born and buried here. I looked at
Grandfather and Grandmother and knew that it wouldn't
be much longer before their spirits and bodies would nurture the earth and give sustenance to the rice fields. I
loved them.

Grandfather then spoke. "Kim Lan, where have you
been and what news do you bring?"

Finally, when I was able to speak, I said, "I went to
see my aunt and cousins in Da Nang. It was my thought

that I might be able to find support with them for demonstrations in the city."

With this, both became attentive, and Grandmother asked, "How are they? We haven't seen our daughter in more years than I should like to count. I pray for her. Ever since she married into the life of a government official in the big city, she seems to have lost her love of our home and her family. Tell me that she still cares."

I paused and looked down. After a moment, I looked back into their faces and said, "I'm sure that deep within her heart she cares for you and her family, but they live in a nice home and have nice clothes and goods. I fear that she is afraid to lose these possessions, and her material security is founded upon the government: first the French, and now Diem and America. These things blind her to the needs and problems of our people. Her husband was not in town but on some official business in Saigon. I spent a night with them and part of the next day. They are well, but they believe lies about us. They have become a part of the French religion. Their world is different. It is almost as if they now speak a new and very different language. I cannot return to them again, and it has made me sad and worried. It is very difficult for me to understand how anyone, particularly a member of our family, can have their lives begin here in the country and then turn from it to aid our enemies."

I could not look into their eyes, but lowered my gaze.

Grandfather's hand slid over to his wife's and held it as she spoke, "My granddaughter, it has always been a sad thing for us. She married just after your mother did and has been gone from here for nineteen years. On two occasions since, she has returned to visit. For many years now though, I've grown to accept that she has gone from us. Her spirit shall never return to this earth. She can no longer understand what it means to be one with the land, where our toil, our sweat, our blood, and even our very beings themselves join with the waters, the earth, and the air around us. Home to her is the house where she lives, her soft bed, her money, and all of her material goods. I hope and pray that her French religion has a place in it for her spirit when she dies. I hope that it is not as cruel a hell as their government was for us in life and that she will not become a Vietnamese slave to a French master in their spirit world.''

She stopped. Grandfather and I both looked at her as tears began to pour down her old weathered and loving face. He held her, and I was at a loss for what to do.

Later that night, I laid in my old hammock in the room I once shared with Ba Can and thought about Mother. I wondered what life could have been like if no Frenchman or American had ever visited our shores. Our people had always been patient and kind. I remembered how normal it was for a person to know poetry and not unusual to answer a question with a quote from an old poem. Things now, however, had begun to change. Families were split apart. Hardness and hatred had crept into our lives. Many were addicted to drink or opium. Life was not just hard, it was dangerous. I cried for a long time before I remembered no more.

The rooster call in the morning found me not wanting to awaken. I remained in my bed unmoving for some time before I felt a hand on my shoulder. Turning, I looked into my grandfather's face. He was quiet, but I noticed a redness in his eyes. The proud old man, the only father I had ever known, stood tall beside me and said, ''Your grandmother has gone to be with our ancestors. I awoke this morning to find that her sleep was more than sleep. I'm afraid I would like your help for a while longer before you return to our brothers in the mountains.''

Shocked, I sat up before he finished. A rush of many emotions poured over me as if I were caught in a sudden great rainstorm with no shelter. My arms reached out and encircled Grandfather. We stood holding each other for a long moment, before he said, ''Come, we have many arrangements to make for the burial.''

Late that afternoon, Chien Son witnessed a long procession of its residents, amid the smell of incense and the chiming of bells, giving tribute to my grandmother who was buried under a mound shaped like the sacred tortoise. It broke my heart to think of Grandfather alone at home, and I spent a lot of time with him just holding his hand.

However, we were afraid that the police would take notice of my being at home, and the next day, he announced that I needed to depart to be with the revolution. Proudly, he said, "Both Grandmother and I need you and Ba Can to bring about victory in this war. We each want you to go and fight. Fight as your mother did. However, I have one word of caution for you, Granddaughter. You must fight out of love for our country, not out of hatred for the enemy. The new nation that we build cannot be based upon hatred. Hatred destroys. I have seen it in the eyes of some of our brothers, although I do not judge them on this account. I know their personal sufferings at the hands of our enemy. I must have your promise now, before you leave. Promise to fight out of love, not hatred, and promise to plant the seed of that wisdom wherever you go."

At that moment, I was overwhelmed by the grandness of this man, my grandfather. I said, "Yes, Grandfather, I promise. My love for you and my respect for you shall always guide my thoughts."

Peacefully waking, I looked around and found myself in the low hills, and my dream faded with the setting of the sun. In its place, groups of former prisoners were scattered around under the trees, and I now recalled last night's raid on the prison. Suddenly, I was startled by a hand on my shoulder. It was Ba Can.

He said, "Come now. We've more work to do."

As I rose to my feet, I glanced into his eyes. In them, burning like a white flame was a driving force that I had not seen in anyone else. Our parents and grandparents all had been taken from us. We had seen friends and neighbors tortured, and the fire-breathing monster that had caused it was still loose in our country. Ba Can's hatred had become his personal demon. It was, more than anything, the strange shining in his eyes that frightened me. I made a quiet resolve: not to let this thing take over my life as Grandfather had warned.

I stood and looked into the night sky. There was no moon tonight. That was good. A few miles in the distance, lights from the American camp at An Hoa flickered, and a solitary enemy artillery round roared overhead to rip into some unknown target in the darkness beyond us. I prayed a silent prayer to Grandfather and continued our march.

CHAPTER 8

Every quantitative measurement we have shows we are winning this war.

—Robert McNamara (1963)

I was back in the fucking armpit of the world. Kicking dust as I went, I walked between tents back to my men. "Day after tomorrow," the battalion CO had said, "I want you to go up into those motherfucking mountains and find out what the hell Charlie has got up there! And I caught enough shit at division headquarters about this bitch running loose down here and me not being able to catch her. Find her, Collins. Bring her ass back dead or alive, and I'll get you some extra R&R." His voice still ricocheted around my brain. The frying pan or the fire, my patrol was being dropped into one or the other. I hoped like hell the morale would stay up. As I walked, my mind wandered to the woman. Twice now she had shown up on the killing end of my rifle. Both times I didn't shoot, and once she had spared me. Who the hell was she? Why was she getting under my nerve endings?

I walked into the patrol's GP tent. Beer cans, empty and crushed, lay where they had been thrown. A couple of guys read perfumed letters from stateside sweethearts. Peterson slept, snored, and unconsciously swatted flies from his face. The tropical misery drove most of these eighteen- and nineteen-year-old men to lie around in

skivvies. Garcia slept in the sweltering heat with a giant
hard-on rising out of his shorts.

I stood just inside the door of the tent and watched as
Sanchez sneaked up on his friend with a towel stretched
between his hands. As I mumbled, "Oh, no!" Sanchez
popped the towel off the head of Garcia's rigid man-pole.
The tent reverberated with a scream, mixed with a six-
pack of heavy laughter. Garcia was up grimacing in pain,
holding himself, and trying to figure out what had happened. Sanchez, convulsing in laughs, with the towel still
in his hands, ran past me out the door.

It took about a second for Garcia to put two and two
together. Then he hobbled out the door screaming after
Sanchez, "*Ai*, you son of a bitch! Your mother's a whore,
your father fucks ducks, and I'm gonna cut off your ear
and eat it."

I watched as the two disappeared around the next tent,
Sanchez still laughing, and Garcia screaming Spanish ex-
pletives. What a crew! I loved every one of the assholes,
even if no one jumped to attention when I walked in. I
lived and sweated too close to these guys to demand tra-
ditional Marine Corps formality. I laughed thinking what
Garcia would have looked like standing at attention with
a hard-on. This was Vietnam, not Camp Pendleton!

I sat down with Williams on his cot and unfolded a
map. "Our next patrol is going in here tomorrow evening," I said, "with this being our objective." My pencil outlined our path.

"We'll fly up Antenna Valley at sunset tomorrow and
find a place to hide for the night. Then we start a climb
that could be a long one, unless of course we bump into
a group of our 'friends' up there and have to run like
hell. The battalion CO thinks they may have a lot of bad
shit up there, and he thinks Charlie's been coming from
there to hit us. G-2 believes they may have some headquarters in the mountains. Plus, our battalion is gonna
start relocating the villages in the valley, and we're supposed to see if anything might be coming out of those
mountains to hit 'em while they're rounding up the pigs,
kids, and whoever in the villages.

Williams looked at the map and drank the last of his
beer. Finally, he said, while studying the map, "*They*

may 'think' I know there's bad shit up in those hills. There ain't no black pajama gang up there. They're the real motherfucking McCoy.''

"Get yourself ready, we're going up for an overflight of the area in a couple hours," I said.

Before leaving the tent, Williams waved a new man over and introduced him. "Sir, this is Doc Israel Jacobs, our new corpsman."

I got up to meet him and said, "Welcome aboard, Jacobs. I've always had the greatest respect for our Navy corpsmen. Doesn't matter what platoon I've seen 'em in, they been Recon Marines as good as any. I appreciate your being here."

"Thank you, sir," he answered. "I'm looking forward to the next patrol."

Then I reminded Williams of our flight time and left for my own tent.

Two hours later we were in the air for reconnaissance, and afterward, I spent a good part of the evening poring over all available maps and intelligence. Finally, I didn't want to think about it anymore and walked out into the dark where at least a little breeze was blowing the swelter off the heat. Artillery boomed not far away, throwing out a round—probably just an "H&I" shot to harass Charlie somewhere.

The next morning, about a quarter past nine, a lieutenant walked up to my tent where I was trying to sort out the worst from the worst C-rats. "They keep saying the old World War II K-rations were worse," I mumbled as I looked up at him. "Shit, I pity those poor suckers. What can I do for you? Come on in and sit yourself."

He pulled his cover off as he stepped in revealing a blond flattop with a few freckles scattered about his light complexion.

"Tim Sullivan," he gave his handle. "The CO sent me down to go out with you. Sort of 'OJT' I guess you could call it. I'm supposed to go up to Bravo Company at Phu Bai, but the colonel thought I could get some good experience down here first."

I sat there and shook my head. "Boy, those people sure as hell give you a lot of time to get adjusted," I said. "You got about nine or ten hours, before we shove off. We better get you outfitted. You know, when we take the local tour of this pristine civilization, we gotta present the right image. We're doing a lot to overcome that 'ugly American' shit.'' Then I laughed and shook his hand.

Shortly before 1900 hours that evening, we had gathered at the battalion landing zone. The choppers were due any minute, and I walked around making sure everybody knew his assignment. I stopped at Tim, whom I had assigned to the rear team, and said, ''Be nervous! Everybody here is. Just keep the safety on.''

Then I could see the birds coming. I thought of the date, August 5, 1966. This was it! We're going to try to work our way into the mountains.

It only took thirty seconds for the three teams to scramble aboard the three 34s, and then we were off with the sun balancing on top of the western mountains. We flew up the valley with our first objective to land as high up as possible, close to the jungle.

Shit, man! My nerves felt like jumping beans. I stared at the mountain heights as they loomed closer. Then we were flying near to the steeply sloping jungles about four thousand feet up. The birds then rapidly dropped toward a shelf of ground with low grasses about one hundred meters from a very distinct line of tall jungle. The valley floor of the Song Thu Bon was a half-mile directly below us, and the map showed a major trail coming out of the valley, up these heights, across the shelf, and disappearing into the jungle. We landed about fifty meters from it, and as quickly as we could, we began to move through the waist-high grass toward the jungle and a draw off to our east. The choppers were gone and we were alone. Alone except for Geronimo and friends, I thought.

I wanted to avoid that trail since it could lead to an obvious confrontation with whatever Charlie was in the area. My goal was to find out what was up here, and that could best be done by not being found ourselves.

With Williams's team in the lead, we moved silently, carefully, through the jungle in the dim light of the early evening until we found a place that offered enough cover for us to ''hole-up'' for the night. It was dark by the time we found a place. Each team was set a few meters from the other. I threw my poncho over my head to cover the glare of my red-lensed flashlight and plotted on-call artillery strikes just in case. We were within range of the 8-inch guns, the best, most accurate pieces that the Marine Corps had.

That night was a little spooky. Every third hour I was up for my watch and couldn't sleep much the balance of the time. We were higher than I had been before, and the jungle noises up here were different. I said silent prayers that no one had seen us.

At first light, those who felt like eating a cold can of C-rations did so. You could never heat 'em out this far, because Charlie could be close by. I wasn't hungry but felt that I needed to eat something since who knew what might happen during the day. I decided on candy and crackers and packed the rest of the unappetizing crap away. Soon we were moving out with freshly painted faces. The brown and green make-up crossed each face like dirty lightning bolts.

As we pushed our way through the jungle, I was stunned by the signs we found everywhere! We weren't using trails, but it looked like we were crossing a very well-used piece of real estate. Small camp fires, cold but recently used, were found wherever we went. The underbrush was cleared out in many places. At one point, under the jungle shadows and to a background of echoing calls of birds and monkeys, we, one by one, balanced on an old tree that spanned a short, but not so shallow, chasm. We carefully treaded our way from one side to the other. My pack was heavy enough, but I pitied Rivers who had the extra weight of the radio. He was sweating when he crossed over and sat beside me in some brush. I had begun to feel like he was a little brother to me. He had pale skin, was heavily freckled, and never knew when to quit. I gave the patrol a break.

Tim Sullivan crawled over, and we very quietly discussed the situation with Williams. "You know," I said. "I thought there might be a battalion up here. I was wrong! It's more like two or maybe a regiment. We gotta be careful, but I think it's just a matter of time before we find something, or it finds us." Much of the undergrowth had been cleared, and the signs of old camp fires gave

the impression of some type of training grounds or biv-
ouac area for a large number of units.

I pointed out our direction on the map and on the
ground, but it was obvious that the map did not adequately plot all these minor draws that we had come
through. Then we were up and moving. Our direction of
travel now was all uphill, and the brush was becoming
thicker. "Just-a-minute" vines snagged at our clothing,
weapons, and even the grenades taped to our pack straps,
provoking more than a few quiet curses.

About four hours of tough work after leaving the abyss
behind us, Corporal Williams stopped the patrol and silently slid back to me. "There's a wide, well-used trail
crossing our front from the southwest," he whispered.

I figured we were nearly four thousand feet in the
mountains and might be on the edge of major shit. I
crawled up close to the trail and burrowed in the leaves
cautiously watching through the bushes. I estimated that
it was ten feet wide and packed hard by years of heavy
use. "This," I whispered to Williams, "must be Charlie
Country Highway 101." Carefully and quietly, we set up
the patrol about twenty feet off the trail, all of us making
like snakes in the grass.

We had waited there no more than five minutes when
two Vietnamese women came walking up the hill each
carrying a sack that must have been two-thirds the size
of the woman bearing it. They were talking and effort-
lessly carrying up this mountain those large sacks filled
probably with rice. We seemed so close to them that I
was sure that if they had not been involved in their conversation, they would have seen us.

The women passed by continuing up the path. I decided to follow. Leaving our third team with Tim to watch
our rear, I moved the other six of us up following the
women. We had gone only fifty feet when a little ahead
of us, they turned to the right on a dog-leg in the trail.
We slowly approached the sharp turn. PFC Peterson, at
point, suddenly froze like Lot's wife. It had a similar and
immediate impact on the other five of us. Like molasses
in January, Peterson sank slowly to the ground on the
edge of the trail. By the time he turned his head to signal
a message, we had all imitated him and were crouching,

partially in the edge of the undergrowth by the trail. He motioned for Williams and me.

Without a sound, we were beside him. Using hand signals, we understood that a large unit of Viet Cong, about thirty men, with weapons were just ahead of us, maybe within thirty to forty feet. I moved forward on my belly about six feet and pushed aside some of the undergrowth to see for myself. I could hear voices but needed to move up more. I was trying to be so damned quiet and yet get closer to see them. I tried not to admit to myself how scared I was. Before I could reposition myself, a hand grabbed my leg. With my heart palpitating wildly, I turned to see Tim crawling up beside me. He quickly whispered, "We've picked up voices moving up the trail behind us."

Things are happening too fast, my mind began to scream. Even before I had finished that thought, I heard noises ten feet in front of my face. Looking up, I saw a soldier moving down the trail across my front, and in about five paces he'd make the turn and be on top of me.

I quickly motioned the patrol into the bush and silently cursed because they sounded like a herd of elephants. In a second Williams, Peterson, Tim and I had thrown our rifles to our shoulders and were confronted by one very surprised Viet Cong. Williams took him out with one quick burst of automatic fire while the rest of us poured sixty rounds through the brush into the VC lounging around the trail behind the first one. A thunderstorm of confusion broke loose.

"Get your men back to the rear team and cut across country back downhill," I yelled at Williams. Then I rushed Doc Jacobs and Rivers out ahead of me while I quickly loaded another magazine and covered the rear. The rear team wasn't very far back down the trail, and in seconds we had picked them up and were quite literally running through the brush that we had so slowly and quietly snaked our way through only a few minutes before.

Doc, Rivers, and I were back in the center of the patrol as we ran downhill. I wanted to get some distance between us and this place as fast as I could and reevaluate our situation. Charlie was obviously on both sides of us, only he may not be so sure what had happened, or what would happen next.

As we ran downhill, I felt something fall from my chest. Looking down I saw that a grenade had been ripped off my pack strap and was bouncing downhill beside me as fast as I was running! As my heart and stomach both deserted my body, I bent down on the run and scooped it up in my right hand. I mumbled a silent running prayer of thanks seeing that the pin was still in it. "Just-a-minute" vines were ripped out by their roots as ten Marines broke the world record in the 440-yard dash and kept going.

Finally, we set-up in some boulders tucked into a secluded corner of the jungle. Rivers tried to reach the battalion on the radio but with no luck. He pulled out his long whip antenna, tried that, and we managed to pick them up, but not very clearly. I reported that we had contact with about thirty VC, and that others were in the area. I added that they had suffered one KIA, and unknown wounded, but that we had taken no casualties. "We have moved away from our patrol route, and I feel that the mission is compromised," I said. "We will keep moving back toward the LZ, but it will be too late by the time we get there to be pulled out this evening. I'll report back when we're there." I signed off, and sat down with Williams and Tim to regroup.

A late summer rainstorm had just begun to thunder through the jungles. This was God-sent, and I thanked Him. "No fucking way can we try to go up higher now," I told Williams. "They'll be out looking for us. Let's get back to the LZ and try again another day. This rain is exactly what we need. Let's move out, but keep low."

We moved from our shelter in the boulders through the rain-soaked jungles toward the valley. We tried to stay low, below the tops of the bushes, and·had about four hours before nightfall to cover an area that had taken us five hours the first time.

Minutes later, Williams motioned me up and pointed to signs of boot prints made in the mud since it had started raining. They're moving across our front, to our left, I thought. Thank God! We continued in the same heading as we had begun, but ever so carefully and quietly.

Another hour later, the rain began to slacken, but it was hard to tell while the incessant dripping from the millions of jungle leaves above continued to lightly shower us. We stayed in the undergrowth, avoiding trails, occasionally burrowing into the wet decaying vegetation of the jungle floor, hiding from some real or imagined sounds.

It was after dark before we came to the jungle's edge, and the grassy shelf onto which we had been dropped yesterday. In code, I reported our position to the battalion and requested to be pulled out at first light. We then set-up for the night, soaked to the bone, and huddling in our ponchos in the mud. I leaned over to Doc and whispered, "Well, Doc Israel Jacobs, I hope you're still excited about this patrol. Did you pack some misery pills in your bag? 'Cause we're gonna have plenty of it tonight. That's provided we're lucky and only have to deal with the weather." A faint smile crossed his lips.

The wind blew hard that evening and made us "what-in-the-hell-am-I-doing-here" cold. I slept very little, not only because the weather was causing such misery, but also because I knew that we must be close to that large trail near where we originally had landed.

Several times during the night, I thought I heard movement nearby. Once Rivers shook me when he was on watch, quietly swearing that people were close. We stayed rolled up in muddy ponchos, wet, silent, and hidden in the brush like some sorry, miserable animals. I doubted that the enemy units we had surprised really knew how many we were, but I was certain that they were looking for us.

First light brought mixed news. The choppers would be out to get us, but I worried about being in the open in waist-high grass just out of the jungle when Charlie could very easily be near. Within thirty minutes, though, the birds—this time 46s—were on station and coming down. In seconds, we were aboard and off. There weren't any more problems. We had taken no casualties, but neither had we been able to push through undetected to our objective area.

Back at the battalion, Williams, Tim, and I reported to the S-3, S-2, and the colonel about our observations. I pressed the point that this was a very large enemy camp. "Colonel," I said, "if anything, we've been underestimating what's up there. There's at least one battalion of permanent personnel and one of transients."

"You're going back tomorrow evening," he said, and

pointed out a location about fifteen-hundred meters from our first entry point.

Tim, Williams, and I walked back to our tents to clean our gear and rifles, and to stand in the cold showers to scrape the mud off our bodies. Later, medicine was put on ripped, cut, and bitten skin, and we all headed for the mess tent. That night, Tim and I got nervously drunk thinking about the next evening. To be a small patrol lost in the middle of the whole Apache Nation is enough to make one's bowels move. I told Tim, "I suppose that there are a few John Waynes out there, but I've never known one."

Still looking into his beer, he said, "John Wayne never wore a uniform, except in the movies."

"Ah, come on," I replied, "I don't have many heroes left. Don't take away the Duke."

The next morning, throbbing headache or not, we began to get ready for that evening's patrol. Williams, Tim, and I discussed with each squad member everything that occurred on the last patrol. I wanted to go over any mistakes, learn from them, and get suggestions.

The hours raced by far too quickly, and we hardly had time to catch our breath before the sun was edging down toward the mountains again. We waited in the landing zone, each of us knowing that we could easily be cut off from the world forever in what we now were unofficially calling "Apache Country."

Tension settled around us like fog. Williams had his point team memorize the map. Assuming it was correct, we would be landing in a small bowl covered by grass two to four feet in height. A small clump of trees would be behind us, and the heavy jungle ahead and above us about one hundred meters away. Williams and his team were to move quickly into the jungle and up around the east side of the hill. I emphasized to them again, hoping not to sound too much like a mother hen, that they had to move as fast as they could and enter the jungle about one hundred meters below the crest of the hill. "This is Charlie's front yard," I added, "so let's not screw around—just haul ass."

I moved over to the rear team with Tim. They had to be particularly watchful of the rear lip of the bowl into which we were dropping. It was covered by a clump of trees, and I didn't want to get caught by surprise from that direction. The expression on Tim's face asked, Is this shit normal? Thirteen months of this, and I'll be a basket case!

Finally, I sat down beside Rivers and Doc. Rivers had checked both radios, and all we could do now was wait.

Sitting in the dirt and dust, I watched a long train of ants working their little asses off. For a moment, I forgot the patrol and became mesmerized by a jillion of those little suckers doing whatever it is that ants seem to do best. The thought of inadvertently, in the semidarkness, rolling up in my poncho in the middle of one of these ant columns in some lost corner of the jungle sent shivers up my spine. I double-checked to see if I had plenty of insect repellent.

The birds came from a different direction this time, and it jolted a body the way they dropped from around the corner of the hill with their sudden, thunderous, wopping roars. They created an inhuman wind storm, turning hot sweat into a fine, grainy mud. I was up the side of the lead bird while the rest of the patrol boarded the three 34s. Assured that the pilot understood our LZ location, I was back down and jumped in beside the crew chief. There wasn't time to be afraid, or maybe fatalism had taken over. In any case, we either sat or knelt in the thundering silence inside the belly of the chopper, steadily covering mile after mile and passing into Apache Country.

I saw the LZ coming up on our right front and grabbed the crew chief pointing to it. Shadows had spread across the mountains as the three birds went in low in a line, landing and leaving almost in the same breath. I wasn't sure whether the crew chief was helping us out or shoving us. They were gone as I was taking my first strides, running through the waist-high grass.

We were alone in the bottom of the bowl. The point team was moving in front exactly as I wanted. The rear team followed mine, closely watching the tree-covered rise behind us. I felt like we were dwarves in a land of giants. In about ten minutes, we entered the shadows of the jungle, hoping that we had not been seen. The jungles only slightly cooled the torrid August heat, and the humidity was almost overwhelming at times. Wiping the sweat off my face, I signalled the patrol to halt. I crawled forward to Williams and his team. Huddling close to the ground, covered by jungle plants and trees, I gave directions to move very slowly around the side of the hill a little farther, and we would set-up for the night on the hillside.

It took us about thirty minutes to find a spot that was totally uncomfortable. If it had been raining, we would have slid down the steep hillside. As it was, we had to use trees to brace ourselves. I was sure there were more than a few private curses at me for my thoughtfulness in finding this cousin to a cliff to lean against all night holding onto trees.

I lay there with my feet against one tree with two others on either side to help brace me and wondered what the fuck we were doing. Remembering the ants, I almost took a bath in insect repellent. It wasn't long before my skin crawled and itched, and I wasn't sure whether one hundred and fifty thousand, nine hundred and ninety-nine ants had become immune to the shit and were preparing to carry me off to their queen, or if I had OD'd on the repellent.

That night, there were no dreams of sugar plums. I stared into the jungle blackness, itching and afraid that if I went to sleep I'd roll down the hill. I totally sympathized with any of my patrol who cursed me as an idiot for picking this site to spend the night. It didn't make a damn that I was sure we were very near to at least two thousand enemy soldiers. I was miserable!

The next morning, the half-can of cold C-rations did absolutely nothing for my sore back or lousy disposition. In order to get our minds off our aching muscles and to do the job we were supposed to do, I made my way over to Williams. My plastic-coated map was out, and I pointed to where I thought we needed to go. Instead of continuing to work through the brush sounding like a herd of elephants struggling along the side of this hill, I directed the point team to move straight up to the top. To the east, the hill apparently dropped back down to a creek and then back up again to the one-thousand-meter level for which we were heading. But I told Williams,

"Move slowly—no noise." The son of a bitch was good, and I knew he would be as silent as death. My hope was that the rest of us might be nearly as good.

I watched him directing his team above us. Watching Williams, I imagined that it was like watching a tiger silently stalking his prey. The jungle was quiet as we slowly broke over the crest of the hill. Williams signalled back to me. I quietly joined him. He had found a narrow trail leading down toward a place where the map showed a creek. The slopes of the hill on either side were too rough, and I decided to use the trail. I had word passed to each patrol member that we would be using it and to be very watchful for booby traps. I whispered to Williams to be damned careful. I then moved to the rear team and told them to keep an eye and ear cocked for anything coming our way from behind.

The point team led us down. We had only gone fifty meters or so when we found a small hootch. We had spent the night only about one hundred meters from the place! The thatch hut turned out to be a rice storage bin. Ever so slowly we continued past and then down the steep hill. Tall trees towered over us, and thick jungle vegetation closed in on both sides and then covered the slopes on each side of the draw.

In another fifty meters, we saw a second hootch. This one was different. I set the patrol in defensive positions and watched and waited. The hut was large and set on a cleared-out shelf of ground before the land continued to drop on the other side. The trees still towered over all of it, but this place was well used. A great boulder sat on the other side of the clearing. But what primarily caught my attention was a bamboo howitzer! It was almost the same as the real thing.

We watched motionless for fifteen or twenty minutes before I felt sure that no one was there. While the other seven of us covered them, Williams led his team in a quick dash to the boulder. They then edged off to the other side. The rear team, minus Tim, was positioned to watch back up the trail we had just come down, while the other four of us searched the place.

The first thing I checked was the 105mm howitzer model made from large pieces of bamboo, bicycle wheels, sheet metal, and nails. It even had elevating and traversing gears. This was the first evidence I had ever heard that there was any artillery training being given to the VC or NVA in the Da Nang area.

Then, as I turned, I saw Peterson coming quickly. He nervously whispered that the trail led down to a creek only about thirty meters away. "There's a bridge across the creek and then the trail goes uphill into a big camp! The hootches are scattered all over. Lotsa VC in there, a whole pisspot full."

I went forward with him and saw that the trail had steps cut into it and was bordered by posts painted white with ropes attached to and joining each post. It looked almost like something that would be seen at Boy Scout camp. Peterson pointed out the camp and its people.

I hid in the brush and told Peterson to snake down to his team, which was too near the bridge, and bring them carefully back closer to us. Then I lay there, pulled out my binoculars, and studied what I could of the place. I could make out about thirty huts before the camp topped the crest of a rise and continued on beyond. Enemy soldiers sat around cooking, cleaning weapons, or just lounging. I swallowed the lump in my throat and hoped that none of these cocksuckers would come over here.

So far I had estimated about a hundred Charlie within my vision. I wanted to get back and check out the "artillery piece" and hut, but I couldn't believe the size of this camp, and it continued out of sight over the top of the next ridge.

I watched the camp through my field glasses while I waited for my point team. Coming over that rise on the far side of the camp was a group of important-looking people. Focusing the glasses better, I watched more closely. My God, I thought, son of a bitch! Those have got to be North Vietnamese officers. Then someone ran into my vision: a latecomer catching up with the main group. It was a woman. I refocused with my interest suddenly even greater.

They were maybe two hundred or more yards off, and in the shadows of the jungle I couldn't see her clearly. She joined the command group and entered one of the buildings. Lowering my glasses, I watched from my hid-

ing place. I couldn't tell if it was my VC lady for whom
I had an R&R bounty, but I kept watching. Then I noticed Williams and his team almost back up to me.

After setting the team in place, I crawled up over the
top of the shelf of ground to join the rest of the patrol,
but with a feeling that I had just found something very
personal. It was almost like all those enemy were only
important in a hazy sort of way, but what stood out was
that I found her home in the mountains.

Tim was busy checking the hut and pulled me over to
show me everything he was finding. There were ten beds
in the basic Vietnamese-style: bamboo and wood with a
thin rolled bamboo slat covering on top. There also were
rifle racks with name plates and underground shelters. I
radioed battalion with the details. Even though the voice
on the other end of the air waves was very cool and professional, the tinge of excitement in his voice came
through clearly.

We continued our search of the immediate area, and
after about fifteen minutes, I began to consider our next
move. To cross the creek and move into that camp area
would be suicide, and to try to slip around the side of it
and continue to press on to the higher ground was almost
as bad.

I knelt inside the hut studying my map when Corporal
Williams quickly came up to me. In a rush he said,
"Lieutenant, they must know we're here; there's an
armed patrol of about twenty VC crossing the creek coming in our direction, and they look like they mean business."

My first thought was, shit, the sons of bitches were
listening to our radio and know we're here. What the hell
now? Should we set-up and fight, or should we get the
hell out of here, if we can?

I decided and told Williams, "Get your team, and let's
move as fast as we can back up to the top of the hill." I
sent Tim to move the rear team up the hill, and got Doc
and Rivers ready to move out ahead of me. We had to
get to the high ground. I whispered to Rivers and Doc to
stay just ahead of me but to start moving up the trail; I
would cover the rear. Coming out of the hut, I saw Williams running across the clearing followed by Rivers and

Doc. I could make out others of the patrol already farther up the hill. Bringing up the rear, I started running to catch the rest.

Suddenly, close behind me, there was a sharp burst of automatic weapon's fire. In the next instant I found myself in the brush on the other side of the clearing and I couldn't remember getting there. I looked down the barrel of my rifle while my heart and stomach both still twitched around higher in the air afraid to rejoin my body. I tried to think and fight off the feeling that had quickly tightened around me like a noose. My rifle was loaded and to my shoulder, and I was ready to shoot anyone who showed his head. Glancing behind me up the trail, I saw my patrol continuing to move as fast as they could up the steep incline, following my directions to get to a more defensible position. That emphasized even more how my situation needed to change if I wanted to continue among the living. To be captured was not a choice— I'd die first! I had to try to catch up with the patrol. My rifle was in my right hand as I positioned myself to jump and run. This was going to be an engraved invitation to any VC to shoot my ass off, but I had no choice.

There was no time to wait. Pushing up as fast as I could, I jumped onto the trail and began running, stumbling, and pulling myself up the hill. Expecting to hear rifle shots and feel fire in my back with each step, I finally jumped to the side behind a tree to catch my breath and look back down. Carefully glancing around, I saw no one, but then I heard people nearby moving up the draws on either side of us not more than a hundred feet away through heavy jungle. Shit, I thought, the fuckers are moving around to circle us. Gotta move quick! Gotta do something quick!

I ran like hell uphill and caught the patrol in a minute. I grabbed the radio and called for the 8-inch guns. My fire mission was given for the coordinates where I stood. We could still hear the Vietnamese voices on both sides, godawful close. As soon as the artillery had the call, we kept running and in another minute broke over the top of the hill. Now we were out of the jungle into the six-foot-tall elephant grass of the bowl that had been our LZ. I grabbed Williams and sent him forward, pointing to some boulders just beyond the crest of the hill, saying, "Let's get there as fast as we can; we're going to be in a world of shit any second." Then Williams was running, swinging his rifle to clear a path through the head-high grass whose razor edges sliced through our skin.

Suddenly, I looked up to see a brown swarm rise from around Williams over our heads. I heard him yell, "Bees," and he was diving and rolling down the slope of the hill toward those boulders. All of us quickly followed suit. For an instant, I thought, what the fuck is next?

The bees in that brief moment, looked large and hairy, but they quickly receded out of my mind as two thunderous crashes ripped the edge of the jungle just behind us. We scrambled, crawled, and rolled into, under, and tried to become one with those two-ton hunks of rock. Rivers, thank God, stayed beside me all the way, and I grabbed the radio and yelled, "Beautiful, fire-for-effect."

Tim screamed, "They're above us. I see a dozen of 'em!" However, in five seconds the world went crazy, as the most accurate artillery in the Marine Corps systematically tore through the outer edge of this jungle from the crest of the hill down into the draws. It was almost within spitting distance, and we crammed our bodies into all the nooks and crannies of these boulders. Shrapnel flew wildly around. At its closest a few pieces came within three or four feet, scaring the hell out of me!

About five minutes into this hellstorm of artillery, I heard Williams yelling at me that there were VC behind us. They were in the clump of trees on the little rise just opposite our landing zone and about one hundred meters downhill from us. The grass was much shorter by the boulders, and with shell fragments flying, I carefully raised my head to call in an additional fire mission. It seemed as if all the artillery in the world was at our beck and call.

White phosphorous rounds exploded exactly, unbelievably, perfectly on target. I yelled into the radio above the roar of the violent explosions, "Fire-for-effect." Again, within seconds a new mini-holocaust descended from the skies precisely on target below us. For minute after minute, the fury of hell tore through the skies and ripped apart earth and trees. We had seen Charlie in front and back of us and had heard him on two sides. I had to depend on the 8-inch guns to clear a path for us, and between my fire missions and a hell of a lot of luck, I prayed we could get out of there alive.

Then I was on the radio talking to chopper pilots swinging around the arcs of artillery. I lay flat under my boulder holding the radio receiver with Rivers lying at my feet. We coordinated the timing with the choppers, the artillery, and myself all on the same frequency. We agreed that as soon as I called for the ceasefire, and the artillery reported clear, one CH-46 chopper would come in fast and pick up the entire team, while the other would fly cover for us. After the artillery stopped, we would have to make a fast hundred meter downhill sprint from our boulders to get to the LZ just ahead of the 46.

It was all set, and I called for the ceasefire. The artillery gave me the word for the last shot out. As soon as it rocked the ground and crumbled a nearby tree, the patrol was up and moving in a low run downhill through the three-foot-tall grass. We got to the bottom as our 46 rounded the lip of the bowl and came in low. The back hatch was down, and I knelt in the grass on one knee waving my patrol aboard. The prop noise of the chopper was too loud to hear if there was anyone using us for target practice. As soon as the last Marine was in, I raced for the open hatch and ran inside where the gunner was located. Suddenly, I saw Tim still outside. Quickly, we helped him jump on board as the bird bounced into the sky.

Slowly, relief settled over me as we gained altitude. I realized we'd get back. I didn't really give a damn how inglorious it might have been. I sat down on the floor of the 46, took off my bush hat, and wiped the sweat and dirt off my face. Looking up at the gunner, I saw him smile. "It's 1700 hours and Friday," he said. "We'll have you back for happy hour." I smiled weakly at him.

I slowly stood and walked around the helicopter to check everybody out. I sat down next to Tim and said, "Shit, I thought you had already gotten on board. We coulda left you! Hell, I'm sorry. What the fuck happened?"

CHAPTER 9

A storm-tossed rose . . .
Such was her future,
All she'd ever be.

—Nguyen Du, *The Tale of Kieu*

I worried about my husband. It seemed so long since I had seen him. Leaning against a tree on the edge of the jungles still high in the hills, I watched the soft colors of the early morning. The Dai Loc Mountains just sat way out there. That's where he was, and they weren't getting any closer. Had he heard yet of our raid on the prison at Hoi An?

Then I remembered the information we had just received that the Americans were evacuating the villagers from their homes and farmlands in the valley of the Song Thu Bon. It sickened me, and I remembered Grandfather's death when they tried to take him from his home.

Except for my brother and myself, he had been the last of our family. The enemy had relocated our people and destroyed our houses. It was their last blow at my home, and it had taken his life. Still alive in my thoughts was the sight, years ago, of Van Thi rushing into our camp with the news that Chien Son, our home, was to be evacuated, and all residents relocated to a camp that they would have to build behind barbed wire. How could any government try to do that? The land was a part of our blood. It was a part of our spirit.

135

Maybe this was the last of the horrors done to us that caused my brother to be totally filled with hate. At that time, I had not been made a part of the fighting force of his battalion yet, but he had assigned me many jobs as a message carrier. I could still see Ba Can desperately organizing the battalion as quickly as possible to try to rescue Grandfather and as many others as possible. We hadn't known if we would be in time.

I thought back and remembered how the darkness of the early morning hours had found us making our way down these same well-used paths to the valleys below. At the foot of the mountains, we had split into the three companies and parted. Ba Can's company headed east-northeast, in the direction of Chien Son and Hoi An. We crossed the main rail line and Highway One. By dawn, we had set up at the Truong Giang River just south of Hoi An and west of Chien Son. There would normally have been boat traffic by that hour, and it was our intention to be ferried across; however, the situation was ominously quiet.

The early morning gray was slowly discolored by the smoldering smoke columns of day-old fires. Like death, it hung in the air over our home.

Wasting no further time, Ba Can directed that we move to a ford in the river about a mile upstream. The company ran the mile, still in the cover of the early morning shadows. In ten minutes, we crossed the river, wading knee-deep, and moved into a tree line about a half-mile southwest of Chien Son.

Cautiously, the company advanced. Our two platoons moved abreast, one at a time. There was no sign of human activity, but I could still smell the smoke and burning embers of a nightmare. Fear gripped my heart as the air was filled with the silence of death. Occasionally a dog would bark, but there were no other sounds, not even the calling of birds. Nor was there any sign of the people.

I could now hear the dying crackling of fires. We paused. Now, very near to the first homes, Ba Can sent scouts ahead. We waited, barely able to control our anger and fear. Deep within myself, I knew the worst had happened. The thought of my grandfather caught in this terror tore through my being. I glared ahead through the gray light and felt hatred. I wanted to kill but had to patiently wait in silence.

Within ten minutes, one scout had returned. The village was empty, and there was no evidence of enemy presence, he had stated. However, one wounded villager had been found, and the other scout had remained with him. I found myself holding my breath, fearing that this person would be Grandfather.

As we moved into the village, I saw the charred remains of the old homes. A few dead animals were scattered around. The remains of some buildings projected starkly out of the earth like parts of blackened skeletons. Most of the trees still stood, but some of them had also been burned. As I walked through this deathly nightmare, I could not truly grasp the fact that this was my home. It couldn't be! I carried a rifle anxious to attack any enemy, but none was to be seen.

Then I found myself on the empty street where I had grown up. Tears came to my eyes as my teeth clenched tightly in anger, and it was with difficulty that I forced myself to keep from wildly racing toward my house. Knowing what I would find and, yet, fearing to find it, I walked at a steady pace.

At first I didn't recognize the house and had to look twice. There was nothing standing. Ashes, gray coals, and an occasional charred post were all that remained. Quickly, I searched the little plot of burned ground, even the underground shelter. He wasn't there. For a moment I sat at the foot of a tree feeling anger and frustration.

Ba Can walked up. His face was cold and expressed little emotion. It was as if he had uncovered a fact of life and had calculated the appropriate response to take. I looked into his face, which was still surveying the destruction, and said, "I have not found Grandfather. What is our next step?"

He looked down at me and said, "We will find the puppet dogs who did this, and they shall know the pain of death." This he said without expression, and then continued, "Before we go, however, two bodies have been found, and one man who is near death. Appropriate burials must be given them, and the wounded and burned man who barely clings to life must be comforted as best we can. He is too badly wounded to live.''

I sat thinking about Grandfather. He wouldn't leave here unless carried away, and I wondered if we had checked everywhere. Suddenly, I jumped to my feet and ran toward the graveyard shouting to Ba Can, ''Grandmother's grave! Ba Can, we haven't checked Grandmother's grave.''

I ran down the sandy path past the few trees into the open, lower area where the village graveyard was located. The unobstructed morning sun shown down on me as I raced into the sacred burial place of our parents. Anger boiled within me, as truck tracks indiscriminately cut their blasphemous way through and across the graves. I ran around and in between graves making my way to the resting place of my grandmother.

I saw his body from a distance away. My pace slowed, and I started to walk, wiping tears off my face, staring at a black-clad, gray-headed figure of a man, facedown on the edge of Grandmother's grave. Trembling, I walked up to him and saw that his crushed, lifeless form lay in the tracks of a truck which had desecrated the grave. Then my stomach heaved, and I was sick realizing that the tracks ran over the top of him, right across the middle of his back. I knelt by his side and cried. Reaching out, I touched his body. It was stiffening in death. Still kneeling, I sat back on my heels and covered my face trying to hold back the tears.

After a moment, I realized that Ba Can had come up. He knelt beside me and placed his hand on my shoulder. Then he moved over to the dead body of the man who had loved and reared us as his own children. Gently, he rolled the body over. Dried blood had smeared the old face, and my brother said, ''His back was broken by this truck. He likely died in only a moment of time.'' Then I saw him studying the tracks made by the truck. Finally, he got up and looked at me saying, ''We have to bury our people and continue our march.''

As I watched Ba Can walk away, I heard Grandfather speaking in death what he had last told me in life, ''You must promise to fight out of love for your country, not hatred for the enemy . . . Hatred destroys.'' I thought of the cold hatred that colored the almost ashen face of my brother. I watched him walk toward his company.

Turning my eyes to the lifeless body of my grandfather, I spoke to him saying, "Grandfather, you must help if I am not to hate. It has already a hold on my heart, and now I believe my brother is driven by it. It is easy to hate. It is my desire to seek revenge. If I am not to, you must reach from your world to mine and help me."

I sat there, staring off in the distance for how long I didn't know, when suddenly I realized someone's presence next to me. Turning, I looked into the face of Van Thi. He knelt beside me, put his arms around me, and said "Cry! Kim Lan, cry. Do not hold it within you."

Little by little, with his arms around me, the tenseness eased, and the barrier within myself began to crack, and then it was like a dam had broken, and for what seemed long minutes, I did nothing but cry and tremble as an ocean of emotions poured out of me. I felt the memories of my mother as well as my grandparents. I could almost touch their warm presence. When I stopped, I realized that Van Thi's shirt was wet with my tears. I leaned back and tried to wipe both my face and his shirt, feeling very embarrassed. He held my hand which was attempting to brush off his shirt, and said, "Do not mind. Tears are human. They are real. To deny them is to deny oneself. Allow them release, and your internal self is cleansed, and you can stand in the world more purely yourself."

The crashing of an artillery round exploding nearby suddenly shook me out of the bitter memories. The destruction of Chien Son was in years past. As I sat and looked toward the distant sea, I watched the great orange ball of flame rise out of the dark, gray-blue horizon ready to climb above and dominate the day. Grandfather's words again echoed across the years, ". . . fight out of love for your country, not hatred for the enemy . . ."

Then I heard myself ask out loud, "Grandfather, I have hated, and still do. How can it be any different? There are only different levels of hatred." Slowly, I got up, wiped a tear away, and walked back into the jungle shadows.

The next day we received new orders. The village of Ap Bon which lay in the Thu Bon Valley was nestled into the foot of the mountains that harbored our headquarters. Its people had recently been removed by the Americans. A battalion of our regular soldiers of the 2nd Division had just arrived from the north, and it was their intent to trap the Americans at Ap Bon. The village had been the first evacuated by the enemy, but it had not been burned to the ground yet. I was to lead a scout team for two of the battalion's companies who were to prepare the trap.

Once the decision had been made, we moved rapidly. My scouts and I went with an advance command team of the division and intended to scout the village and prepare plans for its fortification.

As the sun was setting behind the mountains on the opposite side of the valley, we arrived on the last of the high ground overlooking the village. We were well concealed but could see perfectly the village and valley below. A stream which fed the Song Thu Bon crossed about fifty to one hundred and fifty yards in front of the village. The village was covered by trees, bamboo, and shrubs. Between the village and the stream were open rice fields. The foot of the mountains on which we sat rose immediately from the rear of the village. Small fingers of ground rose several feet above the rice paddies on either side and to the front of the village, and both were thickly covered by the same vegetation. Everything was silent, and there were no enemy soldiers to be seen.

After observing the village from our small hilltop for about thirty minutes, we moved down. Anxiously, I carried my rifle and watched carefully for any surprise. There was none, and the village was ours to explore and investigate. We noted strong and weak points.

That night we sat in one of the abandoned homes and plotted our possible strategies. Although we could make no fires, we covered the doors and windows and lit a small lantern. I dusted off an old table, and the major in charge of the team laid out a large sheet of paper, and we began to map the village. Occasionally, some of us would venture outside in the moonlight and verify distances and locations of pertinent features of the village.

It became obvious that we needed to lure the Americans straight in the front. The village itself was a little more than a quarter-mile wide across its front, and the entire site was well suited to machine gun and rifle fire that could lock the enemy in a crisscross of deadly hail. In addition, the higher ground on which the town was built extended like wings covered with trees and brush out to either side. Each side arced forward and offered an extra opportunity for establishing machine gun emplacements to catch the enemy by surprise from either flank. Remembering a previous success at surprising the Americans with wire interwoven in the thick strands of bamboo, I suggested to the major that the same be done here. He liked the idea.

After finishing the map work, the major made a list of all needed supplies and equipment, and then, in the darkness, we left the village for the mountains. As we reached the top of the small hill overlooking the village, I, with two of my scouts, dropped out of the team to remain to watch over the village. The other two went with the command team on its nighttime trek back up to our mountain base camp. The next evening we expected two companies of infantry from the battalion.

Finally, I began to relax and lay down thinking about the next day. I knew that the 2nd Division's main thrust was being planned for the south side of the mountains in the plains near the village of Que Son, maybe fifteen miles away. I hoped after this action that I could become involved in that battle. For now, however, I directed my attention to the matters at hand and wondered how the major planned to lure the American Marines into our trap.

The next day we spent observing the valley. Portions of it were still being farmed, and a few small patrols of Americans could be observed. About a mile downriver from the village toward An Hoa there was a major roadway which the Marines used. Maybe we could initiate a small-scale ambush at that location and quickly retreat leaving a trail to follow? In my own mind, I was planning operations for the regular army, but realistically, I knew that they had their own sources of intelligence and their own ideas.

Patiently, we waited, and by midafternoon the lead elements of the two-company force had reached my position still in the jungles above the village. As the balance of the force moved in and positioned themselves in the jungle, the major and two captains came to sit with me.

I let them know what we had seen during the day and pointed out the location of the road about a mile away. I said that I thought we might initiate a diversion and draw the Americans to our ambush. I knelt on a bare patch of earth on the edge of the jungle and drew in the dirt my thoughts for the plan. He said he was interested, and then we settled for a while to observe everything below us. I didn't want to wait any longer.

As darkness sank down upon the valley, we moved. Throughout the night, we worked in shifts, two hours working and one resting. By morning we had the village prepared. The entire front was fenced with wire woven through the bamboo and shrubs. Behind this we had built bunkers and fighting holes all interconnected by a six-foot-deep trench. Deep caves were also dug for better protection against heavy artillery and air bombardment. Our fighting positions were all carefully located in order to coordinate rifle and automatic weapons fire. Then we carefully concealed machine-gun emplacements on either flank and made sure that they could cut down the Americans from the sides. These would be employed only after the enemy committed himself in a countermove against our first attack. The six-foot trenches also led back out of the village. Finally, our two companies had several mortar sections attached and dug in toward the rear in the higher ground.

After eight hours of ceaseless toil and as dawn drew aside the nighttime curtains, the major, the two captains, and I sat to finalize our plans. We did not know how long it would take to entice an American unit into our trap. After some discussion, it was decided that by midmorning we would send a platoon-size patrol in the direction that I had recommended. They were to make contact and inflict casualties upon an enemy unit as the opportunity presented itself and to retreat quickly to our fortified village. The Marines would likely respond by sending in a larger force to follow, attempting to destroy our team. They normally were aggressive and often sacrificed caution for speed. If they did so this time, they would regret it.

As we sat in the early morning and developed our potential strategies for the various possible situations, not knowing if we would have to wait days or hours, a faint rumble weakly reverberated through our valley. Instinctively we cocked our ears and froze, silently listening to the growing noise.

The light fog of early morning was evaporating as the sun peaked around the corner of the valley walls. Flying with the sun at their backs came American helicopters. By their numbers it appeared an entire battalion was on its way. The major said, "We may not have to try to lure them here."

A reconnaissance team was quickly sent out to the area where the enemy had landed. We set our men in the prepared positions and waited like a scorpion to attack. Our front was an iron and bamboo wall with fortified positions. Our pincers, with the machine guns' crushing power, extended to the front on either side. The tail end of the village rested on higher ground at the foot of the mountains. There waited our stinger, three sections of mortars. Would the American Marines do us the favor of walking into our lair? We waited.

Two hours passed before our scouts returned. They reported that a battalion of enemy had come. There were two companies at this end of the valley, while the rest had been taken a few miles farther away. The two companies at our end were moving not far from each other but with what seemed to be slightly different objectives. One company was coming in our direction. The question remained: Should we send out some bait, or would they come of their own accord? We watched and waited.

Slowly the enemy Marines showed their plan of movement. One company was moving on Ap Bon. Maybe their job was to burn the village to the ground since it had now been evacuated. With luck they would walk right into our ambush. From our positions, we could now catch glimpses of their lead platoon. In another quarter-mile, they would be at the creek which traversed our front on a slight angle. If they moved across the creek, they would be in a shallow but wide plot of rice paddies which lay from the mountains on our right to the river about a half-mile to our left. The fields in front of the village were open except for the rice paddy dikes. If things worked as we hoped, the Americans would move through the creek into the rice fields directly and immediately to our front.

Our weapons, including our mortars, were plotted to destroy them after they were in the open, one-hundred-yard-wide field between the village and the creek.

We silently watched, and they kept coming. My nerves were on edge. I paced back and forth in the command bunker which was built in the center of the village near the front. We were slightly above our other positions and would have a good view of the Marines as they came. Tensely, I waited. Like tiny marbles, beads of perspiration began to roll down my face. Without my own company to direct, I felt frustrated. All I could do was to watch.

Soon the enemy's lead platoon was emerging from the creek and entering the open rice fields to our front. We waited. The positions of the two remaining platoons slowly became clear. All three were stretched out across the rice fields on a three hundred yard front. Their center platoon was in the lead, flanked on either side and a little to the rear by the other two platoons.

As I stood and watched from the bunker, the major touched me and pointed out that my hair had fallen down to the middle of my back. He smiled and called me one of the *doi quan toc dai*, the long-haired soldiers. Then he quickly focused his thoughts on the approaching Americans.

My eyes surveyed the enemy, and they kept coming. I remembered a part of our training that instructed us about American philosophy and how it affected their military tactics. It seemed as if their history, traditions, and even their concept of manhood and heroes had implanted in their way of thinking that to win they must be bold and aggressive. This had translated itself into military tactics which mandated that they should attack, attack, and destroy. By their individual bravery and the overwhelming force of their firepower, they felt invincible. Consequently, they did not truly understand the art of deception or that their own aggressive philosophy could be the tool of their own destruction. Neither did they value the ability to bide their time, patiently enduring pain, tolerating hardships, and waiting as long as it was necessary before striking the enemy at a time and place of their choosing, not the enemy's. Their acts, which they considered to be daring and fearless, could prove to be stupid and foolish. I watched the Marines as they recklessly came across the fields. The sun shone brightly down upon them. We waited like shadows among the trees.

As they came forward, they held their weapons on the alert. There were about one hundred and twenty of them. When their company was well within the openness of the rice fields, with the lead teams not more than thirty yards from our positions, we opened fire. It was a devastating barrage that hit the Americans from their front. At least a dozen were killed in the first burst of fire, but they reacted with speed and attacked directly at the village front. Our mortars rained down on them. Then they hit the wall of barbed wire-bound bamboo, and their troops began to pile up. Their platoon to our left attacked to the west attempting to encircle us. However, our left pincer with reinforced machine-gun positions bit deeply into their ranks. Their company tried to disengage and pull back. I moved out of the bunker but stayed in the trench.

Then we heard the sound of their artillery on the way. It came like trucks roaring through the sky at the speed of bullets. I clasped my hands on my ears and braced myself against the sides of the trench. The violent heaving of the earth rocked and slammed me. The noise was deafening. The center of the village was convulsing in spasms of pain. Quickly, I raised myself to check the situation. Many of our positions not under the direct assault of their artillery maintained a continuous stream of fire on the enemy. Others stayed below the ground suffering the shattering effects of the heavy guns.

Then I saw enemy reinforcements from the creek. Rapidly, they struck toward the right side of our lines, hoping to find a weak point and relieve their besieged sister unit. No sooner had they passed our right-side pincer, which had been silently waiting, than it struck in surprise out of its ambush positions. The enemy fought and tried to close with our soldiers. They, however, were engaged with the crushing jaws of our front positions while desperately trying to beat off our ripping pincers on either flank.

Their artillery now quieted, but screaming up the valley I heard the warplanes. I watched in awe, seeing the fullness of the American power. A quick thought flashed

through my mind: What would it be like if we had such
power? Then I dove to the bottom of the trench.

A shocking, thunderous roll of the ground lifted me,
and helplessly I was slammed into the side of the trench.
There was an instant of pain and then nothing.

A putrid smell was in the air, and I heard gunshots and
screams vaguely drifting across my mind. I started to move,
but my body ached, and I fell back down. Slowly I opened
my eyes, and my senses began to clear just a little. I was
confused. Darkness was drifting down the valley and settling
around me. I tried to unscramble my thoughts, and finally, I
realized that I had been unconscious for hours. Struggling to
regain my feet, I looked around.

The bunker I had left was a hole filled with debris and
stared back at me shattered in its death. My comrades
were not to be seen. Farther to my left, the white, smoldering fires of napalm had charred the area. I saw bodies
of Vietnamese soldiers burned and stiffened beyond recognition. Stunned, I stood trying to comprehend what
had happened.

As if in a dream, I realized the battle still raged on, but
there were no enemy air strikes. I saw a canteen lying at my
feet and bent over to pick it up. My head was ringing, and I
suddenly became dizzy as I bent down. Then I lost my food,
vomiting in the place where I had just lay.

From my knees, I slowly arose and took a long swallow
of the water. Leaning back against the side wall of the
trench, I poured the rest of the canteen over my head.

Then standing again, I noted almost without care that
the scene of the battle had shifted to the rice fields. Our
companies were battling theirs. The sounds of rifle shots,
grenades, and screams eerily drifted past me as if in another world. With my body aching and my head throbbing, I pulled myself out of the trench. I lay there on the
ground, my strength slowly ebbing into darkness.

When I again awoke, something was different. Vaguely
I could tell that the cool jungle had replaced the bombed
village. I looked around and tested my body.

As I sat up, my heart pounded its beat within my head,
and I sat dazed. Slowly, I looked around. Dead and
wounded were scattered around in a ghastly display of

carnage. Then I recognized one of the company commanders and forced myself to my feet.

The faint light of early dawn trickled through the jungle canopy as I cautiously made my way past the dead, dying, and wounded bodies. I felt sick but managed to get behind some bushes before heaving my stomach inside out again.

Finally, I reached the captain's side. He sat leaning against a tree, half dozing, and I sat beside him. Opening his eyes, he looked at me and smiled, saying, "How do you feel?"

I looked around at the men who lay in front of me and replied, "Like a thousand buffaloes trampled me, but what of these? What has happened?"

He said, "The Americans walked into our trap and suffered greatly. The best I can determine is that one-half of their first company was destroyed, and many more from their second. After the first hour, we closed with them. It is best to fight them in close quarters. That way their artillery and air power cannot hit us without also doing themselves damage. We attacked them throughout the night as they had pulled back near the creek dragging their wounded and dead.

"Then we gradually disengaged. Some of our units carried the bodies of our dead and wounded through the escape trenches back into the hills. We have brought our brothers high in these mountains. Here we will bury those who died. The last of our platoons are now moving up the trails. There's the last coming in now. Excuse me, I must go check with their commanders."

Before he left, I asked, "What happened to the major?"

He looked at me a moment and then said, "He was in the bunker with you. I don't know how it is that you survived, and we did not find him. His body was gone. Everyone in that bunker was blown into pieces by that bomb. It was a huge crater. You better rest. Your eyes don't look right."

Then he walked away through the jungles toward the rest of his men. I sat still and slowly thought, How *did* I survive? My heart continued its heavy beat in my head.

* * *

Within two weeks I felt better. The division was planning a major reorganization of our forces and a shifting of our objectives to the south. We had not stopped the relocation of about five thousand villagers from the Thu Bon Valley, but we still sent small patrols there to execute a raid or ambush. I was given orders to take a team to reconnoiter a part of the valley. There were still a few hundred villagers. We did not know if they were going to be left alone or not.

By evening I had moved a squad of my men to the edge of the valley where we spent the night. The next morning found us carefully following a brush and tree-lined stream toward a village that the Americans had not yet relocated.

At the bottom of the hill we halted surprised by the sudden appearance of an enemy platoon as it moved past a row of hedges in our front and marched on the village. We hid only about a hundred yards away, watched, and waited. They seemed confident and bold. Then they disappeared into the village. It was not a large place, maybe fifty homes, and it lay nestled next to the hills. Many of the people had already gone to work in the rice fields. They stubbornly continued with their work even though they knew the enemy was coming.

I couldn't wait any longer. Even though I wore the shirt of an officer in our army and carried a rifle, I had to risk being seen in order to find out what was happening. However, I dared not risk the entire squad, so I left them with instructions to stay and watch from where they were and, by myself, silently stole into the jungle. I circled just higher in the jungle than the squad and moved toward the village.

As I neared it, I began to hear a rising tumult of confusion. American voices were shouting orders, and fearful and angry Vietnamese replies were ringing through the village. So they've come to take these, too, I thought. It was some time since I had practiced my English, but I could understand what was being said.

I moved within twenty yards of the first home and hid in the last line of jungle. A dry ditch crossed my front just below me and was about fifteen feet wide. Then it climbed back up to a large tree. The village was beyond.

I debated the wisdom of quickly crawling across that open ground to the tree, but before I could decide, I froze. To my right, someone was crying and running. I glanced in the direction of the muffled cries.

Not twenty feet from me, an American soldier had just caught and thrown a young girl to the ground near the edge of the jungle. My eyes widened in horror as he ripped her blouse open and slapped her face. Through my mind raced countless hateful emotions. As the American held one hand over her mouth and knelt on her stomach, he began to pull his pants down, I saw my mother and the whole Vietnamese nation being raped. I couldn't stand it, and I rose from behind the tree where I hid. I prepared to kill and doubtless be killed.

Like a lightning bolt, just as I threw the rifle to my shoulder, a green and black uniform leaped out of the bush near the girl smashing his gun into the side of the American's head! I hesitated.

I watched as the rapist lay unconscious in the ditch and the newcomer carefully knelt by the side of the girl. His hat had fallen to the ground, and he put his rifle aside. Then he awkwardly tried to comfort the girl. He held her as she tried fearfully to hold together her torn shirt. He was an American! His rifle lay beside him, and I cautiously moved closer.

Within ten feet, I knelt beside a tree and looked closely at this new enemy soldier and the girl. His head was lowered looking at her, and he was talking softly, stupidly, to her in words she didn't understand. His short blond hair and soldier's uniform was in stark contrast to her long black hair and dark peasant clothes.

I raised up but stepped on a dry stick making a noise I knew would wake the Chinese. I froze, staring at the two. His head jerked up, and one hand shot out for his rifle. Then he, too, froze.

My rifle was aimed at his heart, but I couldn't fire. His blue eyes locked on me with one arm still holding the girl, and the other fixed in place as it had been reaching for his rifle. We stared at each other, and I knew this was the American! Bound by the past, I stood like a stupid statue, unable to move. The only noise in that short, still moment was a little breeze that gently stirred the bushes. Our eyes searched

and questioned each other. The confusing ghost of so many
past horrors now knelt in front of me!

There was no fear in his face, but I knew that he
couldn't remember me. However, his eyes probed and
searched, questioning me in their silence. I glanced at
the girl. She, with muffled cries, looked at us both and
inched slowly away, sliding on her back.

Slowly, with my right arm holding the rifle, my left
hand went to my head. Without really knowing why, I
took off my cap and unpinned my hair. It fell down across
my shoulders and back. Then I said only, *"Be Dau."*

A wave of disbelief crossed his face, then recognition.
Quickly, I motioned to the girl to be silent and to move
up into the jungle. Then I said to him, "Stay where you
are. Do not follow." I glanced back at him as I turned
to run. He still knelt there watching me wide-eyed.

The jungles closed behind us as I ran with the girl
straight up the hill. A part of me wanted to scream at
him, "Why did you come back? Why are all of you here
killing my people?" There was no time. We kept running, but then she fell.

As I stooped to help her, I heard the noise of someone
running behind us. I swung around and pointed the barrel of my rifle into the chest of the American. He stopped
as if he had run into a wall. His hands went up to his
shoulders, palms out toward me. He said in a rush, "Do
you speak English? You cannot go up there."

I looked at him, angrily saying, "I said, 'Do not follow.' You will die."

"No, you will," he whispered. "My patrol is ahead
of you, not far."

I quickly glanced around and said, "Then we will go
this way. You go back."

"Wait," he said. "What is your name?"

I looked at him a moment before answering, "Kim
Lan. Now go." I grabbed the girl and disappeared into
the jungle toward my squad, occasionally stopping to listen. I heard no one but saw only him. Why hadn't I killed
him? Why had I told him my name? Why?

CHAPTER 10

> When the day comes for me to face my Maker and account for my actions, the thing I would be most humbly proud of was the fact that I fought against, and perhaps contributed to preventing, the carrying out of some harebrained tactical schemes which would have cost the lives of thousands of men. To that list of tragic accidents that fortunately never happened I would add the Indochina intervention.
>
> —General Matthew B. Ridgway (1956)

It's hard to say you're bored when you're in the middle of Apache Country and Geronimo is loose, but I was getting that way. We covered the left flank of the grunts as they swept through the valley relocating villagers. I didn't think much about the reasoning behind all the replanting of people. I suppose it was for their safety as well as ours. Now after about two weeks there wasn't much left, just one more village on this side of the valley and a few across the river. Finally, I leaned over and whispered to Williams, "I'm going to move down front a little. Need to get a closer look. It's only a hundred meters down the hill. No Charlie around here. I'll be back in about thirty or so minutes."

"Remember the fight at Ap Bon," he said. "I wouldn't trust nothing out this far. Shit, Lieutenant, we can't tell if there's any bad guys down near that village. You could get blown away real quick. Let's stay tight up here."

"Williams, there's nobody in the next hundred meters. We'd a seen 'em before now. I want to get a closer look at that village when the grunts move in, but the patrol's got to stay up here and keep on the watch."

With that, I started crawling down the hillside. The

farther I moved away from the patrol, the wiser Williams's words sounded to me. Was I a dumb shit or something? Two weeks fighting only the mosquitoes, leeches, and the humid heat must of been fucking up my brain-housing group. Still I kept crawling.

It was taking too godawful long. Finally, though, I pushed forward on my stomach to the edge of a shallow draw. I hid next to a large rock, screened by the last bush in the jungle. I watched the infantry moving through the village trying to herd up the locals to march them down to the ''six-bys'' to truck them off. It was typical. Many people resisted.

Then I watched one girl slip behind a hut not thirty yards away and try to run off in my direction. I started to feel uneasy. What was I to do if she ran up to my face? Then I saw a Marine jump from a concealed position to my right front and chase after her. Good, I wouldn't have to get involved.

He quickly caught her and threw her down into the ditch not more than ten feet in front of me. Then I saw the look in his eyes. Oh, no, I thought. Shit, you son of a bitch, don't do that!

He slapped her and ripped her blouse open. Young, virgin breasts were exposed, and the Marine seemed to go crazy. He was kneeling on her stomach and trying to unbuckle his belt.

Not thinking, I jumped out of hiding, my rifle in my hands. His pants dropped as he muffled her cries with one hand. I was so close, he didn't have time to look up. My rifle smashed into the side of his skull, and he rolled backward lying unconscious. Instinctively, setting my rifle aside, I knelt down to help her. My God, she couldn't have been more than fourteen or fifteen! I tried to hold and comfort her, feeling like an embarrassed fool.

Suddenly, something cracked in front of me. Jerking up, still trying to hold the girl, I reached for my rifle. In the first split second, I saw an enemy uniform. In the next fraction of a second, I saw a woman, her eyes flashing darkly at me. My God, it was her! I knew it was, even though her hair was pinned under her cap. I couldn't move. She stood there pointing a rifle at my heart, eyes darting from me to the girl. With arms outstretched in either direction, I knelt, frozen, mesmerized by a distant recognition. I didn't even think about the danger I was in. This was the woman! This was her! She stared back not pulling the trigger. My God, she could kill me! Who is she? I know her, but from where in hell . . .

She stood there silently watching me ask without words, Who are you? Then her hand went to her head. Her other arm kept the rifle leveled on me. She let her hair drop. It cascaded to her waist. A slight breeze gently curled it around her uniform. Then her lips parted, and she said, *Be Dau.* A wave—a tidal wave—built up from out of my past and slammed my mind a decade backward in time. I knelt not believing what I was seeing or hearing.

Sweet Jesus, Mary, and Joseph! The girl in that colonel's place in Hoi An in 1956 stood looking down on me. This was another world. This was crazy! I looked at this enemy soldier who could kill me just as easily as she was looking at me, and, instead, I saw a young girl from ten years before. The Vietnamese colonel who had nearly slit my throat back then had been running a bunch of girls for profit on the side. I was to advise his unit on military tactics, but he had been trying to show me a good time instead. The house had been like his little palace of pleasures out of some movie about the Far East. He'd brought this new girl to me. He'd assured me she was young, beautiful, and still a virgin. She had been all that and a whole hell of a lot more!

That same girl stared down at me now with a killing piece in her hands, but in the flood of memories that was pouring over me, I remembered when I first set eyes on her. She had been about 5 feet 4 inches tall; slim, proud, and beautiful with long black hair. But son-of-a-fucking-bitch if she wasn't a girl I once knew when I was in high school. At least she was the spitting image of one.

When I had turned sixteen, in a small town near San Antonio, Texas, a Mexican family moved into our neighborhood. Some people had been upset that some Mexicans had moved in. But me? I couldn't take my eyes off their daughter. Maria Elena checked into my class in high school and checked into my mind all year long. But I was so damn shy it took me a year to ask her out for a date. After that, we dated until we graduated from school the next spring. Some kids didn't like the mixed dating, but for the most part school wasn't bad. At home my parents were supportive and open-minded to a point. There was more than one way to say that it was okay to date, but they wouldn't want me to marry one. "What about the children, of a mixed marriage? They would be called half-breeds! Their lives would be more difficult, and a person wouldn't want to do that to their children." That was Texas, 1951.

Then that Vietnamese colonel, with an ego the size of the Empire State Building, tried to set me up with a fifteen-year-old who looked so much like my Maria Elena that it screwed me up bad. The girl had been frightened, and I remembered the same tearful look in Mena's eyes. There had been no fucking way that I was going to make a whore out of that girl. I paid the maid to help her escape, and then had to pay the colonel a hundred bucks greenback to keep him from having my throat sliced open. I had made up some story about her getting away from me, but that hadn't made any difference to him.

Now she was standing in front of me, only today my life was in her hands. My enemy tigress was that young girl from so long ago. My Vietnamese Mena, with a rifle pointed at my heart! I searched her eyes—did she remember me? She was hesitating, but at the same time she stood confidently over me.

Then she motioned for the girl to leave and surprised me speaking in English, "Stay where you are. Do not follow."

As quickly as she had appeared, she and the girl were gone. The jungle closed behind them as they ran uphill. Her words reverberated through my mind. I knew she recognized me when she first saw me months ago! That's why she hadn't shot me and the helicopter out of the sky! She remembered!

Oh, shit, they'll run into my patrol, I thought. I jumped to my feet, forgetting my rifle, and raced after them.

I hadn't gone twenty feet when, like running into a tree, I suddenly stopped with a rifle barrel bruising a hole in my chest. Her eyes flashed with anger, and I quickly spoke, "Do you speak English? You cannot go up there."

Angrily she whispered, "I said, 'Do not follow.' You will die."

"No, you will," I hurriedly tried to explain. "My patrol is ahead of you, not far."

She looked quickly around and again whispered, "Then we will go this way. You go back."

"Wait," I said in a rush. "What is your name?"

For a brief moment, the look on her face betrayed her feelings. There was some softness in her voice as she said, "Kim Lan. Now go."

The jungle again took her away. She was gone. I returned to get my rifle thinking, That's it. I'll never see her again. God, I need to know who she is. What's her story? All I got is her name, Kim Lan. Now she's gone! That fucking quick. Shit!

I sat down at the foot of a tree. Jungle plants hid me as I tried to control my racing thoughts. Over the last few minutes, I had smashed a Marine with my rifle and then turned around and helped an enemy soldier escape. Did it make any difference that the soldier was a woman I knew? Did it make any difference that we were supposed to be here to protect people that were like her? My mind was confused with conflicting emotions. I didn't like it when the answers weren't easy. I knew that if I was ever to get my head squared away, I would have to find her and find out who the hell she was. Fat fucking chance!

The Marines out in the village were in another world now. The one lying unconscious in the ditch had become almost immaterial. I walked down, picked up my rifle, and checked his pulse. He was alive. I poured a handful of water from my canteen over his face and walked into the bush. I heard a slight groan behind me and figured the son of a bitch would probably be medevaced with a concussion but wondered how he'd explain it.

In two more days, we were back at An Hoa. The village relocation business was done with, but my mind was still back there with her. If part of my mind was left on "No-Name Hill," most of the rest was stuck on her. She was permanently fixed in my head, but I really wanted to have more than sixty seconds with her. Damn it! I had to find out about this shit.

It was hard to think straight anymore. I had been in-country living half in the bush, half out, for too long. If I survived this place and got back to the World, Vietnam was permanently embedded in my skull, and she'd be there. I needed R&R now!

I rated it, I deserved it, and within three days, I was sitting on the hot, dusty flight line at the Marine Corps Air Terminal in Da Nang going to Japan. I definitely intended to put this place behind me for a while. But the wait dragged on. I watched Vietnamese workers hired to clean the air terminal building. Tentatively, they walked around doing menial labor, occasionally faking a smile at some American. It all seemed out of place. We were supposed to be here to help these people, but instead we dragged them away from their natural environment and gave them our own shit-details. I wondered if she knew any of these people, and if they were here really working for Charlie. I just didn't trust them around our camps. Like I heard someone say, "I wouldn't trust one of 'em, unless I had his balls in a vise." I wondered how many VC surprise attacks on our rear base camps were coordinated by the little, dumb-looking, betel-chewing, slow-moving laborers we hired. Yet something about them provoked sympathy in me.

One of them just stared at me. It made me uneasy. Then I remembered the book *The Ugly American*. If we were here to help them help themselves, then we should be out in their villages going one-on-one with each Vietnamese in his own home. That's where "hearts and minds" would be won! However, we weren't, and that little fart kept staring at me.

Shit, my mind argued. It wasn't my fault, man! That's somebody else's decision. I'm going on R&R so I can forget this place—for five days anyway.

I got up and walked outside.

Finally, after a hot six-hour wait, I was on a plane, and we were shoving off back to civilization. Damn, it felt good. As the plane broke through the clouds in the early evening hours, I looked back down on the white cloudy carpet gleaming in the light of the setting sun. Then I relaxed. I actually leaned back, took a deep breath, and relaxed. I promised myself two things: a long hot shower every day and filet mignon every evening.

I slept the last half of the trip, and when I awoke, the plane was descending. I looked down on the city lights and got excited. I made myself another promise and that was to find some American girls. I knew that there were some here as schoolteachers. I also needed to go to the PX and buy some clothes, since I had only one other uniform with me and no "civies." I consciously set my mind to try to forget Vietnam and everything in it.

When we landed, it was the middle of the night, and I had to concentrate on simply getting a quick bite to eat and a place to sleep. There was an all-night Air Force hamburger stand at the terminal, and I grabbed a burger, fries, and a glass of milk—cold milk. It was beyond description to smell the wonderful aroma of frying grease. For the first time in more than a year, I felt like I was really eating.

I got a taxi to a place called the Johnson Family Housing Unit. I was assigned a room in the Visiting Officers' Quarters. At 3:00 A.M. I found myself in front of the door to my little house. I was about to close my eyes and drift through the door to the hot showers when like a rifle shot, a noise cracked the night in the bushes to my side.

When I looked around, I realized that instinctively I had thrown myself into the bush on the other side of the little concrete porch. Streetlights shone down on the yard as I watched two cats streaking across the lawn. Damn, I thought, looking around. I hope no one was watching. Fucking cats! Collins, get your shit together.

I headed straight for the showers, dropping clothes along the way. Turning the water on as hot as I could stand it, I simply sat on the floor and leaned back against the shower wall thinking, How sweet it is! Outside of a few hot water buckets at the Paris Steam Baths in Da Nang, this was the first hot water I'd had in longer than I could remember.

After countless luxuriating minutes, a heavy cloud of steam had filled the upper half of the entire bathroom. I finally got out, dried off, and dragged my limp body to bed. Wondering if heaven could top this, I slid between sheets—real sheets—pulled up a blanket, and immediately felt myself dozing off under the coolness of an air-conditioned climate. Oh, God, how nice.

When I awoke, a sheet lay over my head. I was almost afraid to pull it down—maybe I was dreaming. I'd really wake up and this would be a blanket, and I'd still be lying on my cot in Vietnam. Slowly, I stuck my head out and looked around. I shouted and jumped up and began to think about what I was going to do this wonderful, glorious day. Finally, I opted for a PX run to get some clothes, another hamburger and fries, and to watch for girls, American girls.

I walked to the Air Force Base Exchange and along the way stared at the sites and sounds of civilization: the real world. Maybe I could really forget Indochina.

Walking into the PX, I headed for the civilian clothes and quickly bought some, changing immediately in the dressing room. I felt almost awed being in the presence of all this Americana. There were quite a few ''round-eyed'' blonds walking around the store, and I found myself helplessly staring. Finally, I managed to speak to a couple of these American women, and although they made a point of referring to their ''husbands,'' they were nice enough to point out places where I might best be able to meet some of the single teachers. It was the latter part of August, the schools were soon to open, and teachers had recently been flown in on contract with the government to teach Air Force dependents.

About five hours later, after taking my own guided tour, I made my way to one of the Officers' Clubs. My mind had focused on eating my first juicy, prime cut steak and baked potato. I thought, by God, I'm really gonna forget the war.

I sat down in luxurious comfort and ordered. My eyes wandered the room while I waited, and I figured that I might look like some poor lost soul from the war. Not to worry though, 'cause I intended to work on my stomach and get it back into condition.

When the food finally arrived, I leaned back in my chair and closed my eyes. My entire body seemed to be salivating with the experience of sitting again in a comfortable, air-conditioned O-Club with a thick, succulent steak sensuously stimulating my taste buds. I started slowly, wanting to savor fully each bite. There was no time to drink with my total being focused on this feast prepared in heaven for a starving soul come from hell. Brown and pink juices eased out of the meat and floated next to the potato, which also beckoned my fork, but the poor spud would have to wait its turn. After three indescribably delicious bites of steak, I grabbed a hot roll and soaked up the juices. I sat there for a minute silently relishing the delicacy of the warm bread.

I began to realize that eating could be an art form. After the gastronomical desert of C-rations, I now had happened upon a flowering banquet arising as an oasis on my table. Not wanting to rush and too quickly fill my shrunken stomach, I took part in this pleasure as an event of almost religious importance.

Thirty minutes later, my plate looked as if it had been polished, and I set a new objective during the next days: my stomach would be reprogrammed to progress from the eight-ounce steak just finished to a heartier twelve-ounce. Belatedly, I picked up my Cuba Libre and walked to the jukebox.

After playing fifty cents worth of Ray Price, Eddy Arnold, Johnny Cash, and a few others, I sat at the bar next to the music and ordered another rum-and-Coke—"Twist of lime, please."

I was singing along in my mind, The night life, it ain't no good life, but it's my life . . . when I noticed a young lady walk to the jukebox with a quarter in hand. She was tall, slim, and had fairly long blond hair. Even though the bar area of the club was only dimly lit, she looked beautiful. Get your wits together, I told myself, and see if you can start a conversation.

So turning on my bar chair, I looked at her standing near me and asked, "Excuse me, I'm new here, and I thought that maybe you could help me." Please say something, I thought quietly.

She looked over, smiled, and said, "I'm afraid I wouldn't be of much help. I only arrived last week."

"Well," I responded, "I'm only here for five days, and I guess I'd like to find some places to go to eat and just go out on the town in Tokyo without feeling like I was falling into a tourist trap. What brings you to Japan?'' I felt proud of myself for having been able to converse so far without either using the gutter language of war-time Marines or drooling down my shirt.

"I just arrived from Ohio,'' she said, "and I have to start teaching at a school on the base in two weeks, but I'm afraid I know nothing about the Air Force or Tokyo.''

Not wanting her to leave, I replied, "I got in about three A.M. last night from Vietnam, and I'm a Marine, so I don't know anything about the base, either, but if you're not tied up, maybe we could sightsee a little together? Would you like to have a drink?''

I think she sensed my desperation and took pity on me. Anyway, she said, "Okay, I just dropped by for a quick drink before I rejoin my friends later.'' She sat down at the bar next to me, and I thought, she's smart. Left herself an excuse to leave in case I turned out to be a bummer.

She turned to me and asked, "How long have you been in Vietnam?''

"The better part of a year,'' I said, "but first, what are you drinking?''

"Scotch and soda, thank you.''

I asked her, "Where did you go to college?''

The bartender brought her drink, and I watched her smile at him and then turn back to me. Falling head over heels into her blue eyes, I kicked myself for falling in love with the first pair of "round-eyes'' I sat down with.

She said, "Kent State.'' I vaguely remembered something about their football team, but before I could try to remember their last All-American to talk about, she said, "When I left, there was a growing number of students involved in antiwar discussions. I really wasn't a part of it, but I am curious about Vietnam.''

I thought to myself, Did I really want to talk about the war? After all, I was there to forget it.

God her eyes were beautiful! I was definitely in love. Just in time I brought myself to my senses and said, "I'd rather talk about Ohio, California, anywhere but Vietnam.''

"I'm sorry,'' she said. "That was stupid of me.''

"No, no, don't worry about it. Where are you from? I mean your hometown?"

"Near Cleveland." She smiled. "How about you?"

"Originally, near San Antonio, Texas, but it has been southern California for years now," I replied, feeling better all the time.

"I'm really great. I know nothing about Vietnam, Japan, or Texas. San Antonio? Isn't that where the Alamo is or something big?"

"Yeah, the Alamo's there, but don't feel bad cause all I know about Cleveland is that the Cleveland Indians play there in the summer, the Browns in the fall, and that Jimmy Brown was about the best mother—the best running back in all of football, and they used to give my favorite team, the Lions, fits all the time."

"The Lions? They're from Detroit, aren't they? But have you ever heard of the Cleveland Philharmonic?"

"I guess so, but I don't really keep up with the big bands."

She smiled and ordered a second drink. I felt tremendous—she had ordered a second drink! Maybe this spoke well for our future.

Over the next hour, I found out that she was already homesick, and that this was her first job after graduating from Kent State. I thought that it was just beginning to sink in that she wouldn't see her family for nine months. Her name was Lynn Marie Hartman. We made plans to see each other for lunch the next day, and then she was gone.

After two more drinks, I walked to the base theater and watched a movie, which was another of those luxury items not available out in the bush in 'Nam. Finally, I was back at my quarters and crawling into bed before midnight, again feeling and enjoying some of the comforts of the World: sheets, comfortable bed, and air conditioning.

At noon the next day, I stopped by the Teachers' Quarters anxiously looking forward to seeing Lynn. When she walked out, I knew I was in love. She was so beautiful! She smelled like a lady, she walked like a lady, she talked like a lady, and she paid attention to me! What the hell was I doing in Vietnam?

After lunch at the O-Club, we decided to go to Tokyo and play tourist. As soon as we got there, we began to sightsee and window shop. We walked together in this Oriental-turning-Occidental metropolis, and I felt like I was at the senior prom with the girl of everybody's dreams. After a while, we decided to stroll into the housing area away from the tourist-oriented businesses along the main drag.

We found that it did not take long to get away from the thin veneer of westernization. Very soon, we were walking downhill on a cobblestone street. There was a rock wall along one side, and along the other there were rows of traditional-looking Japanese houses of probably middle class or better status. It was late afternoon and the sun was doing a peak-a-boo dance in and out between house tops and trees uphill behind us.

Lynn then stopped me and said, "Listen!"

There was music playing from one of the homes. It was a beautiful symphonic melody. She held my arm and tears came to her eyes. "My dad plays in the Cleveland Philharmonic," she said, "and that sounds just like them." Looking up at me, she wiped away her tears and said, "Guess I'm being stupidly homesick." We continued walking down the street with the music providing a melody for the receding sun behind us, and she still held my arm.

When we reached the bottom of the hill, there appeared in front of us a small cultured park. Well-trimmed grass, expertly sited trees, and a little pond and stream decorated the landscape. A small white bridge arched across the stream to a flowered path beside which was a swing built for two. We followed the path and sat for a while in the swing.

If music starts playing now, I said to myself, I think that I'll have to get up and look around for the movie director. Music didn't start, but the afternoon was one of those rare moments in life that stays forever beautifully photographed in one's memory.

That night I took Lynn back to the quarters on base. "Would you like to come over to my little apartment?" I asked her. "It'd be nice to talk to you some more."

"I think we'd end up doing more than talking. And I'd probably like it and then live to regret it."

"Well, I think I'd like it a whole hell of a lot. But I like just being with you. I can never describe to you the difference between living in the dust and mud with a bunch of Marines and walking down this street with you."

"Thank you for the thought, but one of your problems is that you need both worlds. I've really enjoyed being with you, too, but I've told myself more than once, 'Lynn, this guy is falling in love with you because you're the first woman in almost a year who has talked to him, and spent time with him, while you've both been in a decent environment.' But don't get me wrong! I want it to continue just like you. Only I'm putting some limits on my feelings. Still, Ryan Michael Collins, I would like very much to see you tomorrow."

I kissed her good night and said, "You're on."

Slowly I walked back to my room. Later, lying in my bed, my thoughts aimlessly wandered back and forth between 'Nam and Japan. A little fatalistic melancholy drifted in, and I wondered whether I would get through Vietnam alive and well in order to enjoy life like this.

Lynn and I spent most of the next day together just getting to know the base and a little of Japan. But I dropped her off a little early and went back to the O-Club to find a Marine I had seen there earlier. I had decided to wander into the nearby Japanese village, which catered to American servicemen in any way they wanted—as long as money was left on the table.

This Marine's name was Cherokee. He was on R&R like me, and we shoved off together. He had spent the last three nights in the "ville" and promised to show me the ropes.

As we drove in the little taxi, I watched the glittering lights of the bars, baths, and brothels beckoning to all the servicemen. The streets were narrow and many were unpaved, but the service was similar wherever you went.

I followed Cherokee into the Bar New York, and then we barhopped to the bars New Orleans, Las Vegas, and California. Finally, we settled at about 2300 hours at the Pussycat Bar, where Cherokee introduced me to his "girlfriend.'' Her name was Meiko. She, along with all the other girls working the bars, made most of their money pushing drinks. They received a cut of the profits on each drink, including the ones you bought them. However, as a general rule, their drinks were Coke, even though you were paying for a whiskey. The girls lavished sensuous attention on you, enticing a guy to empty his drinks quite often.

Meiko seemed to be pissed at Cherokee about his being a ''butterfly'' with other girls, and he decided to split. I was going with him, but in his angry, semidrunken state, he said, ''Fuck no, Collins, you stay. I'm going to find me a piece of ass. I'll see you back at the goddamn base. Just grab a cab and tell 'em to take you to the Visiting Officers' Quarters. You can't fucking miss.''

With that, I watched his lumbering hulk disappear out the door. I looked at Meiko who slid up close to me, placing her hand on my thigh and blinking her mascaraed lashes. She looked up and asked for another drink. She was gorgeous, and I loved every second of attention she gave me. Leaning forward, she kissed me and slid her hand up and down my leg. She excused herself to get our drinks, and slowly glided her hand across my legs as she went.

Returning, she winked and kissed me again. Sitting close, she sensuously stroked my hand, and then picked it up and placed it over her breast. The blood was pounding in more than my heart. I said, ''I'll give you about two hours to stop this shit.''

The jukebox started playing, and I couldn't believe that I was sitting with this dark-haired darling in this little piss-ant Japanese bar hearing Bob Wills singing ''Faded Love.'' I pulled Meiko out on the dance floor, and we danced three in a row before sitting back down. As we sat, I picked up my rum-and-Coke and had a swallow before I realized that this was straight whiskey. Coughing, I looked at her and said, ''Is this yours? When did you switch from Coke to whiskey?''

She smiled and said, ''Three drinks ago.''

''Why?'' I asked.

"Just felt like it. Sometimes I get angry and get drunk."

"Are you angry now?" I asked.

"Maybe."

She drank the rest of her whiskey in one swallow. In the dim light, I noticed scars on the back of her hands that I had not yet seen.

"Where did you get the scars?" I asked.

Without looking at me, she said, "Sometimes the Americans will come in and put a dollar bill over the back of my hand. I get to keep it if I burn a hole in it with a cigarette. Sometimes he puts my hand to his, back to back, and puts a burning cigarette against our hands; in between them, you know. If I keep my hand against the cigarette longer than he can, then he gives me a dollar. Sometimes though I just get angry and take a cigarette and burn myself."

I sat there a little stupefied and asked, "How old are you?"

"Fifteen," she said.

Taken aback by what she had said, I wondered if this was just normal, and I had been so naive that I didn't know what had been going on in real life. But, I wanted to continue talking with her and asked, "How did you start working in the bar?"

By this time, a different waitress had brought us each another drink. Staring into hers, she said, "Two years ago I had to have an operation. It cost three hundred dollars, but my parents had no money. The people who own this bar found out about it and paid for the operation. Now, I must work here until I repay the debt."

"Have you been working here for two years?" I asked.

"Yes, and I'll be here until I'm too old, ugly, or worn out, and then they'll sell me to a whorehouse."

"Why? Can't you make any extra to pay off the debt?"

"No," she said. "It's not possible. Just living takes all my money."

"That's a bunch of shit. Can't your parents or anyone else help?"

She looked up at me with a sarcastic grin, looking like a woman far older than she was, and said, "No, and that's just life, Collins. That's just fucking life."

I saw in her the fate of so many dark-haired, dark-eyed Oriental women. I saw Kim Lan again. Damn it all to hell, I thought. I want to get laid, and I find myself feeling sorry for this girl and contemplating the fate of the human race. Shit!

It was getting late, and she again turned to me with a smile and said, ''In ten minutes, the bar closes. Stay with me. I need you. For love, not money.''

God, Collins, I said to myself, do it, man.

I turned to look at her and said, ''You talked me into it. One more dance first.''

Five minutes later found us walking out the backdoor. There was a narrow, dark sidewalk and a series of side-by-side, one-room apartments. Meiko explained how each girl had a room and on the other side of the apartments was an alley. Only a little moonlight guided us as we slowly walked down the little path, beside which ran the *binjo* ditch, their bathroom. With her arm around my waist, we came to the last door and went in.

One little lamp gave off a dim light throughout the small shadow-filled apartment. It was a room about ten feet by eight feet, with a bed, a small chest of drawers, a small desk and chair, and one window overlooking the alley.

She reached up and kissed me, then began to take off my clothes. Laying them neatly over the chair, she then undressed and told me to lay down on the bed. Then she began to give me one hell of a massage. Gently at first, then firmly, her hands stretched, squeezed, and teased every muscle on my backside. If heaven was physical pleasure, I thought it couldn't be much better than this.

I was rolling over on my back with Meiko kneeling beside me near the wall, when, like an unexpected blast of lightning, a thunderous pounding on the door shattered and sobered my whole state of mind. Reacting within a second and not really thinking, I jumped out of bed, scooped up my clothes in one hand, and was perched on the windowsill ready to leap and run down the alley. All in this same instant there was a booming voice reverberating through the door, stating in very drunken and emphatic terms, ''Meiko, if you're in there with anyone, I'll kill the rotten, no-good son of a bitch.''

My instantly sobered mind caught a note of the familiar in the voice, and I hesitated with one leg out of the window. Looking at the door, which had somehow managed to stay on its hinges, I asked, "Cherokee, is that you?"

There was a silent pause, and then the voice outside, one notch lower in volume, asked, "Collins, is that you?"

"Yes, you dumb asshole," I yelled.

Then I heard him grumbling as he walked away, "Fucking son of a bitch, anyone else, and I'd killed him."

I sat naked on the windowsill, silhouetted by the dark alleyway. For a good sixty seconds, I practiced deep breathing and wondered if it were possible to resurrect the previous atmosphere. Then Meiko was at my side. She kissed me and said, "Come to bed."

"No, Meiko, there's something else I'm gonna do. This fucking world is one screwed up place. It's like one giant whorehouse, and everybody's getting fucked. Well, you've been fucked around enough. There's another woman I've met that coulda ended up like you. But maybe I can do something, and maybe times have got to fucking change. Get your clothes on, we're going for a drive."

She argued some and didn't understand what I was doing, but finally, we were both in our clothes and hailing a taxi. We went to the base, and I had her wait in the cab while I went in to do what I had set my mind to. Then we drove back to the bar, and at 0130 in the dark o'clock, I, with Meiko standing next to me, stood knocking at the door of Mama-san and Papa-san's apartment. They answered the door a little confused and obviously wondering what this damn American wanted.

Getting quickly to the point, I asked how much Meiko still owed them. Mama-san was distrustful of me, so I politely asked if Meiko paid them $300 was she free of her obligations. Meiko stood wide-eyed beside me. I asked for any papers they had on Meiko and showed $300 American money in my hand. Quickly, they produced some papers, and I asked Meiko to tell me what they said. After a little bartering and paper-signing, I handed them the money and gave the papers to a totally bewildered Meiko. I took her to her old room and asked how far her family lived from here.

What she told me was about a two-hour taxi drive. I packed all her clothes in an old bag and partly pushed, pulled, and carried her out to the nearby highway. I stopped a cab, as Meiko stammered and tried to realize what was happening. I told her simply that she had her papers and said, "You're free to go back home, and you better damn well do it. I never want to find you around any bar ever again, or I'll kick your ass."

I paid the taxi driver for the trip in advance and gave Meiko some extra bills. I smiled and waved as I saw her looking back through the rear window, and as the taxi began driving away down the little Japanese highway, I yelled, "Sorry 'bout that Meiko, but that's just life: just fucking life American-style." Then I grabbed another cab and went back to my quarters, where I took another long hot shower, and the world felt a little better.

But is it really better? I asked myself.

I lay in my bed not able to sleep and knew I'd not be able to truly rest until I found out more about Kim Lan. Somewhere in the back of my mind a little voice said, and to find out more about yourself, Ryan Michael Collins!

Yeah, I answered, am I guilty of aiding and abetting the enemy? If a Marine stops and starts to question, he might as well resign!

The world was too fucked up, and I was a part of it. But now that woman in Vietnam, with the long, flying, black hair, and a rifle pointed at my chest again dominated my world. I gave up trying to put her out of my mind. In a sense, Meiko had been Kim Lan; so had that girl at the Paris Steam Baths in Da Nang. My Marines were still there, and that strange world between India and China was still messed up worse than the rest. I knew I had to get back, and I mumbled, "You stupid asshole, Collins."

I packed my bags, wrote a note to Lynn, and called a cab. It was no sweat getting a flight to Vietnam, and I only had to wait an hour and a half. Then I was in the air again. I sat in that silver-winged bird fatalistically not giving a damn. Thoughts about the war, Kim Lan, and me in the middle of it marched back and forth between my ears.

Several hours later, with a crude jolt, we landed on the concrete runway and taxied across the black tarmac. As I stepped off the plane, a blast of summer air hit me like a hot wave. I looked out over the asphalt, concrete, and rows of metal buildings interspersed with tents, and I could see the steamy curtains of heat rising from the dusty earth. I had to psyche myself. This was real depressing! Here I fucking was, back in Indochina. It felt like I was starting all over again! Standing in that airplane doorway, I looked out over a vast ocean of American military. I was struck by what seemed to be the absurdity of two immensely different cultures locked in an embrace of love and death. Yet, they would never be able to mix and work together: what we were doing there was like pouring water on an oil fire. I walked down the ramp and headed for a ride to Third Recon.

CHAPTER 11

> To see only one house—North and South. Harboring compassion, brotherhood. Transforming separate interests. To love's acceptance of us all, I pray . . . forget the hate we bear in ourselves . . . That from the soil of Viet Nam, flowers may bloom again.
>
> Thich Nhat Hanh

We returned safely to camp with the girl, but my thoughts whirled in a dizzy confusion. I needed to hate the enemy, to see exactly who they were, then my direction would follow an easy path. But now this blond-haired, blue-eyed American had come again into my life, and my need for revenge was weakened. Years ago he saved me from being a captive whore, and then he saved this young girl from being raped! How could I hate him? He had shaken me, and I found myself wanting to talk to him. Why was he different?

I cannot, I thought. His interests are not for this country. He has no real compassion for us, otherwise, he would never be fighting in this war. Likely, he has himself killed some of my people. I must bring myself back again. My mind must be cleansed of any concerns but our revolution.

Still, I lay alone on the cot in my little hut, and my thoughts drifted on a sea of emotions. My heart cried out, Van Thi, my husband, come! Put your arms around me. I need you now. Yet my bed held only one. I knew this war could take his life, too. Only my brother seemed truly invincible, but I so needed the touch of my man.

I focused my emotions on Van Thi. There was no man like him, a truly gentle scholar, forced into this war by the barbarity of the Vietnamese lackeys, the French, and now the Americans. I could see in my mind the time I met him many years ago. I was still young. I remembered that morning. It was 3:00 A.M., and a steady drizzle that had not let up for hours had soaked every pore of my body, even though I wore my raincoat. The rain made the early morning so dark and heavy that it felt like a wet blanket around me as I rowed my small, round sampan to the market in Hoi An. The river was black and choppy. I carried fish to sell, at least that was the impression I fervently hoped to portray. My real mission was to pick up a comrade at the main pagoda and guide him to the safety of our brothers in the mountains.

The situation was very dangerous. Both the regular and secret police had been ravaging the countryside, and many cadres had been captured, tortured, and killed. It was nine months past my sixteenth birthday and over two and a half years since my mother had been taken away. My thoughts drifted back and forth between my assignment and the returning horror that had swept over our lives since I had turned fourteen.

It would be about an hour before I could get to the pagoda. All I knew was that the comrade I was to pick up was disguised as a monk. I was supposed to sit on the steps of the west entrance to the pagoda with my basket of fish and quietly recite verses from *Luc Van Tien* while I arranged the fish for sale at the market. The brother I was to pick up was to come to me as if just finishing morning prayers and ask if I knew the way to the southwest. That was my signal to reply, "If the venerable monk would wait until I have sold my fish in a short while, I will assist him in finding his way." If he responded by quoting a verse from *Luc Van Tien*, then I knew that he was the comrade.

After almost an hour of hard rowing through the dark, the rain, and the wind, I reached the banks of the Cua Dai below Hoi An. The rain now slackened and had just about stopped, but I had to climb up a muddy six-foot-high bank with a basket of fish. For every two steps up, I slipped back one, all the while trying to keep from spilling the fish. Finally, a muddy, soaked mess I crawled to the top of the bank, half carrying, half dragging a basket of fish. I prepared to walk toward the city market, which was about a half-mile away down narrow streets, past the rows of low houses and hedges. One block from the market was the pagoda. My heart beat fast, but not just from the physical exertion of the last hour.

I arrived at the pagoda and sat down on the steps in darkness that was only interrupted by the scattered lamps of those who had to come early to the market to set up for the morning trade. There were also some lamps lighting little areas within the unwalled pagoda behind me, and I had noticed several men and a few nuns in quiet prayer. Last year I had nearly become a prostitute in the service of a Vietnamese colonel within his walled domain. That place was not far away in this same city.

Then I thought of the love story between the young scholar Luc Van Tien and the beautiful young woman Nguyen Nga. I had often in earlier times recited to our family and neighbors verse after verse of this novel. It was a favorite, second only in popularity to *The Tale of Kieu*. Without even thinking, I began to softly speak aloud many of the verses I had memorized.

I must have drifted away in my thoughts for a while, when I was suddenly startled by a voice and presence beside me. With a little start, I glanced up and saw the form of a monk. He smiled and said, "That is a beautiful story, and you know it well." The compliment coming so unexpectedly embarrassed me.

I glanced back down and said, "Thank you, honorable sir. I shall move out of your way."

"No," he replied, "it is no bother, besides it is possible that you can give me directions. I am new to this province and am in need of directions to the best road to the southwest."

My heart raced as I said, "If the venerable monk would wait until I have sold my fish in a short while, I will assist him in finding his way."

Instinctively, I continued the next verse from the story of Luc Van Tien:

" 'All around me, rivers have their sources and trees
   their roots,
You bore me in your womb for nine months.' "

Before I could finish, he interrupted and completed the
verse:

" 'And my gratitude and debt to you is boundless.' "

In the lamplight his shaven head shone, and his mouth
barely revealed the presence of a smile. My heart beat
erratically for a silent moment. I was ecstatic. I told him
to remain here for a short while, and I would return.

My fish sale was prearranged. Actually, the cook for
the secret police was a friend, and she would find ways
to communicate to us while buying fish and produce at
the market to cook for the police. She was old, wrinkled,
and her teeth were deeply colored, but while she was
thought slow of wit, she had proven to be very wise and
important. In between the bartering over the price of the
fish, she had warned me that the police were watching
for an important comrade who was rumored to have just
arrived in Hoi An under disguise. I worried that this
might be my new friend.

With the money she paid me from the police food bud-
get, I returned to the pagoda. At first, I didn't see him,
but then one monk in prayer rose. As if he had eyes in
the back of his head, he came to me and again stated,
"And my gratitude and debt to you is boundless." I knew
the flickering lamp on the top step revealed my face if
only dimly, and I smiled and turned to walk down the
street back to the river. He followed, and I thought to
myself that I knew neither his face nor his name, but I
was excited that this possibly could be the very important
comrade for whom the police were looking.

The sampan was barely large enough for two people,
and he took the posture of a monk in prayer. I steadily
rowed to try to pass Chien Son before sunrise. The sky
was already an early morning gray, and I could tell that
some of the clouds had dispersed, which might mean a
break in the rains. It was the end of the monsoon season,
and I looked forward to the warmer and drier spring.

I calculated that it was about 5:30 A.M. when we passed near my home. The comrade had remained deathly silent and motionless, enshrouded by his robe. I admired the discipline required to sit cross-legged like a statue as he did for an hour.

About fifteen minutes past Chien Son, I rowed to the shore on the opposite bank. The river was only about one hundred feet wide at this point, and I pulled the boat into the undergrowth. The brother and I quickly camouflaged it in the heavy brush that reached out over the water. We quietly hid and waited on the riverbank listening for a few minutes. I then led the way out and along the rice paddy dikes. There were no military outposts past Chien Son in this direction, and we walked at a fast pace.

As the colors of the morning edged over the horizon and began to dance their way through the clouds and clearing sky, we had made our way about six miles in the direction of the mountains. No words had yet been exchanged between the two of us since the pagoda, but I turned toward a clump of trees to take a short break and hoped that he would not be angry with me for my wanting a brief rest. We were only another three-mile walk from the safety of the mountains.

We sat in the brush. He pulled back his hood revealing beads of perspiration covering his brow. He took a deep breath and said, "I am greatly impressed. You have guided me quickly and quite easily past the clutches of the police. No one, I suppose, has told you that they are after me and intend to place me on the gallows. I've been in hiding in Hoi An for only two days waiting for a way out and have only managed to stay a step ahead of them. Now I might be able to breathe more freely."

I looked at his face. He seemed a young man. His complexion was light, and he had a face pleasing to look at. "What is your purpose here?" I asked. "I have a brother who is leading a guerrilla band not far away, and before we can go farther, I need to know where to take you."

He smiled and asked, "Would your brother's name be Ba Can?"

I excitedly returned his smile and answered, "Yes!"

He continued, "I bring to him instructions from the

Provisional Revolutionary Government of the Republic
of South Vietnam.'' He looked at me smiling and said,
"Your brother is a very important person, and if he is
anything like his sister, he is a tireless and intelligent
worker. I might add that he must also be a very handsome person.''

Momentarily, I simply took this statement as a compliment to Ba Can, but quickly I realized that he was
really talking about me. I felt my face redden, embarrassed by this man's admiring look.

I was almost seventeen, and many of my friends had
joked with me about my young maidenhood. Some had
already gotten married, and they scolded me for becoming so heavily involved in the struggle for freedom. They
felt that I was neglecting a more important side of my
life as a woman. However, the drive within me, spurred
in large part by the example of my mother and grandparents, had never allowed me to entertain such romantic
notions except in my dreams of a future life after this
fight was finished. But now, for the first time, I felt more
than a professional admiration for this man, and I knew
that I blushed.

"My name is Tran Van Thi," he said.

I glanced up and replied respectfully. "Mine, sir, is
Nguyen Kim Lan.''

"Well," he continued, "Nguyen Kim Lan and Tran
Van Thi must get to the mountains quickly before the
whole world observes our passage."

With that, I regained my awareness of the situation,
afraid that I had taken too long a rest. Carefully, I observed the countryside around us. Already farmers from
a small nearby hamlet were in the rice paddies, but there
were no signs of the enemy. The remaining three-mile
walk could be done in less than an hour.

The dikes were in good repair, and as we walked, trying to act with a normal, friendly attitude, we greeted
the farmers that we passed as our route brought us to the
edge of the Nai Do ridgeline which was the first of the
hills of the Que Son Mountains. The clouds were breaking and in the growing sunlight, we made our way
through the foothills staying in the small, narrow draws
where streamlets and clumps of trees broke the continu-

ous fields of grass. The jungled mountain heights were still far above us and would take another three hours to reach. In the past two years, I had on four occasions been sent on missions to Ba Can's headquarters which lay ahead and above us. However, we now felt much more secure and moved at an easy pace, stopping occasionally to drink from the fresh spring water.

After an hour of uphill walking, I stopped beside a pool of water formed at the foot of a small waterfall. Surrounded by trees in a deeper ravine, I had found this spot on an earlier mission and had fallen in love with it. "Sir," I said. "This place is very beautiful and peaceful. Would you care to rest for a short while?"

He replied by saying, "Yes, Kim Lan, but only if you call me Van Thi."

"As you request," I said.

We sat in silence for a moment before I asked, "How long have you been a part of the revolution?"

He was looking deeply into the pool. His gaze remained fixed in the waters as he replied, "Almost two years."

Daring to ask him more, I continued, "How was it that you became involved?"

His thoughts seemed to be immersed in the water. His stare was fixed on the stream for several seconds before responding. When he did, his gaze turned to me, and he said, "It is not a pleasant story."

"Most of our stories are not," I replied.

Then his eyes returned to the pool, and he began to speak, partly to me, and in part to himself. It was as if his life was slowly becoming one with the water. The stream rushed past as he spoke. Occasionally I glanced at him, but his eyes remained engulfed in the swift flowing water. I became mesmerized. His life seemed to flow past me, one with the stream.

He said that in 1955 he had been the chairman of a student association at a university in Saigon. During the beginning of the government's "To Cong" campaign, several of his professors had been arrested for addressing the classes, encouraging free elections and peace. He spoke about how he had led student demonstrations and then was himself arrested. His story interested me greatly, but when he mentioned that he had been taken to Con Son Prison Island in 1955, I turned, sat on the edge of my rock and listened anxiously. This was about the time my mother had been arrested, and this was the place to which they had taken her.

Van Thi continued, "They beat me continuously for days, especially on the bottom of the feet and on the knees. If I dozed, they threw water in my face and slapped me. Strong lights were held close to my face until it blistered. They wanted me to confess in writing to being a communist, but I wasn't. I kept screaming that at them, but they would beat me until I lost consciousness. Then the worst part came. They attached electrodes to my ears, my tongue, and the private parts of my body. The pain was unbearable, and I passed out again. When I came to, it was with the searing pain of cigarettes being extinguished on the inside of my thighs and on my nipples. I hallucinated with all the pain, and I believe I must have lost rationality for a time. I never knew whether I really signed that confession paper."

I sat in horror, being told stories of atrocities that may have been used on my mother. I realized that in my mind, I had tried not to think of these things, but all along had known that I was simply avoiding the terrible truth. Holding my knees close to me as I sat on my flat rock by the pool, I almost feared to hear him tell any more.

However, he continued. "When I finally realized where I was, my legs were shackled by irons to the floor of a cage built underground. Our ceiling was a heavy iron-barred grate out of which we could see, and it was only a short height above our heads. Four of us were in one cramped cell, and all had suffered similarly. In the next four months that I remained there, I learned that these were the infamous 'Tiger Cages' that the French had used to torture and jail Vietnamese, and now Vietnamese were using them on their own countrymen. Sanitary conditions were almost nonexistent, the food was very meager, and we were often doused with lime and then sprayed with water. The wet lime burned our skin, and yet we had no place to lay, sit, or sleep except in the watery slime in the bottom of the cell."

Then he turned to me and seriously said, "Kim Lan,

you must promise me to never be taken alive. Because as terribly as I and the other men were treated, the women suffered even worse.''

I shivered and cringed at his brief but horrible story of how the men listened to the repeated rape and torture of the women prisoners. He said that when the men would scream out through the cross-bars of the iron grates above them against the treatment of the women, they would again be doused in lime.

I barely heard him say that he had been mistakenly released after four months. I had sat and shivered in horror and hatred in the knowledge of what must have happened to my mother. I prayed silently that she had died before the worst of it, and I even envisioned that her boat had sunk, and she had drowned. I forced myself to believe that she had died early and was saved from the worst of the horrors. I knew that my mother and others had been prisoners of a cruel and terrible people, and we would probably never find out any information about their fate. They simply had disappeared into a hole worse than hell.

Then he had recognized my feelings. While I was being caught again by the horror of my mother's fate, I heard him say from somewhere on my left, ''Kim Lan, I know that I said something that I should not have. I've hurt you. I apologize.'' Momentarily, he said nothing, but, as I in silence was preparing to walk on, he softly asked, ''Do you have someone close to you who has been sent to Con Son?''

I had gritted my teeth, fought back the tears, and turned to continue along the path, now penetrating deeper into the mountain jungles. Without turning back, I told him, ''My mother,'' and strode on uphill. I walked angrily, bushes grabbing at my clothes with him walking behind trying to apologize.

After three days in camp with us, he invited me for a walk in the mountains. I had followed him toward the edge of this small jungle camp that was the temporary home for our then small group of irregular soldiers. It hadn't rained in a day and a half, and while the earth was still muddy, the leaves on the bushes, vines, and trees were dry. At least we could walk without getting so wet. As we neared the edge of the camp, Van Thi looked at me and said, "I was walking out here yesterday by myself and found a very pretty place on a stream, and if you would like, I'll show you."

"I'd like that very much," I shyly replied, finding my interest in him becoming more than a political or military one.

He led, and I walked behind watching him. He was tall and had broad shoulders. I wondered what he would look like with hair instead of the shaven "monk's" head. I guessed at his age, maybe twenty-two. I wonder if he's married? I thought. Then I felt my face warm in a blush at my own thoughts.

A minute later, he stopped and turned to me with a smile. "Look over here at these orchids." He reached out, picked one, and handed it to me saying, " '. . . Her smile a flower, her voice the sound of jade; her hair the sheen of clouds, her skin like snow . . .' "

I glanced down, flustered by this attention and not knowing quite how to handle it, but at the same time, it felt good and I wanted him to continue. I recognized his quote from *Kieu*, and thought of a following verse, " '. . . In the spring flush of youth she neared that time when maidens pinned their hair . . .' " These verses of serious love and troth were, however, too much for me.

I think he must have sensed my feelings and said, trying to be professional again, "Let's go over here by the stream, there are matters of revolution that we must discuss." I had looked at the pale and beautiful blush-red flower in my hand and thought of its fragility and how easily it and love were at the mercy of war.

Then Van Thi jumped down the short embankment, showing off, but landed on a slippery rock and went flying through the air into the cold mountain stream. He lay there with the back of his mud-covered, bald head facing me. I couldn't help it; I started laughing. He turned and looked at me, and I placed my hands over my mouth to try to stifle the laughter. Then he smiled, and we both laughed together. We had laughed our way back to camp never having discussed those matters of the revolution.

But that was years ago, and sometimes I thought that I saw more of him in those years than I did now that we were married. The war had become one of large military commands, and he was miles across the valley with his battalion. Why could he not be with me when I so needed him. I stared at the dark ceiling wanting to sleep and forget so many things.

It had been about six weeks since the battle at Ap Bon. I seemed to be tired so much, and my eyes had dark circles under them. I believed the American bomb had done more damage than I understood. I reflected often about the power of the American bombers that had kept us from overrunning their ground units. The doctor had told me that many of our soldiers had suffered from the effects of chemical bombings, and that I should be very careful. We now were being given gas masks to wear.

However, my strength was returning, and I felt guilty about being away from the battlefield. Ba Can's battalion had now become an operational unit of the 2nd Division. Three of our local battalions from the Quang Nam Province had been organized into the 1st Regiment of the regular forces of the 2nd Division. I was to join them in the area of the Que Son basin south of our mountain base camp where I now was recuperating. Our area of operation extended generally from the village of Tam Ky in the southeast about twenty-four miles to the west near the village of Hiep Duc, and then to the northeast near the village of Thang Binh.

This was a great fertile land that furnished our soldiers with much needed rice and other food supplies. The western and southern boundaries of this area were dotted with a range of low foothills and river valleys.

Even though neither the pretending government soldiers nor the Americans were a threatening presence in the area, it took me about ten hours to make the walk out of the mountains. The summer heat had so sapped my strength that by the time I reached my battalion I was weary to the bone and welcomed a good night's rest.

The next morning my body felt walked upon. But still it was better, and a sense of comaraderie buoyed my spirit in the midst of our freedom-fighters. I reported to Ba Can, and even he seemed more relaxed than I had seen him in a long while. He told me that for a few more weeks he wanted me with him at his battalion command post.

While we were talking in the early morning hours, radio reports came in concerning an enemy assault about seven miles northeast of our positions near the Ly Ly River. Within minutes, messages of several other assaults by the enemy were received. Our headquarters had become a windstorm of activity. All units were now one hundred percent alert. Unlike the enemy forces, we carried the war on our backs and received our supplies locally from the villages. We were highly mobile and used this to our advantage. It was a necessity. To stay too long in one position invited attack by large concentrations of American air power and by their helicopter-borne infantry.

I listened to the brief of the early battle reports. It seemed that there were two American Marine assaults. One was to our southeast about twenty miles, not far from Tam Ky. The second American assault was to our west a few miles from Hiep Duc. The third was by a South Vietnamese Marine unit to our north near the Ly Ly. The quick estimates of enemy strength were from 2500 to 3500 soldiers. Ba Can received orders to ignore the Americans near Hiep Duc and swiftly move toward the South Vietnamese Marine unit to our north. Limited delaying actions had already taken place, but we were given orders to establish positions to cause the enemy to redirect their attack, and then to inflict casualties on them, and to move quickly toward Tam Ky and await further orders.

Ba Can gave his directives, and within fifteen minutes, our entire battalion was on the move. Our soldiers alternated walking and running. All uphill portions of our trek were walked at a quick pace. Wherever the ground was either downhill or flat, we ran. There were no administrative or logistical support units to worry about, and we covered the seven miles in about one hour. We managed to stay in the tree cover where the foothills touched the rice fields.

I was exhausted, but I would never let anyone see it. My physical condition was not quite normal yet, and my willpower and stubbornness would have to fill in.

We reached a low ridgeline that sheltered the Thach Thuong village very near the Ly Ly. The South Vietnamese Marine unit was based in the lowlands to our east. The small detachment of our 3rd Regiment that had encountered the Saigon troops had disappeared into the lower reaches of the Que Son Mountains just to our north.

For the balance of the day, we hid and watched. Finally, Ba Can made his decision. We would spend the night entrenching into this ridgeline and hope to suck the enemy soldiers into attacking us across the open rice fields. He said that he felt his bones speaking to him that tomorrow would be a day of rains. It was August and rains had only infrequently begun to fall. Next month they would pick up more, but this time I prayed for Ba Can to be right. The rain and cloud cover would hamper the American air power, and we might be able to fight the enemy on more even terms. The memory of my last encounter with the American jets was vivid in my mind, and if they began to use their burning chemicals, the rain would be more than welcome. That night we worked in shifts, and by morning, the ridgeline was heavily fortified.

Just before dawn, I was awakened by a loud thunderous blast. I sat straight up but immediately rolled into a nearby trench and grabbed my rifle on the way. I was on my knees, rifle in my hand, heart beating fast. Then the rain began to fall, and I felt a little foolish realizing that it was only thunder. Thunder! I looked up at the clouds on that dark gray morning and thanked heaven for its gift. I pulled my rain jacket on and thought, today may be our day.

Within two hours, as I sat in our rain-soaked headquarters with Ba Can, our small scout teams reported that the enemy was moving on us. It was estimated to be a battalion, and when we could see them, they were coming on line across the now flooded rice paddies. The rainstorm increased, and we could hardly see them until they were close to our positions. Then our firepower ripped into them.

They tried to fight but had lost the advantage of their American war planes in the driving rain, and repeatedly, their futile attempts to slosh through the ankle-deep wa-

ter to attack us were met with more of their own blood.
Finally, with dozens of their bodies floating in the fields,
they withdrew from the battleground.

Their artillery did some damage, but their airplanes
could not reach us because of the weather. However, the
rain began to slacken by midafternoon. Still, the weather
was heavily overcast with light rain, and their American
support had little effect. They attacked twice more, and
twice more withdrew leaving more dead behind.

By evening the clouds were clearing, and Ba Can ordered a withdrawal. We began our twenty-seven mile
march toward Tam Ky. Although we had lost about
twenty-five of our men, the South Vietnamese Marines
had left scores of bodies lying dead in the rice fields. As
we moved with all the speed we could toward the southeast, the noise of approaching aircraft could be heard.
We were not more than a mile away when the first bombs
began to land on top of our former positions. I was
soaked and muddy, but I smiled at Ba Can, and he returned it: a smile of victory. We knew the puppet soldiers
would stand on top of that ridge in the morning and plant
their flag, but in a week, they would be gone again with
far fewer soldiers than when they came, and we'd still be
here.

As we marched with muddy feet, bloodied bandages,
and a fierce determination, my mind wandered. For a
moment I asked myself about the American. What if he
might be lying dead in one of these fields? Secretly, I
hoped that he had gone back safely to his homeland. I,
in a way, wanted to see him, but that could not happen.
It was better that he return home than die here by one of
our bullets. I knew the sharpness of my hatred had been
dulled, and again I heard Grandfather's words: fight out
of love for your country, not hatred. . . .

CHAPTER 12

> All of our U.S. combat accomplishments have made no significant—positive—difference to the rural Vietnamese for there is no real security in the countryside.
> Report by the Long Range Planning Task Group, created by Gen. Creighton Abrams (1969)

With my seabag over my shoulder, I walked across the hot pavement, past rows of glaring silver-metal buildings and dirt encrusted tents. A person could take a knife and cut the air: the heat and humidity drove sanity to hell. Collins, I thought, what the motherfucking hell are you doing back in this shithole? There was another day left on my R&R, and I decided to make the most of it.

I hitched a ride toward China Beach. The little in-country R&R camp of the South China Sea was becoming a favorite watering hole for a lot of Marines. I knew the place. I had been responsible for rebuilding it earlier when I was with the 7th Engineer Battalion. A couple of old French buildings that we had reconditioned served as the central part of the place. Thirty yards in front of the buildings, the sea rolled on and on, never changing. The waters of this part of the Pacific were not at all like the California side of the ocean—no big waves, and the water was as warm as the Gulf of Mexico.

The bar was lonely and that suited me fine. Inside the half-French, half-American building, I watched the afternoon waitress. She smiled and took my order, and without thinking I began to compare the Vietnamese woman in her to that of Kim Lan. I thought of the "might-have-beens" years ago, and the unbelievable fate that had made our paths cross again a decade later! A little fifteen-year-old girl destined for the private prostitution ring of some local colonel is now a tigress roaming those mountains. I began to think that she had more than repaid me. Twice she had lowered her rifle when she could have taken me out.

Vietnam was fast becoming the alpha and omega of my life. It wasn't just Kim Lan. I wouldn't trade my Marines at Third Recon for most people out there in the self-centered, nose-picking land of civilians. Yeah, I reminisced about the California beaches, but here it was different. We were tight. We relied on one another. We sacrificed for each other.

Still, my Vietnamese tigress had begun to overshadow everything! There were at least a hundred and thirty-nine questions bouncing around my head that I'd like to ask her.

About halfway through my drink, a scary thought crept into my psyche: had I endangered the lives of any of my Marines by not taking her out? "Shit," I mumbled, reminding myself, "she's the one who let me off the hook twice when she's had me on the 'Hi-you're-dead' end of her rifle.

After a couple of hours and switching to my favorite, rum-and-Coke, I could tell that my faculties were becoming slightly impaired. Did I give a damn? Hell, no!

A chorus of songs serenaded the evening as it vaguely slipped away from me. The last I remembered I was sitting by the beach singing to the waves as darkness sucked up the final red and gold rays of the sun.

Vaguely, I woke back to life. Steamy heat now fogged my brain, and I attempted to massage the pain away. I could tell it was morning, and I was somehow in my old tent at Camp Reasoner. Whoever discovered aspirin should have been awarded the Nobel Prize. I had only one complaint with the written instructions: they should've read TAKE BEFORE LEAVING THE BAR.

By midafternoon, I was on my way back to An Hoa. From miles away, up in a helicopter, Da Nang looked like an interesting city, shimmering beside the bay, but nothing could help An Hoa. Like a festering sore on the landscape, it was something a person would point at and avoid. So where the fuck was I going?

As we landed in the typical duststorm, I thought, and the housewives of Amarillo think they have it bad. I had no more than gotten back to my tent, which I kicked to shake off the dust, than Williams walked up and said, "Hey, Lieutenant, welcome back. Might as well get your rifle loaded, we're headed for a village on the other side of the mountains—just to check with the village chief. He's screaming to high heaven that there's NVA all around him. So the battalion CO is taking a few people down there to talk to him. You got about fifteen minutes before the birds get here. By the way, how's Japan? Man, I can feel the touch of a sweet woman's skin and the scent of her perfumed body. Um, boy!''

Well, shit, I thought. Nothing like hitting the ground running. A body doesn't have time to feel sorry for himself.

After running to get some ammo and watering my canteens, we were flying above the rail line around the east side of the Que Son Mountains. I sat at the wide hatch watching the jungle-covered mountains a thousand feet below knowing that there were probably a few battalions of bad guys down there who'd just love to shoot this bird out of the sky. I sometimes wondered about my sanity. I looked hard and long at this side of the mountains, knowing that she'd likely be down there with her soldiers somewhere.

The pilot banked to the starboard, and we followed a river to the west on the southern side of the mountains. The South China Sea glistened behind us in the midafternoon sun as we flew into what we had dubbed the Que Son Valley. Looking at my map, I noted the river's name, the Ly Ly, and the main village, which was named, like the valley, after the surrounding mountains.

Our helicopters set down on the edge of the small, but from all appearances, neat little village of Que Son. We were framed by the river close to our south, and the mile-high mountains two miles to the north. The towering masses of land also stared down on us from the western end of the valley about five miles away. The river had its headwaters in the hills up in that end of the valley. The mountains continued cupping around the rice fields to the southwest forming a fishhook and intimidating the valley.

I followed the colonel and his operations officer into the heart of the village. The roads were hard-packed dirt lined by thatch huts with an occasional stucco building. We were led and followed on all sides by curious Vietnamese kids to one of these masonry buildings. It seemed like a store that doubled as a meeting room.

I waited at the door as the mayor of the village, with his half military uniform, assumed the role of commander of the village militia and invited us in to a table. Williams waited on the street leaning against a porch column, rifle resting in his arms. I politely stayed half in the building, half out, trying to keep up with the conversation inside while watching what I didn't trust outside. From my position on the porch, I watched the mayor roll out a map with red marks all over it signifying locations of enemy units.

Good God, I thought unbelievingly. He's got a whole NVA division in these hills and mountains ready to waltz across his face. Sure, I bet they got a couple of battalions but a whole fucking division? This guy is really paranoid.

I began to watch a gathering group of Vietnamese around the front of the building. Mostly, they were youngsters. A couple started playing marbles. How 'bout that, I wondered. Didn't know they had marbles. Edging toward the kids, I curiously watched their style of what I had thought was an authentic American game. They didn't smooth out the ground, nor did they rest their knuckles on the ground with a marble loaded on a thumb cocked under the middle finger ready to blast the opposition to smithereens. Instead they stood or crotched, a marble held several feet in the air, spring-loaded on their middle finger. The free hand pulled the marble against the action finger of the other hand until the finger was almost perpendicular to the back of the hand. When I thought the finger was about to break, the free hand let go. Like the silent swish of a slingshot, the finger snapped forward driving the marble from its height with deadly accuracy toward the ground with its helpless victim. With a crack, a marble succumbed and bounced a couple of feet away and was quickly deposited in the winner's bag.

I looked at the boys, smiled, and with gestures, asked if I could shoot a couple. Within thirty seconds, the people had surrounded us watching the curious spectacle of an overaged Marine lieutenant trying to balance his rifle in the crook of his left arm while he tried for the first time to shoot marbles Vietnamese-style. On one knee, I took careful aim about two feet off the ground and let go. The marble, instead of being propelled with the speed of a bullet in a direct line toward the cat's-eye staring at me on the ground, arched lazily and harmlessly off to the side. I had only one choice: laugh with all those around me who were guffawing the dust off the road.

"Listen," I said. "I admit it. I had a deprived childhood. Never learned the proper way of shooting marbles. But let me have another chance."

They all laughed louder, none of them understanding a word I said. I knelt carefully on one knee, rifle in my left hand, and I did a little leveling job on the ground. The marble was cocked American-style behind my thumb. My knuckles were poised just off the ground. I felt the pride of every American marble-shooter resting on my shoulders. The two-hundred-year tradition of the red, white, and blue was at stake. Carefully, I lined up on a smirking Vietnamese agate and blocked out of my mind the surrounding giggles. I focused and shot. *Crack!* I hit it! That enemy marble must have flown and bounced six feet. Proudly, I rose to my feet, tipped my hat to the audience and walked back to Williams.

I sat on the steps of the porch as the small crowd now gravitated to me. One young boy came up, pointed into the hills, and said, "VC, VC." He aimed an imaginary rifle at the mountains making the sounds of rifle shots. It mattered not whether he was trying to impress me, or if he was seriously afraid, but I was struck by his features. About ten years old, he looked a whole lot like a brother of mine back home who was that age. I had to bite my tongue to keep tears out of my eyes. A momentary flash of homesickness had unexpectedly hit me.

This kid and the others were caught between an M-16 and an AK-47. If there were half as many Charlie in the hills as the mayor was noting, there was going to be bigtime shit hitting the fan in this valley before long. What would happen to these kids? I reached out and held the boy's hand and said, "I'll call you 'Johnny.' Okay? You 'Johnny,' okay."

"Okay, Johnny," he said, pointing to his chest. He walked away saying, "Johnny, Johnny, Johnny."

God, I wanted to go pick him up and hug him. Would the kids survive? Whose bullets would rip out their eyes? Would the bullet be stamped, "Made in Michigan," or "Made in Moscow"? Would the kids really give a damn?

"What's up, Lieutenant?" Williams was asking me. "You look like you know that kid from somewhere."

"He just looks like another kid I know back home." I watched "Johnny" run off playing, and said, "Sometimes it seems like a real small world, Williams."

As I sat there drifting into melancholy, I heard the meeting breaking up behind me, but didn't pay much attention. Ten minutes later I sat in the chopper rising up and over the village, waving to kids we were leaving below.

In a short three days, I was preparing to lead my patrol to the western end of the Que Son Valley, while the grunts were going en masse into the rice fields and low hills below. Actually, it was to be a combined assault between the South Vietnamese and US Marines, a pretty big affair. Not more than five miles from "Johnny," we were to screen their flank closest to the mountains. If there were a division of NVA around, our asses would be in a real tight squeeze. Hell, just a battalion or regiment would've been bad enough. On the other hand, it had been explained to me that we had four ships off shore, a battalion of artillery from the 11th Marines, and unlimited air power. Our supporting arms really had the muscle this time.

By sunrise, the morning of D-Day, we were standing by for our ride. Monstrous packs, crammed with ammunition, water, C-rations, and assorted military gear rode heavily on our backs. Brown and green camouflage greasepaint angled across our faces under soft bush hats.

Magazines filled with twenty rounds each were inserted
in each rifle, but all safeties were still on.

An Hoa was a beehive of activity. Our battalion and
another from the 5th Marines, along with a regiment of
South Vietnamese Marines, would be hitting the valley
and low hills looking for the 2nd NVA Division. My
Lord, I thought glancing around in the semidarkness.
They really believe something big's out there.

Ten minutes later, we were in the air. Recon was pre-
ceding the grunts, but our patrol area was higher up in
the hills. Again, we flew east and circled around the
mountains to come into the valley with the sun just grabbing a handhold on the eastern horizon at our backs.
Ahead of us, the mountains loomed up like a wall, and
we flew past others on our right as they reached higher
than our helicopters only about a mile away. Then we
were flying into the cup formed where those land masses
"fishhooked" to our portside. High in the jungles, there
was a shelf of rock on top of a cliff near the birthplace
of the Ly Ly River, and that was our destination.

I watched the village of Que Son pass beneath us and
thought about the kids, their marble games, and
"Johnny." To our left front was a small friendly outpost
called Nui Loc Son. It rested on a small hilltop near
Highway 534 at the pointed end of the fishhook to the
south of the river. Then we passed over the little hamlet
of Thach Thuong and began to drop to make our one and
only run at the cliff. It was the sole patch of clear ground on
the jungled hillsides. I caught a glimpse of a waterfall on
the Ly Ly glistening in the sun's first rays not far off, but
my attention was not on aesthetics at the moment. The
adrenaline was pumping.

Then the choppers were suddenly down. We leaped
and landed running, as the birds quickly got the hell out.
Alone again, we lumbered as fast as we could toward the
jungle cover, each of us carrying the weight and bulk of
an eight-year-old child on our backs. We huddled quietly
under the green canopy listening, hoping no one else was
around. Faintly, off in the distance, the sounds of the
waterfalls hummed a tune—background music for the
jungle birds.

After a couple of minutes silently listening and watching, we moved uphill to the west. The main body of the Ly Ly was a thousand meters down to our left, and I thought we'd work around its headwaters and then into the barbed end of the fishhook.

For ten hours, we struggled higher through virgin jungles, climbing rocks and logs. I hoped to God that I wouldn't step on a snake or round a tree and run into a tiger. But there were no signs of any human beings, just us, the jungles, and the monkeys. However, in the valley below, the initial assault waves had landed. From where we were, we couldn't see them, but radio reports indicated the South Vietnamese Marines had encountered heavy small arms fire when they landed between Que Son and Thach Thuong. Several prisoners gave evidence to the presence of the 1st Battalion 3rd Regiment of the 2nd NVA Division. The enemy battalion had apparently maneuvered away from the three South Vietnamese Marine battalions into the mountains somewhere below us. I knew they wouldn't climb the cliff but might move up alongside the river and wait for orders in the protection of the hills and jungles—about a half-mile through steep mountains and forests somewhere down below.

By late afternoon, we had crossed the river where it was hardly six feet wide. Now we were on the downhill side of our patrol route. Not far from the stream, we found a good location to wrap up in our ponchos for the night. No other action had occurred on this, the first day of the assault. If there in fact were an enemy division around, I felt sure they'd hit somebody soon. The time and place would be of their own choosing. I, however, had found no evidence yet of their being in this part of the hills.

I had the last watch from 0500 to 0600. It didn't seem to be getting lighter as sunrise neared, and I wondered. Suddenly, a roll of thunder rocked the mountains and the rain began, and the rain gods of Vietnam punished the landscape. Like shrapnel, the rain ripped the jungle. A heavy wind drove the storm and whipped the trees. Even in the jungle, it was blinding.

My poncho was awkwardly draped over my pack and body as I attempted to keep a part of me dry. I knew better. First, it was a small rivulet of cold rain running down the middle of my back under my poncho. I shivered at the beginning of the total misery that was coming. Within an hour, I was soaked. My lungs felt waterlogged, and I sniffled. I glanced around at the patrol, each man huddled inside his poncho; every man miserably cold and wet. We all looked like big lumps of wet, green, plastic rocks scattered about our little spot in the jungle.

Finally, I thought, We've got to move. The misery of the situation could only be relieved by putting our minds to some other equally despairing task. So we pushed on trying to find our way downhill while the rain quickly was turning the ground into mud and our skin into prunes.

We began to work up a small incline before turning toward the valley. Thick undergrowth gave us handholds when our feet slid out from under us. Silent curses followed falls. Occasionally, a rifle smashed a tree or rock as some Marine slipped heavily. Like wet, slimy creatures of the mud, we labored up the short rise from which I planned to patrol downward again.

It took thirty minutes to move about fifty meters to the top of this finger of the mountain that pointed down toward the lowlands. The rain still did not let up. Then the point team stopped, silently gesturing. Williams waved me up.

They had found a huge trail. Williams had found steps, framed with wood, cut into the trail. Benches were placed on either side of it. "Christ Almighty," I mumbled through the stinging rain. "Suppose that battalion of NVA got orders to move up this way. They'd be using this motherfucking trail. Shit!"

The storm still drove through the jungle, and it was hard to hear what Williams was saying, but we finally understood each other, agreeing on a course of action. We did not want to run into any Charlie up here—no one would be able to help. We were on our own. If we could find them from a distance, great, but no way did we want to walk down a trail that a battalion of enemy soldiers might be walking up. Four hundred to nine are not good odds! So, we turned around and slipped and slid back downhill.

Knee-deep in the rushing water, we continued our downward trek in the middle of the little stream. The bushes closed around us, and we carefully made our way toward the lower elevations in the tunnel formed by the juvenile river as it cut its way down the hillside through thick jungle undergrowth.

An hour later we began to hear the sounds of battle over the pounding, pulverizing rainstorm, which still had not let up. Somewhere below us, Charlie had decided to take on those South Vietnamese Marines. This weather was good for Charlie. It hampered or eliminated our ability to call in our air power. Maybe that NVA battalion that was thought to be coming this way had turned back on the South Vietnamese. We didn't know, but we kept stumbling downhill, wading in the rocky streambed. My feet hurt, but if they ever went numb, I'd start to really worry.

Five hours downstream, I motioned the patrol to hold up. My feet had stopped hurting. It was time for everybody to hide in some wet bush and massage their feet. If it were possible, we'd try to eat cans of wet C's. The rain kept pouring, and I thought that it was not humanly possible to be any more wretched than I was at this very moment.

I leaned against a tree not far away from the river which had now swollen to about thirty feet wide. Misery was spelled M-E. I managed to drop the pack after a minor struggle and just sat in the mud and rain. As I pulled my boots off and looked for my second pair of socks, Williams sat down next to me.

We looked at each other for a few seconds before I finally said, "Williams, do I look as bad as you?"

"Except for your lily-white skin, Lieutenant, I'd say you look like I feel. Better put some more camouflage paint on your face cause it looks the color of your backside, sir. Shit, I could give a rip about the motherfucking NVA. Williams just wants his black, motherfucking ass back inside a dry tent. Lieutenant, can your motherfucking bones get waterlogged?"

I almost laughed as I looked at my feet. They were white as ivory and made prunes look smooth. We sat shivering like sorry, wet dogs, rubbing our feet, trying to get some warmth back into them. My second set of socks needed to be wrung out before I could even put 'em on. At least they weren't caked with mud like the pair I'd been wearing. I slipped down to the stream and washed the mud out of the first pair, feeling like a fool in my mud-encased uniform.

After "airing" our feet in the continuing rainstorm, occasionally listening to the battle as it raged in the valley, and trying to eat a portion of the cold, wet, sick crap we called our rations, we packed up again. "Please, God," I prayed, "let this shit pass."

In another three hours of struggle, the rain had slowed to a drizzle, and I calculated we were down somewhere about two to three hundred meters above the rice fields. The heavy jungles had ended, and the Ly Ly was coming into flood stage not far away. We could see the fields below. Everything was covered by a shallow sea. The inundated rice fields were one continuous lake with which the river seemed to merge.

We moved to a vantage point, if there was such a thing, and I pulled out the binoculars to try to see what the hell had happened. It was about 1700 hours, the skies were still overcast, and a light drizzle fell. Yet it was much better than before.

Less than a mile in front of me was the village of Thach Thuong. Just to our side of it was a battle-torn hilltop, but it was the flooded paddies in front of the hill that told the story. "My God," I mumbled, grabbing Williams and pointing. Scores of bodies literally floated in the water.

"Holy Jesus," Williams said, surveying the battlefield with his glasses. "Shit, we thought we had it bad. Look at those poor suckers. Who's who?"

"There's a yellow flag floating out there, and look over to the left, Williams. There's the regiment. Those South Vietnamese Marines must have charged the hill in that rainstorm. Shit, how could they have even seen through the rain? Charlie cut 'em up and spat 'em out. But where's Charlie now?"

We scanned the hilltop. There were a few bodies, but no signs of life on the muddy mess. Then I heard the planes. The clouds had drifted up and a beam of sunlight shone through. The ceiling was maybe three thousand feet, and the jets were coming. For the next hour we watched as F-4s, F-8s, and A-4s from Da Nang cremated the hill. Never, however, did we see any live enemy. We stayed where we were that night.

At first light the next morning, we watched the South Vietnamese Marines charge and slosh through the flooded rice fields, and this time they took the hill. It was a bombed out and vacated piece of real estate.

We had seen no evidence of any battalion moving into the mountains. I contacted the 5th Marines' regimental command post at Tam Ky, and reported my opinion: the NVA had maneuvered away to the south. There was a chain of low, rolling hills south of the Highway 534 that extended to the southeast and Tam Ky. Instead of escaping into the Que Son Mountains, where we were, the enemy was moving toward our regimental nerve center.

The sun actually shone that day. Our socks were carefully hung on bushes just inside the jungle to dry some, while our feet got the greatest drug possible: fresh sunlight. For the entire day we lounged around the edges of the jungles, keeping watches posted in all directions. I began to feel human again.

The next day found us continuing on our trail, but this time back to the west on the lower south side of the mountains toward Hiep Duc where our 2nd Battalion, 5th Marines, had been searching the countryside for enemy units. We spent the entire day patrolling about five miles to the west and back again. We found trails and evidence that the hills were used but saw no soldiers. However, our radio was picking up transmissions of another heavy battle. This time it was farther away toward Tam Ky, near a place called Ky Phu about ten miles or more southeast of us. I wondered whether it was the same enemy unit that had hit the South Vietnamese at Thach Thuong. They sure as hell didn't seem to be running away from us, although they didn't stay long in any one place.

By the end of that day, we pulled our ponchos over us again as the rain clouds we had seen near Tam Ky was rolling our way. The day after next we were scheduled to be extracted, and we wanted to relocate to the very end, the point, of the hilly fishhook. We would be near

Nui Loc Son and could watch the roadway to the west where Hiep Duc lay about six miles off. In addition, we would command a great view of the valley to our north, and the South China Sea was only about fifteen miles away to the east. It was ideal as an observation point, but it was also dangerously close to the battlefields where there was a good part of an enemy division that wasn't showing much fear of us.

Again, the rain lashed out. Cowering under my poncho, this time without the protection of the trees, I was pummeled by a waterfall that smashed through my raingear and stung my skin. In Texas there had been a saying about this kind of storm: ''It's raining like a cow pissing on a flat rock.'' But I was the flat rock! It was almost like several people were pounding my poncho with baseball bats. However, this storm only lasted about two hours and was gone. Finally, I dozed off about thirty minutes before my first watch.

Only scattered clouds greeted the sun at daybreak. Our wet bodies were already on the march again. We moved into our OP positions while early morning shadows still stole across the hilltop. Three clumps of trees within a fifty-meter circle were to be our positions for the next twenty-four hours. At least, I hoped we wouldn't be disturbed and that we might be able to dry out during these next hours until we were picked up.

I grabbed the point of the three positions on the most easterly side of the hilltop. South Vietnamese Marine Regiment, minus their casualties from the Thach Thuong battle, were now marching eastward on Highway 534. I could see the village of Vinh Huy about six miles from us in that direction. The South Vietnamese would pass it on the north. Low hills spanned the area between the site of the now silent Ky Phu battle and Vinh Huy. Forests covered most of those hills and extended to the main road that the Vietnamese Marines were using. I was concerned that our South Vietnamese friends were asking for trouble using the road like they were.

''Williams,'' I said, ''watch that line of trees just south of the road. Those South Vietnamese are getting close to that village out there, and I'm not sure what their objective is. But if you were Charlie, where would you be?''

''Shit, I'd come out of those hills and follow the forests to that bend in the road just this side of the village. There I'd set me a big motherfucking ambush.''

''Keep your glasses focused out there, Williams,'' I cautioned him.

Exactly one hour later, it hit the fan like a three-ring circus. The forest spit fire and man-made thunder rolled, but this time the skies were clear. The South Vietnamese column buckled and backed up. This time, however, our jets came screaming out of the sky to their rescue in minutes. These weren't exactly fifty-yard line seats, but I watched an unbelievable demonstration of American air power. I was impressed that the South Vietnamese held their ground, but I doubted they could've done it without the tons upon tons of bombs dropped on Charlie.

I shook Williams, pointing and saying, ''Look at those people, Williams, look!'' Charlie was attacking the South Vietnamese right in the face of our bombs.

''Those people got balls, Lieutenant.''

''No, see what's happening now. Going hand-to-hand like that means the jets can't hit 'em without also wiping out the friendlies.''

The NVA had charged out of their positions, not running from the bombing, but instead into the teeth of the South Vietnamese Marines. When they closed together, eyeball-to-eyeball, our jets could only blast away at their rear elements, avoiding the South Vietnamese.

For several hours, the battle ebbed and flowed. I had been radioing all I could report. It looked like there was only one battalion of NVA committed to the fight versus three of the South Vietnamese. We watched one of the three battalions get aboard armored personnel carriers and circle to the NVA's right flank. They came down on the enemy from that side with .50-caliber machine guns mounted on the APCs firing nonstop.

We watched in amazement as the South Vietnamese never got out of their machines. The APC gunners continuously swept the battlefield with their heavy machine-gun fire, locked as they were behind the metal shields of their vehicles.

Williams caught my attention and noted, ''The APCs

are firing past the NVA into their own lines. Son of a bitch, they're just running crazy down there.''

He was right! We watched as the enemy forces used the confused firing of the APCs to cover themselves and then disengage, sliding back into the forests to the south. I tried to yell over the radio what the hell was happening, but nothing seemed to be organized or working. By mid-afternoon the battle was over. Technically, we claimed the battlefield and the enemy was gone, but I began to feel that the objectives of the two sides were different. Maybe the NVA were achieving their goals all along while we thought the bragging rights were ours.

Over the past few days, we had not once detected any enemy units leaving the valley floor. A week had gone by. There were no resupply and medevac helicopters for them like there were for us. How much food and ammunition did they have stored around the countryside? How much did the villages help them? Did they have medical teams or hospitals hidden down there somewhere between our 3,000 US and South Vietnamese Marines?

That night I prayed for no more rain. It wasn't even the bad part of the monsoon season yet, and I was sick of it. It had rained fifty inches in the one month of December the year before. I dreaded a repeat. The mud on my poncho and uniform was like dry-caked dirt. I tried to sleep with my body and mind torn between pain and nervousness. The moon eased its way across the sky, and I debated with myself where those enemy units might be headed to now.

It was the early gray-light before dawn when Rivers shook me whispering, "Lieutenant, I know I've heard people moving. Sometimes it's like hearing a rifle hit a rock. Then maybe once or twice there's been a sound like a human voice. I'm not sure, but I'd bet there's a group of NVA out to our west somewhere."

I woke everyone up, and on a hundred percent alert, we listened and waited. Occasionally, a muffled sound in the distance, now higher in the mountains drifted down to us. Then there was only silence.

Just before daybreak, I grabbed the rear team and began to do a high crawl through the bush in the direction

the noises had come from. We had about an hour before
the choppers would be coming to pick us up.

About a half-mile away, on one of the trails we had
earlier crossed, Sanchez motioned me over to him. He
had found a boot. It was ripped and looked like it had
dried blood on it. Then we found signs of the passage of
a whole pisspot full of people. A couple of sandals,
bloody bandages, one rifle, and the boot were scavenged
to take back to intelligence.

I was beginning to have more respect for these enemy
soldiers, and I wondered where Kim Lan was. I was due
to go home before long, and I wondered if I had seen the
last of her. Shit, how the hell was it possible that I'd ever
run into her again? Did I think that I could just pick up
the telephone and ask her out for dinner or something?
Dumb ass.

CHAPTER 13

Great Potter's wheel, arch foe of womankind,
You've spun me enough . . .

Nguyen Du, *The Tale of Kieu*

We marched all night, and I was exhausted. The fourth time my sandals were sucked off by the endless mud, I just put them into my pack and continued barefoot. By early dawn, we arrived near the town of Ky Phu about four miles west of Tam Ky. It had not rained as much here, and we knew there were American units nearby. We hid in the tree cover of the low hills, rested, and ate. The skies still were partly possessed by dark clouds, but, at least, for a while, I could sleep, and sleep without the rain.

The next day was spent trying to resupply our energies as well as our food and ammunition, and by the end of the day, we were sending our reconnaissance teams. The villagers at Ky Phu helped, and Ba Can waited for further orders.

On the following day, I went into the village with one of our resupply teams and met some of the people. In the town, we began to talk and laugh about the possibility of leaving a message for the Americans should they come into the village, as we all expected they would. Since I had learned English, I was selected to write a message on the side of one of the old stuccoed French buildings.

I wrote carefully in my best penmanship. It took me a long time, but finally I finished and stood back to read out loud to the others: "Stop spraying noxious chemicals in South Vietnam. 250,000 Expeditionary French Corps were routed. Don't follow their footsteps." They all cheered, even the gathered villagers.

The following morning our reconnaissance teams reported the arrival of an American Marine battalion near a small hamlet about a mile and one-half from our positions. They had begun to deploy their forces in order to drive back toward Tam Ky with us in between. Obviously they knew we were somewhere near and intended to destroy us.

Ba Can sent one platoon out to harass the enemy with sniper fire. They were to locate near the hamlet of Cam Khe. The battalion then moved into a position to the west of Ky Phu to engage the enemy battalion from the right flank when they were occupying themselves with our sniper platoon. As we began to move our units forward, the rains began. Maybe, we would again have some heaven-sent protection.

All morning our sniper teams delayed and harassed the American battalion. By midafternoon, the enemy had reached and moved through Cam Khe. There was a quarter-mile between the eastern end of the village and our positions in tree lines near Ky Phu. I could see our sniper platoon emerge out of some trees near a small creek. They began to move quickly into the open ground toward Ky Phu and us. The rains were beginning to increase in intensity, but it was not enough cover for them. The Americans charged out of their positions, their fire ripping into our platoon. Angrily, I watched our men falling. Desperately, they tried to set up and return fire only two hundred yards from our positions. Finally, Ba Can could wait no longer and ordered our units to open fire on the American right flank.

Three enemy companies had moved into attack positions and were bearing down on our lone platoon when we hit them from their side. Through the rain, we could see the Americans begin to turn their companies into positions facing ours and start to maneuver across the fields at us.

The storm so far held off their attack helicopters. Ba Can ordered the company on our left flank to advance and hit their right. We still outflanked them, and this maneuver locked our unit into close combat with theirs.

The battle raged on, and for the next two and one-half hours, the rain alternated between a light drizzle and a pounding thunderstorm. It was sometimes hard to distinguish between the battling forces.

By early evening, the skies had begun to clear, but the battle was still violently ripping men and machines. Both sides had suffered casualties, but Ba Can now saw the incoming American air power and decided to execute his previously planned withdrawal. Each company was moved back in phases down the tree lines, and everyone acted quickly. Wounded were taken with us, but fifty dead were left behind. Most of those belonged to the sniper platoon that was caught in the open. I heard Ba Can reporting that he estimated eighty to one hundred Americans were either dead in the rice fields or evacuated from the field of battle.

In the first four days of the attack against us, Ba Can had lost about one-fourth of his battalion, but he didn't once stop to grieve the losses. I never saw him rest. He now led his battalion in a circle around the Americans, and finally we again turned north. I wondered if the enemy could possibly have such determination as my brother. I tried to compare Ba Can to the American. The two times that I had seen him in the last months seemed like impossible acts of fate, but now that we had actually met face to face, I wondered and worried if someday I'd find him dead on the battlefield.

Then I looked around at the wounded and tried to help them. There was a large hospital hidden below ground not far away. We left our seriously hurt there, and then, again, our commander pushed us overnight. Only this time, we did not have far to travel. Past the American battalion that we had just fought, we marched five hilly miles through the darkness. About two o'clock in the morning, my brother allowed us to collapse and sleep near the rice fields surrounding the village of Vinh Huy. I did not know what our orders were, but I was too tired to care. Finding some grass under the now clear, star-filled skies, I lay down.

Instantly, I was awake with someone shaking me. My mind was confused and alarmed, and I tried to gain my senses. Finally, I recognized Ba Can's voice. He was saying, "Kim Lan, wake up! It is time to get ready. The day awaits us."

I just sat holding my head in my hands. It was dawn, but I felt as if I had only fallen asleep a moment before. I was so tired, I could hardly think. I said to my brother, "Ba Can, you amaze me. I'm still exhausted. It couldn't have been more than five minutes ago that I lay down to sleep. That must be the moon you see, brother. The war has finally gotten to your mind. Go back to sleep."

He just smiled at me, and standing at my side, he looked around at his men. My body ached, but finally I said, "You're really convinced that this is the day? Well, what do you propose to do? Your soldiers need some rest."

He laughed and said, "My sister, you still are not up to your full strength. The spirit of the revolution keeps us going, and you, too, will feel it bring you to your feet. Here, take a drink of this and come over to the command group."

With that he was gone. I looked at a flask in my hands and drank. It was a warm and strong rice wine. Slowly, I got to my knees and then onto my feet. As I wavered slightly, I thought, the spirit of the revolution must also be having a hard time awakening this morning. I half-walked and half-stumbled toward Ba Can's command group.

The South Vietnamese Marine battalion that we had battled earlier was now advancing in an easterly direction between the Ly Ly River and Highway 534. I heard Ba Can saying that when they neared the village of Vinh Huy at a certain location along the highway we would strike.

Within an hour, Ba Can had his men on their aching feet and on the move again. He was their example, and as long as he could keep going, so could they. I was marching on willpower, ready to collapse but not allowing it to happen. We moved into our positions in an area heavily overgrown with trees and brush. The hills were to our rear and the highway to our front. We set the ambush. Our withdrawal route was thoroughly noted, but this time it did not appear that we would be blessed with rain. For this battle, Ba Can had placed me in charge of the communications. We communicated by wire. It was more difficult, but the enemy could not intercept our messages as we did theirs sent by wireless radios. Our mortars were set in the hills behind us. Our communication wires were laid, hidden in the ground or brush. Between our infantry companies, we needed those who were brave and fleet of foot to help carry messages and check radio lines for repair or replacement. Then, after the battle, the lines must be reeled in while on the move. There had been much debate about this, but the prevailing thought had been that no matter the effort involved, secrecy was of paramount importance. The enemy must not be able to find and monitor our messages.

By midmorning the South Vietnamese Marines were on the march and very near. We hid, waiting tensely. Then they were in front of us, and just as the viper striking quickly and unexpectedly from the tall grass, we launched the ambush. Our rifles, machine guns, and mortars lashed out at the enemy. They returned fire, and we closed in bloody battle. They outnumbered and outgunned us, but we had the advantages of surprise and position.

After the initial onslaught, we rolled back the enemy's right flank, and he tried to regroup. Within minutes, American aircraft were streaking out of the skies on us. I knelt behind a tree and screamed in anger at the planes that raked us with bombs and cannon fire. We held on and closed with the enemy. Battling hand-to-hand at least kept the aircraft away, but they still smashed into our rear units.

The fighting was fierce, and if it had not been for the bombers, we could have driven the South Vietnamese off. However, men fell wounded, often mortally, on both sides, and for hours through the afternoon, the warfare tore bodies and land apart.

Both sides seemed close to exhaustion by midafternoon. Then enemy reinforcements arrived from our right flank. They came in armored vehicles and slammed us with heavy machine guns.

Ba Can was everywhere, running from one unit to the next shouting commands and ordering companies to reconsolidate and face the new attack. The Saigon troops

continued their attack, but I noticed that their infantry
was not leaving their vehicles. They attacked in an un-
organized manner and much of the ammunition seemed
to be ripping the air over our heads and smashing into
their own forces with whom we had spent all day locked
in combat. I ran to Ba Can and listened. He radioed his
company commanders and called for a gradual withdrawal. Without realizing it, the new enemy force gave
us the covering fire we needed.

We disengaged slowly through the trees. Finally, by
dusk, the battalion had completely removed itself from
the field of battle. One hundred more of our men had
been killed or wounded and would have to be placed in
hospitals. Ba Can, however, boasted that we had proven
ourselves again. The enemy, he felt, must have lost a
battalion. Yes, we withdrew, but my brother noted that
our bases of support were positioned throughout this area,
and we could return anywhere at anytime. The enemy
would leave, doctoring its wounds and would not be back
for some time. Again, at night, we marched through the
foothills, making a swing first to the south, then to the
west and north. Our seriously wounded remained behind, hidden in the hospitals underground. The enemy
had marched and searched through this area and missed
our medical units dug in several levels below the ground.

At one point, I stood beside the trail and tried to watch
for those who needed the most help. Bloody rags circled
the arms, legs, and bodies of so many of our soldiers. In
the moonlight, I would see an occasional tough grin
quickly flashed at me, and my heart went out to these
uncomplaining brave ones. Some collapsed from a com-
bination of exhaustion and wounds, and others would help
them back up.

We trooped on into the lower ranges of the Que Son
Mountains. Just over two hundred soldiers out of our
original four hundred marched out of the valley and into
the mountains before sunrise. Uniforms were ripped and
torn. Bloody bandages were still wrapped around many.
We all were filthy with the sweat, mud, dust, and stench
of a long week of war. This was but one week, however,
in a twenty-one-year-old war.

The skies were beginning to lighten as night was slowly

turning into morning. Pink and blue rays were shining over the sea far to my left, and under an easy gray that became lighter by the minute, the valley floor sprawled across the face of the land in front of me. I stepped out of the column of soldiers as they struggled up the mountain and sat on a large rock and watched the scene as it slowly marched in front of me. From my pack, I pulled out my notebook and pencil, and I began to try to draw on paper the emotions I felt. Looking into the faces of the tired and bloodied soldiers, mostly men, but here and there a few women, I was more than a little overcome. Soldiers helped one another. Someone, someone could be heard shouting encouragement, and that someone would be a different person in a different part of the column. More than a few had bloody bare feet but kept marching, and some even smiled.

I should have collapsed and not been able to get back up, but at this moment, I was proud to be Vietnamese. I sensed two thousand years of history, tradition, and culture invisibly weaving strength into the soul of each soldier. They would march on, and if one died, another would step forward to take his place. Destiny was manifest in the very root source of our cause. The tide of a long history flowed in our favor.

I looked at my sketch. It was so rough. I knew that I could never vividly paint life into the blood and glory that was stamped on the faces of my comrades. I prayed that someone, someday, could paint this picture more adequately than I. I folded the paper and put it in my pack and rejoined the column.

The sun was just coming out of the sea far to the east when we stopped to rest at about the first line of jungle, maybe three thousand feet over the valley floor. I dropped to the ground and knew now I'd never get up. I hazily watched the pink and purple clouds drift across the sky and felt myself sinking into softness.

The next thing I felt was Ba Can shaking me. I didn't know how long I had lay there. My brother looked at me and said, "Kim Lan, you are not well yet. When we get back to our camp, I'm putting you on leave. In fact, I hope to make arrangements for Van Thi to come and spend some time with you. But before he gets here, you need to cure the dark circles under your eyes.''

For the next month, I was forced to pamper myself, and I felt like I was being given special treatment. Despite the guilt feelings, I longed for the coming of my husband. Daily I found myself torn between my need to be with the soldiers on one hand, and yet the desires to be with my husband—I felt guilty. So many thousands of others were without their families. But I was also plagued by thoughts that he wouldn't be able to come.

I now felt rested and the doctor said that soon I could return to my unit. Van Thi still had not arrived, and I had about resigned myself to his absence. Faintly, I held out the hope that he could still make it, and with the rains now starting, he might do it more safely.

Then on September 15, unannounced, he was there. The rain had stopped for a brief few days, and shafts of sunlight shone through the trees as he walked past soldiers and into the clearing in the center of the base near Ba Can's headquarters. He carried a pack, rifle, and worried expression. I had just walked out of Ba Can's headquarters and stopped where I stood, almost afraid to move. Was it really him? Since our marriage five months before, we had not seen each other. He smiled when he saw me and walked forward. My feet were frozen to the earth. He came up and held me. Tears flowed. I couldn't help it, and I cried, clinging tightly to him.

He said, ''You are still so beautiful. How are you? No, wait. First show me where I can place my pack and rifle and let us find some place alone to talk.''

He was every bit the handsome soldier I had known before, and I walked holding his arm. Within me, I felt as if I were going to explode. Emotions spiraled on emotions, and I wanted to shout from the top of the mountain across the valleys below. I wanted to dance in my happiness. Instead, I walked, quietly holding tightly to his arm back to my little house.

For the last month, with more spare time than I had known since I couldn't remember, I had been transforming my rough shelter into more of a comfortable little home in the middle of this busy camp high in the jungled mountains. Secretly, hopefully, I had also been noting private, secluded little corners of the jungle dreaming of the day Van Thi would come, and I could manage to take him away from this busy place. Now, he was here, but I could not find my voice.

The mountain streams, after reaching a low point brought on by the summer dry season, were beginning to recover in the rains. About a mile's walk from the perimeter of our base, I had found a place where a stream had cut deeply into the side of the mountain. Cliffs about twenty feet tall had been formed on either side of the stream. It was overgrown with jungle bushes, except that at the bottom of the little falls that the stream had created, a small beach of sand had been built up on either side of the water. It was here that I wanted to take Van Thi.

He dropped his pack and rifle in my hut and held me. I began to relax. I could feel it. The tensions eased out of me. Then I said quietly that I had found a nice place about a mile away. He smiled and said, "Let's go." I quickly put some sweet cakes in a bag, grabbed a blanket and teased him out of the little thatch roofed home. He carried his rifle, and we walked past the soldiers and past the base perimeter. My emotions steamed their way throughout my being, and I wondered what Van Thi was thinking. I wanted his thoughts to be centered only on me.

After walking quietly for about several minutes, I finally asked, "What are you thinking about? You're so quiet."

He stopped. Turning, he pulled me to him, and I dropped what I had been carrying and melted in his arms. He kissed me, and the flame from his lips lit fires in my thighs. I held him tightly, knowing the passion that I had only dreamed about for months. Then he stepped back a half step holding my hands, smiled and looked into my eyes. Still I couldn't find the power to speak.

At last he spoke, "Kim Lan, I'm so sorry. I'm still, at least in part, at war down in the valleys. It's hard to switch so quickly from the battlefield to the gentle arms of my wife."

Then he placed his hands on each side of my face and kissed me softly on my lips and asked, "How much farther to the place you were telling me about?"

For a moment, I stood with his arms around my shoulders, staring into his eyes, not really thinking about his question. Then he asked again, "Kim Lan, let's go. How much farther?"

Embarrassed, I started out of my love dreams and answered, "It's right in front of us. We just push past these bushes and follow a pathway back upstream about two hundred yards." He held my hand and led the way.

In a few minutes, we had gotten to the small beach and pool. The water tumbled down over boulders and crashed noisily and beautifully into the head-end of this small narrow gorge. Trees leaned out overhead like a roof. The sand was cool and beckoning under my bare feet, and I dropped down to my knees. Sitting back on my heels, I breathed deeply with my eyes closed. I stayed like that as I heard Van Thi kneel down behind me. He put his arms around me and whispered in my ear quiet, sweet, love things. Involuntarily, I shivered.

Then he got up and stripped off his clothes as he walked toward the water. Naked, he waded waist-deep before turning around and calling for me to follow. My body burned with love's fire as I stood up and followed my husband. He dove under and swam. As I walked in, the water rippled against my bare skin, and I longed to be next to him.

He surfaced near the other bank and laughed, saying, "I must offer thanks to the heavens above. I needed this. With you, the battles, the blood, and the bruises fade away. If you could do me another favor, please unpin your hair and let it fall."

I stood with my breasts barely riding the water's surface and reached back to fulfill his request. Then I stood smiling at him and slowly sank to my neck in the water feeling refreshed and aroused. He dove, swimming across the pool under the water coming in my direction. Laughing, I dove and swam to the side out of his grasp.

When he came up for air and looked around, I was swimming to the deep end. Then I stopped, turned around, and treaded water. He swam after me and I waited. As he came close, the two of us were slowly water-dancing, trying to stay afloat while we flirted with each other. Then I swam over to a shallower part and called for him to follow before he became too tired.

We stood hardly waist-deep, and I threw my arms around his neck. He pulled me tight and hungrily kissed me. I felt him hard and throbbing against my body, and a teasing fire swept its way though my flesh. My breasts thrilled to the touch of his wet hands.

I wanted him too much to wait any longer and grabbed his hand, leading him from the water. I turned to look into his face at the edge of our blanket, but as we stood together, our wet skin lightly touching, I was overcome by shyness. He leaned forward and kissed me, and my knees trembled. We knelt down without pulling apart from one another. I wanted to throw myself on him but could only bring myself to lay down side-by-side with the most beautiful man that I had ever known. Our fingers touched and softly stroked each other. He looked longingly at my breasts and kissed them. His lips stung; it had been so long. My skin tingled and nipples hardened.

I felt him hard against me, and he raised his lips to mine. He kissed my lips, my eyes, my neck, and slowly his tongue touched and caressed my body. His manhood throbbed between my legs, and he said, ''I'm ready to explode, and I want to be in you when I do.''

I rolled over pulling him with me. Kissing me again, he easily slid on top of and into me. We moved together, slowly and then faster and faster. He cried out and his body quivered, but he slowly kept moving in me. I couldn't stop. On the edge of ecstasy, my body pushed upward, harder and harder until something warm and wonderful struck like lightning throughout my body. Our bodies throbbed rhythmically together, eagerly anticipating every sensation of love. Slowly, easily, we relaxed and lay together quietly. After a quiet minute tightly in each other's grasp, he whispered, ''I love you.''

I squeezed him tightly and said, ''I love you more!''

He leaned back and looked at me with a mock frown and said, ''Do you insult me? Is my love not good enough? How could you love me more?''

We looked at each other and finally broke out laughing. I reached up, put my arms around his neck, and said, ''It's not the quality of your love; it's just once every five or six months that is less than enough.''

He smiled and leaned forward to kiss me quickly on

the lips and ducked down to suck on my breasts. A slight
moan of pleasure came from my lips, and I locked my
legs more tightly around his, not ever wanting to let go.

We lay together for a long time just holding each other.
After a while, he pulled out from me and got up, and I
wanted him back. He went to the water, slowly walking
out and then diving under and swimming. I watched him
for a while and then pulled the food out of the bag and
set up our little banquet of desserts on the blanket. He
came out; his body now gleaming in its wetness. His
long, lean muscles shone. His manliness hung down,
no longer hard and erect, and I wanted to ask him, "How
long before it can be hard and within me again," but it
was only my unspoken thought. Then we sat together
naked and ate. I wondered about the warmness I felt. He
looked at me after a while and asked, "What's the matter? You're so quiet."

I answered, "I'm not sure, but there's just a feeling
within me. It's new and different. I think that maybe
someday we shall have a baby."

He looked at me quietly and then moved closer. Setting his food down, he hugged and just held me without
speaking. I felt loved and warm. Some internal clock had
just started to tick.

The days went by, and too soon Van Thi had to return
to his unit. When I saw him off, the rains had started
again. On the edge of the jungles, still high in the mountains, we stood in our raincoats holding hands. He kissed
me, and said, "Take care of yourself. I love you. I'll
return before long. Depend on that. I will."

Then he was gone, walking in the mud downhill. The
rain increased, and he hadn't gone far before he was almost totally obscured by the storm. Faintly, I saw him
turn and wave one last time. I waved with both arms,
and my tears flowed with the rain. Alone, for the first
time I felt afraid. It was an undefined sort of fear, and I
wanted to run after him. Instead, I simply stood in the
same spot with the rain pouring. My hair felt like a
long, wet mop, and I didn't know what I wanted to do.
Slowly, finally, I turned and walked back.

Returning to my hut, I sat down in my wet clothes,
and my mind aimlessly drifted. Something in my soul

knew a child had been conceived within me. Then I
feared for my husband. Everyone close to me had been
killed except for Van Thi and Ba Can. Now clouding my
mind, a vague darkness followed my husband. Waves of
anxiety engulfed me. I stared through the doorway at the
storm which blotted out the light. As the wind wrestled
with my hut, verses from *The Tale of Kieu* called to me:

> A hundred years—in this life span on earth,
> How apt to clash, talent and destiny!
> Men's fortunes change even as nature shifts;
> The sea now rolls where mulberry fields grew.
> One watches things that make one sick at heart.
> This is the law: no gain without a loss,
> And Heaven hurts fair women for sheer spite.

"The sea now rolls where mulberry fields grew." This
was the American's quote. Ten years ago, he said it was
the one Vietnamese saying he knew: *Be Dau*. No matter
the strength of our labors, time has a way of shifting and
undoing the product of our hands. Unless a person can
become a part of the eternal current of life, his legacy
eventually will be lost. Words, thoughts, and principles
of life, whether passed through the generations by word
of mouth or by pen, will live and multiply in the lives of
others whether a name is remembered or not. However,
be it next year, or a thousand years, most of man's mon-
uments to himself will be no more.

I thought of the American again. In his way of thinking, the sea could be challenged and the tide turned. I
would have liked to say to him, "Maybe, with all your
wealth and machines, you can change the tide for a time.
There, however, will come a year when you will give up
the relentless battle. Then what will be, will be."

Did the American have a wife and child back in his
home? I wondered about him for a moment longer.

CHAPTER 14

If there is anything that makes my blood boil, it is to see our allies in Indochina . . . deploying Japanese troops to reconquer the . . . people [Vietnamese] we promised to liberate. It is the most ignoble kind of betrayal.

General Douglas MacArthur (1946)

There was only a slight wind, and the ship rocked gently in the South China Sea. The dark had gone by now, and the sky was at that point somewhere between light gray and early blue. For a moment, I tried to block out the tension that was developing below decks, and I became mesmerized by the water as it flowed in limitless waves over a million miles and slapped nonstop against the sides of this giant, gray hulk called USS *Duluth*. I was nearing the end of a six-month extension in 'Nam. Two monsoon seasons had come and gone since I had been here, and now not only my friends and family back in the land of the living, but my Marine buddies also wondered about my sanity. In a month, I'd have over a year and a half in-country, but there would be no extending again—I was going home this time!

But I wondered if subconsciously I had requested to stay this last six months on a chance of seeing her again. I hadn't though, and I felt a let down. Not since last fall had I seen anything of her. There were no reports about any VC woman. She had disappeared. Maybe she had been killed. The war had blown sky high down in this south-country in the last year. She could have easily gotten caught up in the shit. However, there was just one more month for old Number One! Hell, all I wanted was to get through the last thirty days. A nineteen-month tour of duty in 'Nam was enough! When I got back to Pendleton, I'd have just a few months, and I'd be out again into the land of blonds and Chevy vans. I hoped for good. I was tired—just wanted to squeeze some California sand between my toes and not worry about anything. Maybe I'd sit on the beach at night and talk to seals. Then I supposed I'd have to go back to college and figure out what to do with my over-thirty self: become a confirmed nose-picking civilian like everybody else. Shit, I'd probably fall incurably in love with the first pair of gorgeous round-eyes I saw and screw up the rest of my life! But I would be forever able to know that I did my time with my Marines.

Then behind me the noise of the helicopters gearing up for take-off intruded across my thoughts. I turned around and watched my platoon commanders get their men ready.

This, I thought, is a long fucking way from Recon. Four months back I had made captain and was transferred to the infantry. It was a whole new bag of tricks being an infantry company commander. My old nine man, "swift, silent, and deadly" squad of Recon Marines, had turned into one hundred and fifty grunts packing enough gear to blast a hole in the Great motherfucking Wall of China. I was even going to have tanks with me! Instead of soft bush hats, we were wearing the heavy, metal helmets and flak jackets that everybody cussed.

The helicopters were ready, and I watched the company prepare to board each bird. I climbed down the ladder to join Gunny Kershaw. We'd be in the lead bird, while my EO would bring up the rear. We were the lead company in Operation Whitestone Canyon.

As I ran, or rather tried to keep from stumbling under the heavy pack, across the gently rocking ship's heliport, the familiar nervous anxiety pumped through my being. This was my first ship-to-shore assault since we had practiced them off Norfolk, Virginia, ages ago. We, however, weren't going across the beach, but were flying deeper inland.

I grabbed the gunny and said, "Let's go." We ran up into the wide back hatch of the CH-46 followed by our Marines. I turned at the entrance and watched my men run past me. When the last of the group going in my bird was in, I clumsily sat down beside the gunny, trying to make like I could carry my pack like Fred Astaire. My covey of radio operators sat nearby. Then with more than a little straining and shuddering, we were off the ship's landing deck and over the sea. I began to feel the sense of excitement heighten. Our war birds muscled their way into the sky and were off racing like green-winged quarter horses over a cloudy track. As many as we were, it would take two waves to get the battalion reassembled on land.

After a noisy five-minute flight, in the early dawn light, I could see below me a long, narrow, brown lifeline tying Hill 55, now close on our right, to An Hoa, farther out to the front. That was Liberty Road, and it was built by a lot of blood and sweat through Apache Country. I knew more than one Marine killed by enemy mines on that road and had traveled it once myself. Being up in the mountains with Recon had felt a lot better than driving down Liberty Road.

Then I felt us quickly dropping from the sky. We came in low, and Vietnamese began to scatter as a pisspot full of helicopters rapidly descended into the recently harvested farmlands near the road. Then we were bouncing in the fields. As fast as possible, the companies spread out over the dried-out paddies to secure a good-size perimeter. The spring rice harvest was over a short while ago. One of our objectives was to root out the VC and keep their hands off the food. The Arizona Territory was behind us to the west, and ahead of us lay the Dodge City area. But less than a mile away was the Thu Bon River, and just across that was the home of Geronimo himself—Go Noi Island.

The merciless heat of the tropical sun had baked the empty rice flats into dry mud-rocks. The nearest tree was about a quarter-mile away. The paddy dikes were two to three feet tall, and dozens of Vietnamese resumed their walk along the road behind us starting their day's work. We lay waiting for the rest of the battalion and reinforce-

ments from Hill 55 to link up with us. I hated it. The
rising sun would expose the hell out of us.

I studied the map and tried to match it with what I
could see of the ground ahead of us. The Song Thu Bon
forked into two branches to surround what was Go Noi
Island. The island was only about three clicks across,
north to south, but stretched out over twelve thousand
meters, twelve clicks, to the east. The north fork of the
Thu Bon was called the Ky Lam, while the south was the
Ba Ren. This latter one, during the dry season, was nothing more than a series of intermittent, narrow finger
lakes. It was already well on its way to being that.

Only a few scattered tiny hamlets lay between us and
the river. I turned and looked at the Vietnamese on the
road behind us about the length of two football fields
away and at the several crossing the paddies on all sides
of us. A strange feeling, like being on another planet,
swept over me. All these people wearing black pajamas
and conical-shaped straw hats seemed to have eyes peering out from under all sides of those bamboo cones. I
felt their indirect attention and get-the-hell-out-of-our-
lives looks.

Then the words of our S-2 came back real hard. I had
never had it put to me in that manner before. "Gentlemen," he had said. "In this one province alone, we estimate there are over one hundred and seventy thousand
Vietnamese civilians giving aid, comfort, and supplies to
the VC. That is three times the number of all US Marines
in I Corps. Only three percent of the hamlets can be
considered secure. I don't need to emphasize, gentlemen,
that you should assume that any civilian you encounter
is not friendly."

Again, I looked across the silent distances at the Vietnamese going about their business, ignoring or plotting
against us, and thought, so ninety-seven percent of you
little assholes are against us. And I'm supposed to protect you from the VC! I bet you can't wait for me to turn
my back. You've got a different version of the fire-team:
three of you work in the fields with dumb looks on your
faces, while one guy hides in the bush and plants mines,
booby traps, or takes potshots at us. Then you rotate,
giving the guy in the bush a break so he can stand in the

fields with a dumb look, too. Well, you can kiss my ass, fellows. George Armstrong Custer this Marine ain't. One potshot at us, and a fucking 90-millimeter cannon from an M-48 Sherman tank will blow you a new asshole. You all, and the "water-boo" you rode in on, can go right straight to hell. Old Number One here is going home in a few weeks, and I intend to make it back in one healthy piece.

But we just had to lie there watching sunlight rise for another half-hour. During that time, the rest of the battalion and tanks from Hill 55 began to link up with us. Not far out to my front, I could see the burned-out wreckage of a Marine amphibian tractor from the last attempts to seek and destroy the enemy around Dodge City. But we didn't care whether headquarters designated the areas by that name or the Arizona Territory or anything else, 'cause it was all just Apache Country to us.

The sun rose higher until it hung just above the horizon. The magnified orange orb carried in its youthful glare a distinct warning of what it intended to do to our poor bodies in a very short time.

By 0700 the battalion had consolidated and organized its position near the road. Then six hundred Marines began to move out in long lines across the dried out fields. My A Company was on the right flank, along with the three tanks attached to us. In order to accomplish my personal objectives of not getting the company blown to hell in a handbasket, I set up the tanks and two platoons ready to blast anything that spit at us, while one platoon advanced by squads on line. They ran and maneuvered from dike to dike, as if Charlie was just in front of them. As soon as they reached the covering protection of the tree line, they dropped behind it to set-up cover for the next platoon. Then I moved the second platoon, not following directly, but to the right front. After that, I took the tanks and the third platoon across.

Within an hour, we were on the banks of the Song Ky Lam. Across the river in front of us and in the fork of the two rivers was the village of Tuy La. Battalion ordered me to ford the river and swing to the right of the village, between it and the Song Ba Ren. My company would be moving down the right side of the island, while

Bravo Company would sweep through the villages, and Charlie Company tied its flank to the Ky Lam on the portside. Delta came in reserve with the battalion CP.

By noon we were all across the Ky Lam and marching down the island on a line that was over a mile wide and a little bedraggled. For the next three days, we fought the energy-sucking heat, mosquitos, boredom, and razor-sharp grass that sliced our skin.

The battalion had passed through the village of Tuy La without event, and then Phu Tay had loomed in front of us as if a tree-lined island in the middle of dead rice fields. Grass huts with occasional stucco buildings left over from the days of the French fell behind us, and the battalion marched on. Old wrinkled men and women sat next to their homes on dirt streets and seemingly ignored us, chewing betel nut and cleaning farm tools. Little kids played in the dirt with their bottom-halves naked, occasionally pointing and giggling at us. The young men and women were not to be seen. But the battalion was pushing for the rail line. Maybe some VC unit was staying ahead of us just out of our way. We'd eventually push 'em into some open space and pound their hides with artillery and bombs.

On the fourth day, we were close. In front of B Company was the village of Phu Dong. Just beyond it, was a sea of the damnable grass. Its cutting edges gleaming in the sun, the tall devil-weed silently waved at us. From my position about ten feet above the fields, I could barely make out the half-hidden village of Lanh Dong lying in the tall grass next to the tracks. There crossing this river-island, and across our front, was the old French rail line built high on a dike to keep it above the seasonal floods. C Company had drawn the short straw. Their job was to swing from their flank position on the left, after we had reached the edge of the lake of weeds, and sweep across our front pushing any enemy toward the open sand flats of the Ba Ren in front of me.

Then the companies of sweaty, dirty, insect-bitten, irritated Marines continued their advance. Bravo was in Phu Dong, while we watched the half-open land between the village and the shallow, drying river. About a half-mile short of the railroad tracks, we halted and pivoted our flank so that two of my platoons now faced the shimmering open sands of the Song Ba Ren. My Marines set themselves in an L-shape to give some cover to C Company as they pushed through the grass and Lanh Dong and to be ready to blow apart anything that moved like enemy across the river.

Again, I studied my map. Bravo Company was in the village to our left. Charlie Company was starting its miserable trek through the high grass, and, to the right side, was the drying-out Ba Ren. We had positioned ourselves on the last bit of semihigh ground before the sands opened up and sloped down to the dying river. There was about a hundred yards of exposed, hot sand between us and the fingers of the river that were still pooled with water. Then there was only a short hundred feet or so to the banks on the other side where the ground rose about ten feet in most places. On top of the flat shelf above that side of the river was a roadway that linked Hoi An farther away to the east and An Hoa to the west. It crossed the rail line less than a mile away to our left-front. The flat shelf disappeared there. A long ridgeline began at the junction of the tracks and the road, just at the river, and angled across and away from us to the southwest leading into the Que Son Mountains. I hoped that battalion would blow the hell out of those hills before any of us had to cross the open river sands. According to the map, the ridge was called the Nai Do. It stared down at us from the not-so-distance and almost laughed. I remembered the problems we had on the other side of these same mountains and what must be up in there and looked again at the Nai Do as a highway to the Que Sons. And I knew that we would have to cross the river in front of that motherfucking ridgeline. Charlie Company would have to go right into the teeth of it with us a little off to the right flank.

I watched the heat rise in steamy waves in the miserably hot afternoon. Looking at the sands and the Ba Ren water holes, I felt that I was watching one of the TV specials about the drying landscape of the African veldt. I almost started to look around for the wild animals cautiously coming in for a drink. This time it wasn't lions and leopards—but VC and NVA.

It was late afternoon before Charlie Company had pushed through the hellhole of dry, hot, stuffy, humid air of the razor-grass sea and then the village. Nothing moved. The only stupid ones killing themselves in this heat were us. Now two companies of Marines faced the Ba Ren sand flats and water holes. Bravo Company had occupied the village with its advantage of trees, brush, and the highest terrain on the island. Delta still waited in reserve. The tree-lined bank on the other side stared out of its shadows and dared us to come over. The Nai Do stood behind the bank and the road, silently waiting.

I looked over at C Company and Capt. Tom Diggs, or "Digger" as we called him. He had the worst of it by far. It just wasn't his day. Five- to six-foot-high weeds had just cut his people to hell in that stuffy hole, and now he faced the Ba Ren with the ridge rising up steeply above the opposite bank.

Digger had been like me. He had gotten out of the Corps, and then this war in the Oriental tropics had started. He had never felt right being a civilian while his buddies were still fighting in Vietnam, so he had re-enlisted. Now he was in the middle of it. Sometimes we talked about it over a few beers. He didn't regret his decision, but the memory of his wife and new kid sometimes made him feel that he hadn't done right by them. He and his Nancy had started on big plans. He had been working on his master's degree when he dropped it all and put his uniform on again. He had shown me pictures of his wife and child, and sometimes he would sit for an hour smelling her perfume-scented letters. It made me want to be married, have a girl, or maybe just a pen pal.

But I had to quit worrying about Digger and start planning how I was going to get my Marines across the open sands and safely to the bank on the other side. Again, I placed the three tanks in firing positions with one platoon in the rear to cover us. The section of 60 "Mike-Mikes" were dug in near the tanks. These, our light 60-millimeter mortars, and the three 90-millimeter cannons on the tanks were to be ready to blast the hell out of anything that tried to mess with us.

Then, with two platoons on line, I took command of the "sprint" across the Ba Ren flats. We expected there to be some enemy at least to try to harass us so we advanced by fire and maneuver. Digger was doing the same. Marines were throwing out a light rifle fire into the banks of the opposite side of the river and running, rolling, firing, and running again. I could hear a few men start to laugh at the invisible silence that faced us and absorbed our sporadic rifle fire. Then I heard more.

Someone screamed, "Incoming."

We all made like sweaty, green, sand-snakes squirming into the river's beach, as enemy 82-millimeter mortars blasted and showered us with sand. The ground heaved and my ears rattled. My experience fought against the momentary fear and tried to take command and figure out what was happening. Cries of pain echoed down the river valley along with the accompaning call, "Corpsman up!" But the impact of enemy mortars was almost petrifying. I felt myself wanting to burrow in the sand, afraid to move and get blown to hell.

Not only my ears but my brain was also ringing from the explosions. The last round was like dynamite blasting within yards of me. Cautiously, I raised my head. Sand showered my body as another exploding round almost rolled me over. Then I finally figured out that no one was shooting at us from the bank, but the mortars were coming in from the ridge less than a half-mile away. I called my platoon commanders to move out of these open sands as fast as possible. I radioed for all the supporting arms I could find to blast the ridge. Then we ran and hit the deck and ran again, but most of the time, I think we had our butts so low to the ground that we were dragging the sand from the river. Teams stayed behind to help pull the wounded to the safety of the riverbank. Then, just as I was almost at the protection of the bank, a blast knocked me off my feet. I struggled to my knees. My neck was scratched where my helmet strap had raked it as my helmet was blown off my head. Bare-headed, I looked around trying to get my wits together. The bells of hell pounded their beat on my eardrums. But above it all, the cries of wounded men drowned out all else.

One Marine lay near my feet holding his head. I touched him, and he looked at me in a daze. I could find no wound and told myself, A concussion maybe. Then I

saw Staff Sergeant Liverette, 3rd Platoon Sergeant, trying to call for a corpsman while puking his guts out. A
Marine lay in front of him, and the doc was running up.

Half running, half crawling, I made it to Liverette.
The corpsman was talking to himself, working on whoever was wounded. There was a lull in the enemy mortars, and the call for medevacs had gone out.

"My God! Shit, damn, fuck!" I mumbled as I knelt
almost in shock. In front of me, the wounded Marine lay
exposed. One arm and one leg were gone and lying in
pieces around the sand. The others, ripped to shreds
themselves, hung only by a few strands of flesh to the
body's trunk. But it was the face that destroyed me. The
front, from eyes to jaw, was a bloody hole. The eyes,
nose, and jaws looked like they were gone. Blood
pumped out of the hole. The corpsman was in tears, talking to himself and tying tourniquets everywhere. The
Marine, I didn't know who the hell he was, still, somehow, lived.

I turned and saw the medevac bird on its way. It took
every ounce of discipline I had to keep my stomach from
turning inside out. Then the helicopter was there to take
him and others out. I watched and wished that he hadn't
been wearing the flak jacket and helmet. They somehow
spared his heart and brain, but he would have been far
better off otherwise. I prayed he'd die and asked God to
forgive me if that was a sin. But I didn't really give a
damn, no one should have to live like that. Then the VC
hit us again.

My forward two platoons were now in the semiprotec-
tion of the riverbank. My radio operator, Corporal Powell,
came up to me crawling with the radio saying, "Charlie
Company's catching holy hell out there, Skipper!"

For the first time, I looked at Digger's plight. He had
run into a fucking hurricane. Not only was he hit by
mortars and the shit that had rained on us, but he also
had run into a full-scale ambush. Overlooking the riverbank, the enemy had entrenched himself in the ridgeline
directly in front of Charlie Company's advance. At a distance of a hundred yards, they poured out a calculated
fire into Digger's men who were caught in the open hell
of the Ba Ren sand flats.

Then the "Battalion 6" was on my radio. Delta Company was being ordered around my right flank and the two of us were to push up to the road and attack down the An Hoa-bound highway and rail line to hit the VC from the western flank and try to save Charlie Company. Suddenly, screaming Phantom 4s dived out of the western sun and came roaring over our heads driving their bombs into the ridge as they climbed up to the clouds and rolled over to do it again.

My last platoon and tanks had now run the gauntlet and pushed across with Delta Company. Now we were racing to set up a line of attack that stretched from the river south to the tracks. I found Capt. Charles Rowe, the skipper of Delta Company, and we had about sixty seconds to coordinate an attack. He would be on the right with me next to the river. Just as we were going to run back to our people, he grabbed me saying, "Listen to the fucking radio, man. Digger is dying out there."

Over the green box, I heard static, rifle shots, and screams. Then I heard Digger. I knew it was him. For a hateful moment, all I wanted to do was kill! But I could only listen to Digger's plaintive cry, "Every time I move, they shoot me again!"

"God help him," I screamed and began running.

Then two hundred-plus Marines, in a ragged, bloodied line, walked, ran, crawled, and did everything they could to reach those sons of bitches on the ridge. The Phantoms screeched out of hell over our heads and plowed five-hundred pounders into the ridge. But as much as we threw at them, the enemy hurled back at us. The ridge looked like fire mountain. Then just short of what would be our final assault to the hillside, we waited for the last runs of our jets. The enemy fire had quieted.

Over the next two hours, we climbed and fought scattered snipers into the lower slopes of the ridge. Medevacs had taken our dead and wounded, and Charlie Company was down to thirty-five people. Digger's body had been flown out along with the majority of his company. Maddeningly, the enemy seemed to have evaporated with the darkness that now settled over us.

The sunlight of the following morning revealed a

scarred and eerily quiet ridge. Trees and rocks had been blown in half, and, occasionally, a body or parts of one, would be found. The smell of burned flesh incinerated by our napalm saturated pockets of ground. A few bodies, starkly pointing toward nothingness, were found painted a ghostly gray-white by the jelled-gasoline bombs dropped the afternoon before. We counted forty enemy bodies, and the rest had simply hoofed it back up toward the Que Sons.

I looked at Gunny Kershaw, who had stayed with me all the way. The tough old salt appeared battered as he sat exhausted with no sleep and stared through the tree in front of him. I wondered if I looked as bad. I remembered Digger and thought about Nancy and their new kid. And then the thought of the Marine back on the riverbank shuddered through my body. No face, no arms, no legs, and yet he lived, pumping blood out of his torn body. I prayed again that he had died.

Later that day, the birds came to take the rest of us back. I wondered what would be next for our worn-out bodies. Would I be able to skate by these last days without having to go back into the bush?

A quiet, beat bunch of dirty and bruised Marines sat staring through the inside metal walls of the CH-46 on our way back to the ship. I felt like they looked but decided to get up and walk around looking at wounds and try to be concerned in spite of my own exhaustion.

In the distance, the Navy ships began to come into view. I knew morale would lift with the showers, sleep, and food. Then my mind began to drift back again to the living, bleeding but breathing, and mutilated body of that one Marine. Back on board ship I checked the reports from the Da Nang hospital. He was still alive! The first sergeant had gone in to see him before we had gotten back. He told me that it was useless for anyone to go see him. He lay comatose in his ICU bunk wrapped like a mummy without arms and legs. They thought he had a chance to live!

Shit, somebody's got to have the courage to slip him some quick-acting poison or something, I thought. Fuck, how can anyone live like that? My God! No face, arms, or legs!

However, in the wisdom of the Marine Corps, a person was not allowed time to mull over that kind of crap. Very quickly, we were to be hitting the beach again. We would be without Charlie Company for another couple weeks while they brought in new cannon fodder to rebuild the company. But this time the South Vietnamese Army would be working near us. Hot shit!

We were told the place of our new assault was named "Breaker Island." I wondered if someone up in division or Third MAF headquarters was assigned the important job of coming up with the names of these operations. Maybe it was important to be able to give the next of kin a name for the place where their son, brother, or husband had been killed.

NVA were known to be on Breaker Island, and South Vietnamese intelligence reports outlined how it had been a hotbed of communism for years. The village there had even been relocated once, but many of the people had managed to filter back and crudely reconstruct their houses. We had been told to expect mines, booby traps, and a confrontation with NVA units.

Well fuck, shit, and damn! Mines and booby traps and the NVA? In eighteen days I'd be leaving for the World, and I felt myself getting a bad attitude. It was called, "Short-timer's disease." Man I don't want to get fucked up now! Let me just get off the motherfucking bus right here, and I can look any person or Marine in the eye and know that I served my country.

That afternoon I was again having my eardrums massaged by the sounds of a helicopter. It was one of the routine administrative runs back to Da Nang. I was going with it, and my plans were to find my SeaBee friends at MCB-10 to make probes and grappling hooks. My imagination was working on methods to find mines, booby traps, and other unfriendly situations buried beneath the ground.

Then before four days had passed since Whitestone Canyon, we were shoving off again. The cold milk and hot meals had been great, but now, C-rats and Charlie were waiting for us. The first one we would eat, but I didn't know about the other. This time we were to land across the beach, and I prayed the enemy wasn't locked and loaded watching through the gunports of beach bunkers expecting us.

Too quickly, D-Day was on us. We were waiting in the well-deck of our LPD. I watched in nervous awe as the monstrous back hatches of the ship opened. The gray light of early dawn rode the waves of the dark sea and washed in lapping at the sides of our little amphibian tractors. Our small boats prepared to methodically charge forward out of the ship's backside. I imagined that the mother ship was giving birth, and we, like a bunch of newborn tadpoles, would shortly be swimming for our lives.

As the last of my company finally loaded into their respective amtracks, I boarded mine. Then the hatch closed behind me, and I felt almost overpowered by the confined darkness. The air was heavy with the trapped sweat and body odor of Marines who shared this quasi-coffin with me. Adrenaline was pumping as I made my way to the rear and found myself a temporary seat. The motor of our vehicle was idling. In the dark, there was some shuffling of bodies and the occasional clank of a rifle or E-tool against metal, but no one spoke.

The air was so thick, you could almost touch the silence, the smell, the heat, and the emotions. In fact, you didn't have to reach out to it. It settled on you.

I felt the driver shift into gear and begin to move. A little top-hatch above me was opened and some light and fresh air trickled in. The splash of the waves was heard, and every few seconds a spray of saltwater lightly showered through the two-foot opening. That hatch was our only opening to the world. Ninety percent of our vehicle rode and hid under the water. The Marines, all burdened with helmets, heavy packs, flak jackets, and weapons remained sitting on little benches lining the dark insides, and the silence was creepy. We felt the shuddering movements of our tractorized tomb as it plowed through, almost under, the sea. Although we couldn't hear 'em, the Navy guns continued to pound the beach to our front.

In the limited light of the top hatch, I studied the map for one long, last minute. For the first time, the name of the village really jumped out at me: Chien Son. This wasn't far from Hoi An. I thought it interesting that I was ending my final stay in Vietnam near where I first served as an advisor eleven years before.

Then, the amtrack shifted into high gear. I knew that in a few minutes our vehicle would hit the sand barrier of the beach, and we would all lurch forward in our seats as our driver downshifted. I sat hoping that we would land in the right place, and that I would be able to get the company coordinated after being separated in the different vehicles.

"And Jesus," I prayed, "don't let any fucking Charlie be sitting in some bunker on the beach with a machine gun waiting to blow us away as the hatch opens."

In the dark, I smelled the odor around me and wondered whether this was the smell of fear, and then thought that a little fear was good. But there wasn't time to think very long as we collided with the underwater beach. I braced myself as the amtrack geared down and plowed up the sand for about four long seconds. Then there was a yell and the front hatch dropped.

We all raced madly forward, with seventy-odd pounds bearing down on our backs. The naval guns had ceased their firing, and there was none from the enemy. In fact, everything seemed abnormally quiet. As I ran, I felt as if the sand was swallowing each of my legs. Every step was sucked down at least six inches. I said a quick thanks that no one was there to shoot our butts off because it would have been easy.

Reaching a five-foot-tall sand berm line about fifty feet from the water, I dropped behind it with my radio operator. I grabbed the receiver and began to talk to my platoon commanders. We had to quickly reorganize and move off the beach into the scrub tree growth and the village to our front.

This village, hamlet, or whatever it was, looked different than any I had yet seen. There were no thatch huts, only crude shelters and lean-tos. As per our plan, 3rd Platoon would move through the place pushing toward the west. The 1st Platoon would secure the immediate area including the hamlet, while 2nd Platoon swung to the north up the beach and prepared to move parallel to the sea. The battalion command post would come ashore at the location of the 1st Platoon when all was secure.

Lieutenant McAdams reported that he was ready with the 3rd, and I gave him the order to move to the opposite end of the village. Lieutenant Spaulding's 1st Platoon was already into the first half of the place.

Lieutenant Morris with the 2nd Platoon had moved his people to cover our right flank and was prepared to move up the seaboard. I wanted to be positive of the area's security before telling the colonel to come ashore with his command post. I knew that both B and D Companies had been heli-lifted to more northerly and westerly sections of this quasi-island and were themselves now moving into their immediate objectives.

Together with the gunny, my radio operators, and naval and air gunfire liaison, I moved into the village to find Spaulding. The 3rd Platoon was now moving west pushing through the 1st. We began to notice Vietnamese. They were all kids and older people, mostly women; not even many young women were to be seen, much less men. No one offered any resistance, but one woman was found crying and screaming. Her little boy, who looked like a five year old, had been killed by the ship's guns. His side was torn wide open by a piece of shell fragment. That was the only casualty we found. But regardless of the fact that so far we hadn't found any enemy soldiers, the ninety-seven percent unfriendly civilian population figure again popped up in my mind. Still, I felt like saying to the lady with her dead child, "I'm sorry." I didn't though.

The 1st Platoon was charged with the responsibility of clearing the village and peacefully removing the villagers to a central staging area. The battalion had South Vietnamese intelligence and interrogation units attached to handle both the villagers and any captured enemy. I felt the area secure enough and now informed the battalion headquarters that they could come ashore.

With my headquarters following, I went forward about a quarter-mile to find Lieutenant McAdams. He was sitting with his platoon sergeant, Liverette, inside an abandoned shelter reading their maps. The gunny and I joined them, and together we decided our next steps.

There was another quarter-mile of this same sandy, brushy terrain, but then the map showed a couple of hun-

dred meters of rice paddies out ahead of us before we
reached the western end of the island. That side was
bounded by a river. But I wanted to personally see things
ahead of us. So I asked Gunny Kershaw to organize Corporal Powell, Doc Garcia, and a squad from McAdams's
platoon to move the next four hundred meters by ourselves to recon the area. McAdams argued that to move
forward like that was his responsibility. I told him,
"Mac, no doubt you're right, but I'm going ahead. You'll
have plenty of time to do your thing; we're just going to
the end of the sand and trees and not out into the paddies.
In the meantime, you secure your positions here, and
we'll be back in a little while."

Before moving out, I spoke with the gunny. "What do
you think about swinging to the right and sort of looping
across our front from that direction? I know we haven't
run into anything yet, but the dozen of us moving straight
ahead could be asking for problems."

We were by ourselves, and I was trying to look ahead
through the scrub trees, sand, cactus, and shelters. He
turned, and I glanced at this feisty fighter I had for a
company gunny. He was about five feet, nine inches tall
and maybe 150 pounds if he were soaked in beer. His
mouth was always getting him in trouble.

There was a time I remembered when the first sergeant
was cussing him, yelling, "But goddammit Gunny, why
the hell did you stand up in the middle of a hundred and
fifty fucking sailors and start singing, 'Bell-bottomed
trousers, buttons made of brass, loose around the ankles,
tight across the ass'? And then, you dumb shit, you
screamed for all the cocksucking swabbies to line up to
suck yours as you had enough for them all. If there hadn't
been a squad of fucking shore patrol walking in the front
door, you and me would be dead. Motherfucking dead!
Do you hear me, you shit-for-brains?" Well that was the
gunny—old Corps, through and through. I didn't know
how he was still alive.

Now he looked at me and said, "With all due respect
to the captain, sir, I hope he doesn't mind me saying he's
a dumb ass for doing this, but regardless of that, I think
it's great. I get damn fucking tired of sitting in the back

of the company. Getting to recon out ahead like this plum excites my ass, Skipper.''

I thought to myself, You're right! I am a dumb ass. Why am I doing this?

So, we took one of Mac's squads and headed out as quietly as possible to the right for a hundred yards and then back across our front. In ten minutes we were past the last of the village huts and didn't see any more people. It took about fifteen more minutes to cautiously cross the sandy terrain covered by these half-ass trees with patches of cactus before we found ourselves at a sudden drop of about five feet to a large field of rice paddies. Paddy dikes broke the irrigated land into squares to our west. They hadn't harvested here yet. To the north a few miles was Hoi An. I wondered what had happened to this little village called Chien Son. It looked like it had once been quite a nice little place, but the ruins of many houses spoke about some bad shit happening there in years past. Maybe, I thought, they had burned this place to the ground to relocate the village. But it didn't keep the people away too long, and I'd bet they'd have to kill 'em all to make them stay gone.

We silently set our positions and continued to signal by sign language only. I positioned the patrol at the edge of the paddies in a tree line, and then walked around by myself. I had gone only about twenty or thirty yards when, while looking back toward my company's area, I stared into the backs of three Vietnamese men not more than thirty feet from where I stood. They were looking away from me back toward the company. One was in a hole at the base of a tree with only his head sticking out. One other stood beside the tree, and the last sat on a limb. Some bags were at the feet of the one standing by the tree, and the one in it had a rifle.

I hadn't time to think when the one standing casually turned and saw me. By the look on his face, you'd thought that he had just seen a ghost, and I didn't feel a hell of a lot different. I quickly threw the rifle to my shoulder, pointed at him, and yelled for the gunny. All three Vietnamese were now staring at me, frozen in place, their eyes fixed on me.

In a couple of seconds, when my patrol had reached

me and had finally gotten these, our first prisoners, tied together, we opened their bags. There were grenades, trip wires, and other explosives for making booby traps. I said to the gunny, "Jesus, Mary, and Joseph! Thank God they hadn't planted and rigged this shit yet."

"Their tough luck," he mumbled, as he shoved the prisoners with his rifle.

By the time we returned, the battalion CP was ashore, and the 1st Platoon had rounded up a hundred or so villagers. There were no males between the ages of nine and fifty-nine among the group. I knew there had to be some more around. Even if their army had left, all the men couldn't have gone with it. With our prisoners turned over to South Vietnamese interrogators, I began to move the platoons into action.

An hour down the beach, we sat on a mound of sand, and the three-foot probe I had shoved into the ground stared back at me sticking ten inches out of the ground. I looked at the gunny and Corporal Powell, who were nearby, and said, "I can smell 'em! I'm probably sitting on top of 'em." Powell walked over and stepped on the probe, driving it to its hilt in the sand, but suddenly it stopped, hitting something very solid! Powell yelled for a couple of others to come to help dig.

Three marines dug three feet into the sand and found concrete. A hole was dug revealing what appeared to be a 36-inch concrete culvert. Powell grabbed his E-tool and began banging on the concrete, trying to break through. Finally, a hole big enough for a man to get in was chipped away.

Powell was in his T-shirt, sticking his head in the hole, and I warned him, "Before you go in, drop a grenade." I couldn't believe that anyone would volunteer to jump into an underground tunnel by himself without anyone even asking or ordering him.

He dropped the grenade and retreated a little. When it exploded, a cactus "pot plant" jumped into the air about eight feet away. The line of sand dunes that rose up and overlooked the entire beach was crowned by a cactus field that resembled Southwest Texas more than Vietnam. It was in the middle of all this cactus that one little pot plant had been blown about a foot into the air before falling back into its place. Surprised, I walked up through the cactus to the top of the berm and looked down at the outline of a wood-framed hole, big enough for a small man to fit through. The pot plant of cactus sat a little skewed since it hadn't fallen exactly back into its man-made position. Carefully, I picked the plant up by a couple of ears and set it aside. It was just a hole, dark and spooky. I looked up and down this long five-foot-tall row of dunes paralleling the water. Most of it was covered by cactus, and its position gave anyone in it a good command of the beach. The Navy's guns hadn't penetrated these sand piles. Whatever type of bunker network that existed before the shelling, still existed now. I was very glad that Charlie hadn't wanted to man the bunkers that probably lay beneath my feet. We would have had a damn high casualty rate before we could have gotten off the beach.

By the time I walked back down to the others, Powell had taken his pistol and was slipping into the hole. His ears were stuffed with cloth to keep from rupturing his eardrums in the tunnel if he had to shoot.

After about two minutes of crawling in the dark with a flashlight, he poked his head out of the hole and said, "There's a culvert running perpendicular to this one under the dunes, and it parallels the beach. Charlie could have been crawling through these things as we hit the beach and been under us all the time. But this one runs a few feet inland, too, and then there's a wall, but it looks man-made. It's about where the skipper was sitting a while ago. I'm going to check it out."

The gunny said, "Be careful, Powell. Keep that forty-five ready." Powell's head disappeared again, and we heard him moving up to and then digging at what he had told us was a wall.

Within a minute, there was a muffled, "Son of a bitch!" Quick as a spooked jackrabbit, Powell was scrambling out of the hole looking like he had seen the devil himself. He yelled, "There's Charlie in there! God-damn Charlie's in there!"

Then the gunny was grabbing his arm, asking, "Where and how many?"

"Inside the wall, underneath us! I punched a hole in

the wall. It looked a little makeshift, and I knocked a hole in it pretty easy. But son of a bitch, there were about six pairs of eyeballs looking back at me. Scared the piss out of me. I don't know why they didn't shoot me through the fucking running lights. There's a bunker right under this mound of sand.''

No one seemed to want to go back into the tunnel, so while one guy watched the hole with his M-16 at the ready, the rest of us looked for a hidden entrance. After a few minutes, it was found, and we cleared the small doorway. Since no one wanted to go in, the only options were either to frag the place and pull out the bodies or throw in a smoke grenade and make 'em come out. We decided to smoke 'em. So while the rest of us set-up with our rifles aimed at the opening, Powell threw in a red smoke. We waited.

It wasn't long before Vietnamese began to crawl out coughing, half-blinded by the smoke, and almost painted red by it. There were four men and two women. We tied their hands behind their backs and marched 'em down the beach to the South Vietnamese.

Now that we had found how they hid themselves, we pushed on looking for more. Over the rest of the day, we located five more bunkers and twenty more Viet Cong.

The next day, we continued finding enemy hiding in these underground holes. About noon one of our teams returning from delivering prisoners brought back reports that these people we were pulling out of the ground were not the regular army types, but belonged to their political and medical units, plus a scattering of others, like saboteurs. My returning Marines also described the torturing of the prisoners being done by the South Vietnamese interrogators with the Battalion Command.

"Shit," I said, "those fucking little assholes will do that when they're protected by a lot of American firepower, but I've seen 'em run otherwise!"

"Yes, sir," the squad leader said, a little matter-of-factly. "I saw 'em pumping their stomachs full of sea water and jumping on 'em. Sorta messing with their bodies real good.''

I put it out of my mind and concentrated on business. Lieutenant Morris came over to coordinate with me.

Gunny Kershaw also walked up. Morris was from New York, the gunny from Georgia, and Kershaw had not shown any friendliness toward Morris in the four months I had been with them. I figured that part of it had to do with the gunny's dislike of lieutenants from "the north."

Morris took off his helmet and gazed out to sea wiping sweat off his brow. Then he asked, "Skipper, do you hear the stories about the prisoners being tortured?"

"Yeah, I heard."

"I've seen too many wimp South Vietnamese who aren't worth a fart in a windstorm when it comes to fighting, but they do this shit. What do you think about torture, Skipper?"

Gunny Kershaw interrupted, "Lieutenant, what the fuck does it matter? These assholes we're pulling outta the ground would do the same to us. Look, I was in the Pacific in forty-five, in Korea in the fifties, and this shit now, and I fucking well know this: the only goddamn way to walk through the Valley of Death is to be the meanest, toughest, motherfucker in the Valley. They want this war won? Just put the Corps on line, and we'll march through this shithole of a country and blow every swinging-dick in it back to his ancestors."

Morris spun around and angrily said, "Goddamn it, Gunny, I've been over here for nine fucking months. I don't trust one little, slant-eyed asshole in this place. But what the fuck are we doing in this screwed-up place you call the Valley of Death? Let the motherfucking place rot in its own blood. This goddamn war will ruin the Corps."

The gunny wouldn't let it die. "Lieutenant," he said, "you got a bad problem. You think too much. Don't ever forget you're a goddamn Marine. If every Marine did what you're talking about, we'd all vote on whether we wanted to fight or not. It'd be a fucking Chinese fire drill. The Japanese would have a capital in Los Angeles, and Hitler'd be in New York. For months now, you been acting like you think war is evil 'cause people get screwed in the butt hole. Hell, yeah, it is! That's why you need a war machine that doesn't question, but goes out and kicks ass and takes names. That's so you're not the butt hole that gets screwed, and that's why you got the fucking US Marine Corps. We're the fucker, not the fuckee. And

damn it, Lieutenant, you're going to get some of my Marines killed if you walk around thinking we're fighting
for nothing. Your commandant says do it; that means
you're fighting cause you're a Marine. There ain't no
fucking right or wrong. It's live or die. It's stick together
and do what you're told. Otherwise you will die.''

The lieutenant glared at Kershaw. But before he could
say anything else, I grabbed Morris and said, ''Go back
to your platoon, Jack, I need to talk to the gunny.''

He walked away about ready to explode, and I turned
to the gunny. ''That boy will get somebody killed 'cause
he's too fucking much into philosophy,'' he muttered.
''He tried to tell me the other day that Ho Chi Minh
worked with our secret service in World War II helping
to rescue American pilots from the Japanese. I told him,
what the shit do I care what Ho Chi Minh did twenty
years ago. It's him or me now. Kill or get killed. Fuck
philosophy.''

I sat down in the sand and began to dig a hole to nowhere. ''Gunny,'' I asked, ''do you remember the poem
'The Charge of the Light Brigade'?''

''Only the name,'' he said.

''Well, that's what we are, Gunny. Into the Valley of
Death they send us, and not only do we go in, but we go
with that gladiator bravado saying, 'We who are about to
die salute thee.' ''

He looked at me and said, ''You're not gonna get
philosophical on me, are you, Skipper?''

His voice carried with it a note of a challenge, and I
replied, ''Shit, Gunny, since when do I have time to get
philosophical on you? Let's get back to finding holes and
pulling out Charlie. Remember one thing though: you
believe in the tradition of the Corps, and a part of that
means to show respect for officers no matter what you
may think of them. Show more toward Morris.''

He glanced at me and said, ''Aye, aye, sir.'' Then he
got up and moved back toward the cactus. I watched him
move out with the confidence—and wariness—that only
years of experience can bring.

No longer did I feel exhilaration, but the heavy weight
of nineteen months in this war began to settle on my
shoulders. Feeling too tired to question things like Mor-

ris did or get pysched-up like the gunny, I just sat there near the beach.

Suddenly, to my right, a man started screaming, not forty feet from me. I jumped to my feet and moved over watching Marines pull another Vietnamese out of a hole. He was yanked out with a Marine on each arm.

From six feet away his chest grotesquely stared at me. As he continued screaming, I grimaced, watching his chest pump red, smoke-smeared blood from a hole seared deeply into his flesh. I didn't understand. It looked like he had thrown his body over the smoke grenade that had been thrown in to drive him out! It wouldn't have killed him—what the fuck did he do that for?

"Come help me," another of my men yelled as he tried to pull another one out of the same hole.

The crying man had been pulled off a little but continued to scream as a corpsman tried to pour something on his deeply burned chest. Finally, the second person emerged, being half dragged. It was a woman. We were only about a hundred feet from the sea, and I was about to tell 'em to carry her closer to the water, away from the man who continued to cry and scream. But before I could say a thing, she rolled over.

The first thing I saw was that she was very pregnant. Oh, shit, I thought. Damn it, I don't want to get involved with a childbirth! Then her long, black hair flowed to her side as her bewildered and fearful face turned to stare hatefully into mine.

"My God, Kim Lan!" I stammered in shocked disbelief and knelt in the sand beside her.

CHAPTER 15

> The war is finished. I feel only sorry that all our American friends have to leave so soon . . . I believe that your sympaty [sic] and the sympaty [sic] of the great American people will always be with us . . .
>
> Ho Chi Minh in a letter to
> Mr. Charles Fenn (1945)

The days, weeks, and months went past, and I felt changes within my body. The rainy season meant a slowdown in enemy activity against us, and we concentrated on filling our ranks with replacements, training them, obtaining and distributing supplies, and continuing our efforts to maintain contact with the people in the villages. Through it all, I worked hard at those jobs assigned by Ba Can, but a new life was growing within me. I had felt it when I was with Van Thi, and now I knew it was so. Often, I would go alone down the path to the north side of the mountains on the edge of jungles and just sit down. Gazing across the miles of fields in the valley below, I could see the mountains where Van Thi was, above Dai Loc in the distance. I wanted to reach out and touch him, but I sat there quietly. Occasionally, a tear would come to my eye. I worried about rearing a child in war, and I wrote Van Thi often. His return letters didn't come as frequently as I sent mine, but maybe some never made it to me. I always looked forward to receiving them and eagerly consumed each, rereading them so many times that the pages were becoming crumpled. Then often times, I worried about the child's health but would drive myself in work to keep my mind off those terrible things.

Throughout the rainy season we reconditioned our army. By spring, the rains were abating, I was six months pregnant, and we were on the move. Ba Can had brought our battalion, with me, out of the mountains, his anger and hatred fired anew by more recent bombings and atrocities committed by our enemy. We focused our work in the Que Son Valley.

Then one day Ba Can stood before me and announced, "Kim Lan you must now go back into the mountains and the safety of our camp. You are becoming a problem. I do not want any of the soldiers to worry about a pregnant woman. You are my sister, and I am responsible. So I must tell you to leave this evening. It will be for your own good and also for the baby's."

He stunned me! I had been sitting, but now got to my feet, looked at my brother, and said, "I cannot believe what I hear. For all these years I work as hard as anyone, and you now speak to me like this! Yes, I am pregnant, but that will give me some protection from the Americans. They are not as likely to suspect a woman who is only three months from having a child. I've already been thinking of how I can best help you! As a liaison with the villages would be perfect. But please don't dismiss me like this."

"It is my decision." he said simply. "You must leave by this evening." Then he turned on his heels and started to walk away.

"Wait!" I yelled and walked after him.

However, he turned to me with more than a small note of anger in his voice and sternly said, "I am now speaking as the commander of this battalion. Go back to camp. You are to return this evening. You are a danger to yourself and these soldiers. Do not argue."

He turned again and left me standing alone under the trees. I wanted to scream at him. I knew my body. I knew what I could and could not do. It was his problem if he didn't like the thought of me being out here. But others were nearby and had heard how he had ordered me off the battlefields because I was a danger. I felt humiliated.

But what choice did I have? By evening, I was slowly walking up the path into the mountains. I felt anger and frustration. The few people who were going my way suffered the brunt of my rage.

When we finally reached the camp, I immediately set down and penned a letter to Van Thi. Line upon line I gave vent to my irritation. There were too many things happening, and I felt I was losing control of them. I wrote my demands that my husband come to me by the end of May. I wanted to go home to have my child. It would be born near the beach as generations of my family had been before. Emphatically, I made sure that Van Thi knew that I wanted him there, and that we would go home for the baby. The letter went off with the next messenger going to the headquarters in the Dai Loc Mountains. It went with a sharp prayer that Van Thi would receive it.

Daily, I found work to do, and, daily, my emotions were building till I wanted to explode. The weight I carried bothered me, and as the heat of the summer came, my irritability increased even more. I was angry at Ba Can and angry at Van Thi. As the weeks went by, I sometimes stood on the edge of the jungles, still high in the mountains, screaming at my husband across ten miles of valleys and hills. I knew people around talked about me and at times stayed out of my way, and I didn't care. I was fat, angry, uncomfortable, and alone.

But two months painfully went by. I hadn't received any message from Van Thi in six weeks. The last I had read from him was, "I'll try my best to get there."

Try his best indeed, I thought! He had just better be here.

Finally in the last week of May, I angrily packed my bags and prepared to walk by myself back to Chien Son. I was mad at all men: my brother who had become so distant and driven by hate, my husband who had not come to me, and all the foreigners who had come to our land to destroy our culture and freedom. The fate of women was fragile and in the grip of heavy-handed men! Just once, just once, I'd like each of them to have to carry a growing life within them. Maybe then our world would become a better place in which to live!

Then my thoughts wandered to my destination. Chien Son wasn't the village it had once been, but some of the townspeople had returned. Our homes had been rebuilt with temporary shelters, not the nice homes they once were. Life was very temporary, but it was home. I had returned once a year since its destruction just because it felt good to do so. It was in an area that could be fairly safely traveled, although certain places had to be avoided.

On May 25, 1967, I set out alone with my small bag. As I got to the line of tall jungle trees that so abruptly stopped at an elevation of about three thousand feet, I looked over my shoulder miles to the north toward Van Thi. I did not scream. I just quietly, almost pleadingly, looked. Then I set my face to the east, the sea, and home.

For eight hours I walked, and my anger rose as my body ached. Where was my husband? My legs couldn't move without rubbing each other raw! With one hand, I held my bag of clothes. With the other, I had to hold my heavy, awkward, and protruding middle. My long journey found a much needed rest when I spent an exhausted night in a small hamlet of four homes with some friends. The next day after breakfast, I continued my misery. By noon, I was only three miles away from home, but it was taking so much longer than I had thought. I sweated in the sun, and it seemed that my whole body was one giant heat rash. Uncomfortable was not an adequate description for what I felt. Finally, I came to a little place that I remembered, and I sat to cool my body in the shade.

I glanced around inside this little tree-covered nook in the middle of the farmlands and remembered how, so many years ago, I rested here with Van Thi when he was disguised as a monk. Then, for the first time, I had gotten to see his face clearly, and even with his shaven head, he had looked so handsome. I sat and daydreamed under the small group of trees.

Suddenly, I was shocked by the touch of a hand. I sat straight upright, startled out of my semisleep. There, squatting in front of me, was my man. I cried and tried to lean forward to hug him, but my heavy belly got in the way. He quickly moved over and hugged me. I buried my head in his neck and cried. Somewhere I heard his voice saying, "I'm sorry. I'm so sorry. It seemed like everything was working to keep me from coming. When I finally got to your camp, you were gone. I think I lost five pounds running out of the hills trying to catch up.''

I pushed him back and wiped away the tears. Looking at him, I shouted, ''You lost five pounds? You lost five pounds? Why you poor soul! I waddle down the mountains like a hot, fat duck. I have to go through more than eight months of a child growing within me, and you're not around. Rainy season and hot season, mud and dust, it's me alone. My friends avoid me because I scream at you from the edge of the jungles. Now you say your poor body lost five pounds trying to catch me! Look into my eyes and see if you can find any sympathy. You won't find any for a man who loves and leaves his woman!''

I pushed him away. He sprawled on his back and lay there. Quietly and then more loudly, I heard him start to laugh. I yelled loudly at him, ''What are you laughing at?''

He continued laughing and said, ''I was trying to see my beautiful Kim Lan as a tired, fat duck, waddling down the mountainside.''

I yelled at him and picked up a stick to try to hit him and then finally started to laugh myself.

He looked at me and came close, kissed me, and said, ''I guess we should be careful. How much time do you have left?''

''Probably about two or three weeks,'' I answered. ''But I just don't know. In any event, this time you better stay with me!''

''I will, I will!'' he answered.

With one more rest stop, we at last arrived in Chien Son. A little, but only a little, had changed since my last trip there. I relaxed. It felt good to be at home. As I stood in the sand and looked at the old village that was only a skeleton of what it once had been, a tear rolled down my face. I sensed the presence of my mother and grandmother, and I could almost see my grandfather working in the rice fields.

One new thing that had happened was that our army's presence in the area had become stronger. Another battalion of the 2nd Division had this as well as surrounding areas in which to patrol and gather supplies. But they had just moved out of Chien Son to patrol neighboring villages. Now only some of our political and medical people had remained behind, although a special unit might go through once in a while.

Over the next days, Ba Can and I built a shelter on the plot of ground where my old home had once stood. We often sat alone on the beach. With only about three hundred people now living in Chien Son, we did have the opportunity for some time alone. Sometimes I would sit for an hour or more at the graves of my grandfather and grandmother. I would cry wondering at the fate of my mother; she was the one beautiful woman of such heroic proportions who so inspired my life, but who was so horribly missing in the course of this terrible war. But she was only one of many who had disappeared. I tried to remember Grandfather's admonition. It was beyond Ba Can and beyond so many others driven by the hatred inspired by the enemy. It was very close to being beyond my abilities. Hatred, anger, and revenge are easy thoughts.

Van Thi and I explored the old village in the days that followed. Our people had built underground shelters and tunnels. There were about one hundred of our cadres here. Some reconnaissance teams came and went, but the main effort was to establish a political presence and a basis for a medical station. It was hoped that with the village being kept with rough shelters only, and at a reduced population, that the enemy would not bother with Chien Son. I had heard that with the next rainy season a huge offensive was to be launched at the enemy, and that Chien Son was to be a major hospital area during the attack. But it was too hard to think about that right now.

As the days went by, Van Thi explained to me some of the bits and pieces of the early plans he had heard of for an offensive to liberate our country during the next Tet holiday. He started to quietly tell me about it, but as he went on he had to get up, walk around, and wave his arms. I listened intently. The plans and his hopes sounded too good to be true. In just about a half year, the whole country would be engulfed in the flames of an explosion. The climactic battle of the revolution was close. Therefore, this growing season was critical. Supplies of food, ammunitions, weapons, and medical needs all had to be gathered and pre-positioned. Just after the height of the rains, we would attack during the New Year's festival. Van Thi became more emotional than I had ever seen him. His face was animated, and his voice, almost agitated.

But as I listened, the baby moved. He kicked me hard! Van Thi noticed that my attention wasn't on his explanations any longer, and asked, "What's wrong?"

"He moved." I said. "I think he will come soon."

My husband came and sat next to me. He held me, and I placed his hand over the baby to feel it. Van Thi became very sentimental. He said, "Our child may not be born in a free country yet, but he shall grow up in one." Tears came to my eyes as I held my husband's hand over my own body to touch the product of our love. That night we slept quietly in our shelter near the beach.

Suddenly, thunderous blasts ripped through the sand. I was shattered out of my sleep. The skies were the color of early morning gray. Crashing through the air from the direction of the sea was a devastating series of thundering whistles exploding around our beach, shaking the ground on which we lay. I could hear babies and children screaming. Van Thi was at my side. He yelled, "Naval attack. Get into the bunker."

We crawled and rolled into the underground shelter built by our soldiers not many months ago. It was well constructed and vented. We pulled the camouflaging over our entrance behind us. Van Thi grabbed my hand and reassured me that all would be fine. We held each other in the darkness, and I felt my body contract around my baby. The pain passed, and I hoped and prayed.

We huddled in our disguised bunker for what seemed at least an hour. The enemy's naval guns unrelentingly pounded but did not touch us. Finally, the thunder and ground-shaking stopped. Van Thi looked anxiously at me. Then he said, "I'm going up to see what's happening. You stay here. Everything's going to be okay."

Another contraction came and went. After about ten minutes, my husband hurried back into the hole. Our hiding place was a big enough room, and if the enemy came, he might never see it, but it was becoming hot. I looked hopefully through the semidarkness at Van Thi. The tiny bits of light coming through our two small air vents revealed little, but I could tell. "They're coming, aren't they," I said.

He said, "Yes, but don't worry. Everything will still work out. We have food and water here."

Finally, I pulled out of him that it looked as if the American Marines were making a beach assault. A wave of fear rolled over my whole being. I feared most for my baby, and then I grew angry and shouted, "It's not fair! It's not fair! My entire family except for Ba Can? No! No! Not my baby now!"

Van Thi was reaching out for me when another pain gripped me. I trembled as he said, "It will all work out. They won't find this bunker. Lie down and rest."

As the minutes turned to stifling hours, he tried to comfort me, but my anger was turning to hatred. I thought to myself, Ba Can is right. He and his hatred will live. Our battles will be won through the strength of those who become fanatics in their hatred of the enemy. The Americans and their Saigon lackeys do not fear me, but it is the likes of Ba Can that they fear.

Van Thi, as if reading my thoughts, held my hand and spoke softly. "You will live. Our baby will live. I have seen it. I know it. After the revolution, he'll grow strong in our country, and you will watch over him. This I know as firmly as I have ever known anything."

In the dark, my mind was only half focusing on his words, but slowly I began to hear them. Turning quickly, I asked, "What do you mean, 'I have seen it, I know it.' What about you?"

He looked at me as a small shaft of light glanced off his forehead and eyes, and calmly, assuredly said, "Simply that. It is as if one page of the future has been opened, and I saw it, if only for a brief moment. You were there, along with our child."

Anxiously, I asked, "What about you?"

"I don't know," he responded, "I saw the both of you as through the eyes of the observer who does not see himself."

I reached out to hold him. Love and tears were again enveloping my soul. Then the hours turned into night, and I fought against the coming of the baby. He couldn't be born yet! Then another day came, and the bunker became hotter again, and my pain increased.

I lost track of the time and found that my thoughts were not always organized. Then I heard noises: the sound of men and machines. Another contraction gripped me, and this time it was harder and with more pain. Van Thi felt me tighten my grip on his hand, and he stroked my hair, which was now wet with sweat in this hot, humid hole in the ground. In our underground blackness, I held tightly to him.

Then men's voices, American voices, could now be heard just outside the entrance to our hiding place. I remembered my English, and I could occasionally understand their words drifting down from above. Suddenly, a terrifying shaft of light pierced our darkness and the shouts of the enemy were almost in our faces. For a brief second, I sat petrified in fear, and I saw Van Thi easing away from me toward the hole. Then in the space of time that would take lightning to reach from the heavens to the earth, I saw an enemy grenade bounce into the hole only a few feet in front of my husband.

In that flash of time I heard him yell, "Kim Lan, I love you," and he threw his body forward covering the grenade.

I heard myself screaming, "No!" as I reached out for my husband. As my hand grabbed his leg, there was a muffled explosion underneath him and a simultaneous scream from his throat.

Agony ripped my heart! Words of terror vaguely trembled past my lips as I tried to reach my husband crying in pain. A crashing, swirling confusion screamed around me like a life-sucking nightmare.

Then I saw the arms of soldiers reach down and pull on my husband. Gritting my teeth, I held his legs. No! This could not happen! But it did, it did! And he was wrenched from my grasp. I had to help him and awkwardly tried to push my heavy body forward. Then I felt arms grab me and roughly pull me also.

The light of the day blinded me. I tried to twist out of their grasp and heard Van Thi scream not far away. Heaven above, help me! my heart pleaded, but my mouth remained still. I turned in the midst of enemy soldiers trying to see my husband. I felt myself being engulfed in fear, and I fought it. No, I shall not show weakness! Then anger and hatred filled my being. Teeth clenched, I rolled over out of the grasp of the soldiers and looked into the face of an American. I would spit poison at him.

Then his eyes went wide. He dropped to one knee beside me and threw away his helmet. It was him! It was the American! I heard him say my name. No! Why him? Why did he have to do this? I hate them all! I hate them all!

Through eyes without tears, I made his soul a target of my hate-filled thoughts. Our eyes locked, and his emotions mixed with mine as east and west winds collide, unite, and spin in all their fury. Then I heard him again say, "Kim Lan," and his eyes glazed. Screams behind me tightened my fists and ravaged my heart. The American touched my hand and yelled at others, while I feared again for my husband.

I was lifted and carried toward the sea. No! I didn't want to be taken from my husband! Then I was placed under a tree. The American took my hand and tried to speak gently. With a wet cloth, he wiped my face. Only my eyes spoke the hate I felt. Then I thought of my child, and I feared.

Looking softly into my eyes he said, "Kim Lan, forgive me, please. I'm sorry. You're pregnant." He looked away toward Van Thi.

I hatefully thought, Yes, I'm pregnant. Yes, that's my husband. Is it the intent of you and your people to kill us all, even my baby? But I spoke not a word.

"I've called for a helicopter to get you to the hospital at Da Nang: the American hospital. You will not go to the South Vietnamese. I will do what I have to. You and your child shall live. I'll come. I'll help. I promise."

He continued as he sat on the sand beside me. "After we leave this place, I'll come to the hospital. Don't say anything to anyone. I'm putting a tag on your wrist that simply says 'South Vietnamese woman from near Hoi An in labor with child.' No one will know."

I angrily stared at him hardly hearing what he said but torn by both the pain of the coming baby and the screams of my husband. Then the noise of the helicopter drowned out everything. Enemy soldiers were lifting me, and we went through a sandstorm to the enemy machine. Inside the helicopter I looked at a strangely helmeted enemy, his face covered by green glass and felt a twist of fear. Then again my heart cried out for my husband. As the plane lifted into the air, I rolled my head to one side and looked out the door. But my husband was not to be seen. Only the American. He still stood there, watching, with his helmet lying behind him.

Van Thi! Van Thi! my soul cried in confusion. But now standing between my husband and myself was the American. Between me and everything, he was there. In a strange machine, I was flying through the air being taken to an enemy hospital. Fear gripped me. My lower body tightened and hurt. I knew my time was very near, but I swore not to show my fear to the enemy, ever!

The rough metal floor of the aircraft vibrated through an eternity of terror and I felt ripped into pieces by the horror of this nightmare. The winged monster of my vision breathed its hot breath on me while it clawed apart the bleeding body of my husband. My lips trembled with the fearful words of my heart, My baby! My baby! They cannot take him, too! Then in my mind's eye I saw again the American: the helmetless blond soldier with soft eyes saying, "You and your child shall live. That's my promise."

I knew I'd never see him again, and I knew my husband was gone to his death. Then I remembered Van Thi's vision of my child and myself, and I held onto that as the only promise I had left in life.

We bounced, suddenly on the ground, and I closed my eyes and prayed. I felt hands lift me, and I saw large metal buildings toward which I was being carried. Pain again gripped me, and I held my body.

Rushed inside one building and placed on a bed, I anxiously watched as two women and one man began to work around me. This time, I twisted when the pain came. I tried to remember advice I had received and breathed deeply. A friend had told me to stay on my feet as long as possible, and I remembered. Struggling to stand, I pushed past the nurses and began to walk up and down the aisle. They argued with me to get in bed, but I made signs to them to wait. I didn't wish to speak and let them know that I knew their language.

I must have walked for a half-hour; occasionally grabbing onto the wall or a bed to hold myself as I felt my body tie itself into painful knots. Then a wrenching ache dropped me to my knees. A nurse helped me to bed. For another hour, I breathed through the pain. My clothes were wet with sweat. Finally, a doctor made motions to me trying to encourage me to push on the baby from within. The signs he used were stupid, but he was speaking English, not knowing I understood his words.

Minutes, painfully, fearfully, passed by. A sudden terror shook me, Would they take my baby from me? They are the enemy!

Then with a last ripping pain, I bit my tongue and pushed again, and I felt the birth of my child. It was over! Then out of the depths of exhaustion, I struggled to reach him. Only I would have him.

Him? I thought. I looked at *her*! I had given birth to a daughter. Feeling tears on my face, I held my crying girl, and whispered to her, "Go ahead, scream, fight, and live. It is in your blood. Do not deny it. Our revolution shall live on in you."

The days went past, and I gained strength, and my daughter became more beautiful. For me she was like a flower blossoming in the midst of a metal building built on the hot sands of an enemy camp. I named her Xuan Hoa, "Spring Flower," after my special friend in An Bang.

After a few days, a Vietnamese interpreter was brought in to speak with me. He asked, "Where are your identification papers?"

"Lost in all the confusion," I lied.

Still, I acted ignorant of English and listened as they debated what to do with me. Remembering what the American had said, I would only say that I was from Hoi An. They then agreed that I would be placed on a helicopter to be taken to the military headquarters there in two days. There they would determine what to do with me. What could I do? How could I talk my way out without identification? Where would I go with my child? The

fate that had torn the life from my husband was all too
real and again threatened me. But now it wasn't just me.
Every night I cried myself to sleep, only to be awakened
by my baby wanting to nurse at my breast. But a new
feeling was growing within me. It was strange. Now I
was a mother, and a small, defenseless child depended
on me. My mind felt scattered, and I was so often concerned. How could I protect her? How could I give her
the love and everything she needed? Love for my child
held me constantly. The hatred that had so overwhelmed
me was, little by little, being replaced by the attention
demanded from me by my daughter.

The next morning, holding her, I walked outside the
building and tried to think. I had to figure out how to
escape this enemy camp. Tomorrow was the day they
were to take us away.

I looked around at the hugeness of this place. Maybe
I could just walk out the gate acting like all the other
Vietnamese workers. No, it looked like they all carried
identification cards, too. Then I sat down and looked
around. Mine was not the only building, and walkways
built with boards connected them all. The wooden paths
had metal roofs to shield away the sun and rain. I was
amazed at the enemy hospital and compared it to our
rough underground medical shelters built several levels
underground. My daughter started to get restless, and I
began to nurse her. The two of us were marooned in the
middle of an enemy camp, in the midst of a typhoon, but
somehow still safe. That, however, might soon end.

I sat underneath a porchway in the shade and watched
Americans as they walked everywhere. A few Vietnamese workers were doing busy-work here and there in the
glare of the sun. Some nurses occasionally paused,
smiled, and said how pretty my child was. Behind a mask
of silly smiles, I nodded, but wondered what their reaction to me would be if they knew the truth. I began not
to pay attention to the swirl of activity around me and
drifted in my own worries.

Soon though, I realized that a green uniform was
standing beside me, and I heard, "Kim Lan." Frightened, I quickly glanced up. It was him. The American
had come. Even though he said he would, I had never

expected it. Fear and anger knifed through my soul. I wanted to strike out at him but remained frozen in place.

He sat down on the walkway and looked at me and then at the ground. His voice was almost pleading as he said, "I hope that you can forgive me. I don't know if that was your husband, and, believe me, I didn't want to have this happen to you, with your baby and all. Can you just understand that I'm only a Marine. I follow orders. Governments fight governments. I never wanted to hurt you. And I don't understand what has made our lives cross like they have. Look, after everything that's happened, I wouldn't blame you if you wanted to kill me, but let me try to help."

He paused and looked at me. I felt the hatred begin to boil within me, and I could feel my heart being tightened in the grip of a nightmare again. Then I realized that others would notice that he spoke to me in English as if I understood. I began to become nervous.

Then he said, still almost pleading, "Please walk with me. I would like to get you out of here. If you will just act normal, I think I can get you away. Would you come now, while we have a chance?"

I felt self-conscious sitting there with him. I wanted to leave, but didn't know where to go. Then I remembered what he had done eleven years ago, and how he had rescued the village girl last year. Maybe heaven was answering my prayers once more. I didn't understand why, but I followed. Xuan Hoa objected as she was taken from her food, and I walked after him with her. He took me to the opposite side of the next building where an American jeep sat in the sun. Helping me into a seat in the front, he quietly asked me to trust him. Then he started the motor, and we drove away.

With anxious thoughts, I watched the buildings and people pass by. Neither of us spoke. After a short distance, he stopped and said, "Around this corner is the main gate. It might help if you were nursing your baby."

I did so and held my breath as he drove through the gate patrolled by armed guards. No one challenged us, and, quickly, we were outside on a paved road. Looking around, I watched as we passed alongside a giant American helicopter base. Waves of heat shimmered off the big airstrip, and he drove on. Then after a short drive, he turned just beyond the helicopters and directed his vehicle toward the sea. I felt anxious not knowing what was to happen next. Fear for my baby's life was my biggest worry.

In five minutes, he stopped under a tree near a wide sandy beach. The airbase was behind us, and this part of the sea front was empty, although not far away, there were many Americans on the beach. I felt him look at me, while I watched my daughter fall asleep. Then turning to him, I allowed my anger to cry out.

Embittered I asked, "Where is my husband? Is he dead? And what about me and my child? Do you wish to kill us, too? What is it that causes you to come to my country and destroy my family?"

Tears rolled down my face, and I didn't care. He looked away from me, ashamed. I cried out again, "What is your name so that I can remember who killed my husband?"

"Collins," he answered, "my name is Collins."

"Collins! Collins, why?"

Then he looked back at me. We sat in the shade, and the steady rhythm of the waves ebbed and flowed a short distance away. Finally, he said, "I'm a Marine. I obey my orders. I don't intend to hurt anyone who is not trying to hurt me or others."

"Those others killed my family," I screamed. "What about my husband? He threw his body over a grenade to protect me and my child. But it didn't blow up and kill him. Where is he?"

"I don't know, Kim Lan. He was taken to the command post to be doctored and questioned. It was a smoke grenade. It wasn't meant to kill anyone. It was just to make you come out of the hole. I'm sorry." His voice was quiet, and he glanced from me to the sea, saying again, "Believe me, I'm honestly sorry!"

I watched him and knew he wasn't telling the whole truth. It was well known that the US forces brought with them South Vietnamese interrogators, and their torture techniques had been reported to all of us. I grabbed his shoulder and turned him to me again. Looking directly into his eyes, I asked, "He was sent to those puppet soldiers from the Saigon government's interrogation teams, wasn't he?''

"Yes, they were there. I know that. But I couldn't do anything for him. I didn't even know who he was, and I still can't do anything for him. For Christ's sake though, I can do something for you and your child before I go back home. Let me help you. Don't just sit there and yell at me. I'm sorry for your family. This whole war doesn't make much fucking sense anymore. I'm just a Marine. I'm here following orders. At least until now. Now I'm in deep shit if anybody finds out about this.''

"Wait! You say you're sorry for my family, but you don't begin to know what has happened to my family. You don't know how my father died, or my mother, or grandparents. How can you sit there and believe that you're 'just a Marine,' and that that relieves you of any responsibility? How can you? In the name of heaven, how can you?''

He stared a hole through the floor for a long minute. "Why," I asked, "should I believe you after all this? Answer me!''

Finally he said, "Maybe you shouldn't. It's just that I don't know what to do except that I want to help. Maybe I can't help other people in your country, but maybe I can help you.''

He looked back to the sea and watched the waves for a moment. Then he turned to me and said, "Look, I've got a friend who's a helicopter pilot at this base behind us. I've already talked to him. He's going out in two hours to An Hoa on a supply run. He'll take me and 'a friend' for a ride to drop her off somewhere. I didn't say where. I just let him talk his way into believing that the friend was my girlfriend who had a child. He thinks I want to take her home before I leave for the States. I didn't have to say much, he just believes that.''

"You said what?'' I shouted, but he quickly interrupted.

"Please, just listen and let me finish,'' he almost yelled. "I've got my orders. I'm leaving to go home tomorrow. My friend, the pilot, thinks I'm trying to get you back to your home village and your mother before I leave. It's the only way, and he's doing something that he shouldn't be doing and could get in a mess of trouble for it.''

"You've got no right to say such things," I blurted out. "You make a prostitute of me and my child, a half-American bastard. You have no right to say such things. You Americans are sick, evil people. You kill my family and—''

"Stop it. Stop it, please!" he interrupted. "It's the only story anyone would believe. Listen, you didn't kill me twice when you could've. I got you out of that place a long time ago, but I still owe you. Let's just say that, between you and me, this helps even the score.''

Angrily, I began to speak, "I don't know what 'even the score' means, but my mother said a long time ago that America had prostituted itself with the French and had gotten the 'whore's disease.' I never knew the full meaning of that until now.''

"Shit," he mumbled, and then said, "I know I can't bring your family back. If I could, I would, but I can't. But let me take you and your child somewhere. Let your family live on through you and your child. I know it would be what they would want. Please.''

I could see the sincerity and guilt all over his face but said, "Is this to make your conscience feel better?" He slumped back into his seat and just stared at the sea. Then my baby moved in my arms and cried just a little. I looked at her and knew I had no choice.

I asked, "What happened at Chien Son?"

"There's no one there. They've relocated the village," he responded without looking back at me.

I clenched my teeth. "Then there is only one place where your helicopter can fly with some safety," I said after a moment's thought.

He leaned forward again and looked at me. "Where?" he asked.

"It's a little village named An Bang, not far from An Hoa.''

"Is it west of An Hoa on the edge of the mountains?"

"Yes, it is!" I replied, wondering how he knew.

"Yeah, I know it."

"How do you know?"

"I patrolled near there, remember. By that pond when I saw you."

I felt myself blush, remembering how I had stood naked with only a rifle while he watched me.

He continued, "I have wanted to ask you ever since, what you were doing there, and why you didn't shoot us out of the air. Do you mind my asking?"

"I was married the day before in An Bang, and my husband and I spent the night by that pond—the husband you have now sent to be tortured and killed."

"Oh, my Lord, was that your honeymoon? Shit!"

"Honeymoon?"

"That's American for those few days after you get married when just you and your husband go off to be together. You know, there's no one else around, and you can enjoy yourselves, forgetting there's a real world out there. I'm sorry for what we did to you, but why didn't you shoot us? Your rifle was pointed right at me."

"Because I remembered your face. I memorized it a long time ago, and then you were there. I was shocked."

I looked at him for a moment trying to reorganize my thoughts. Then I asked, "Are you going to take me and my daughter to An Bang?"

"I'd like to. That's not far from An Hoa, but how safe is it?"

"If I were there with a rifle, yes, I would try to shoot a helicopter down. But I don't think any units of our army are there right now. Besides, I am willing to take the chance, and you owe me that much and more."

"You know," he said, "I'm a stupid son of a bitch. Nobody in his right mind would do this. I'm gonna get myself blown to hell. This helicopter ride is stupid. I got a ticket home tomorrow!"

My temper began to rise again. "This land is my home! Just drop me off somewhere so I can kill an American on my walk out of here. Why can't you *all* leave tomorrow?"

He breathed deeply as he stared off into the sea. I just watched him. Xuan Hoa then cried in her sleep. I cuddled her closely and began to sing an old song to her that I remembered Grandmother singing to me. After a minute, I glanced back at him. He was watching me intently.

I directed my look into his eyes and silently challenged him.

Finally, he said, "I can't believe you. Here you sit holding your baby, and yet I remember you on that hill overlooking the coal mines. Your hair blew around your uniform, and you shouted orders and charged into American bullets. Hell, I even saw you kick a grenade away into a hole. I admired your courage. But now, you sit here holding a baby!"

I looked questioningly at him. "How do you know about the coal mine battle?"

"I was there," he said. "I had a patrol just to the west, and when the fighting started, we ran across the paddies and up the hill to reinforce those Marines there. Their officer was dead, so I called our artillery. That saved us, but two of my men were killed."

Staring unbelievingly at him, I blurted out, "That was you?" I shook my head saying, "I don't understand how our lives have crossed so often." Then I gazed at the waves wondering, feeling his eyes still resting on me.

"If there is some kind of fate to this," he said, "I can't explain it. Look, Kim Lan, I'll convince my friend, the pilot, that it's safe to drop you off quickly at An Bang. It will have to be a little way off in the open, but I can convince him to do it. He owes me from a long time ago. I'll get you back. I don't understand either how our fates have put us together, and I suppose I never will. But there's something else I'd like to ask you.

"You know there's no way you can win this war. Even if I'm tired and ready to go home. Even if I've got out of my system whatever I needed, there's million more that'll just keep coming. What are you going to do? What is your future?"

I felt the pride of being Vietnamese. Two thousand years of history and tradition straightened my back. I proudly looked him in the face. "My mother told us stories about American beliefs, and I've come to see it also. Americans suffer from two, no three, problems that they will never defeat. First, you do not know patience. Second, you are not truly interested in this small country across many miles of water. And thirdly, you may have a few million Vietnamese on your side, but there are

thirty million others against you. It is good that you,
Collins, are leaving. Soon now, the country will erupt in
war far beyond anything you have yet to see. If you are
here, you may die.''

He shook his head in disbelief and just looked at me.
Then he leaned back and said, ''I wish there was no war.
I wish I could know you. You are an intriguing person—
a beautiful and mysterious woman. Maybe someday
there'll be a story in your own history books about 'Kim
Lan—the enemy tigress.'

''You know this is war, and we are supposed to be
enemies. But this thing is real screwy—you and me, I
mean. You sit there, sometimes wanting to kill me and
sometimes knowing that I've helped you in the past and
want to do it again. You don't know what to do about it.
And me? I'd probably be court-martialed if anybody
knew what I was doing, and I don't even know what I'm
doing.''

I watched him and finally said, ''I don't understand all
your words. I don't know what 'court-martialed' means.
I don't know what 'screwy' means. And maybe you are
right that I've wanted to kill you. And maybe the only
thing that keeps me from trying is what you did years
ago. I think I want to hate you, but sometimes I think
that I shouldn't. You just do not understand all the years
of pain, and how you people are destroying my homeland. I cannot understand why you do this. And then why
has this between you and me happened?

''You said you are tired, but you have been here only
a short time. Think about us. We are tired from many
more years than you, but we can't stop. Our freedom is
too important. You don't even know our language. You
don't know how it used to be, and sometimes still is, that
the farmers come home in the evenings and watch some
of the townspeople act out one of our old plays. We still
do that in the mountains with our army. You don't know
that before the French our government leaders were selected based upon their knowledge of our history, and
their ability to write poetry and literature. With the
French, and now you, leadership became based upon how
much money you had and with whom you had influence.

Do you not understand the corruption that you have brought?''

I paused and looked from him to my sleeping daughter. Then I added, "There are many questions I'd like to ask many people."

Softly he spoke while he watched me and then the sea, "There are questions that I have, too. Some of them I'd still like to ask you. Like about your family. Is there anyone you can turn to?''

"No. But I would like to ask you about some things that have gone unanswered for a long time. When you appeared in my life for the first time, why did you do what you did? Why did you help me?''

I watched him turn his gaze back to the sea. Finally, he looked again at me and answered, "You were innocent. You were young. You were not a prostitute. Your tears sobered my mind and washed my soul. I felt for you and loathed myself for what I had thought of doing.''

Then he glanced from me to the sea for a second and added while staring off a thousand miles, "And there's one more thing. I loved a girl a long time ago but was not allowed to be with her. When I saw you eleven years ago, I thought I was seeing her. You looked very much like her. It—I don't know how to say it—it made me feel a special tenderness for you.

"Kim Lan, this whole situation is more than I can put together in my mind, but there's a story I remember seeing in a movie years ago. It was about the Korean War, maybe fourteen years ago. An American officer and a Korean girl grew to like each other very much, but he had to return home, and she stayed. As they were parting, she told him about an old Korean folktale of two pine trees. It was about how each grew straight and tall very near to the other. The wind whistled through the branches often and they sang love songs to each other, but their branches could never touch. They could never reach each other until the day they died. First she fell, then not long after, he. Finally in death, their branches intertwined and their skin touched.

"Sometimes in my stupid nostalgia I think we may be a little like them. Kim Lan, I'm going ten thousand miles away across this sea tomorrow. But my prayers shall always be with you and your daughter. Whatever happens, I pray God will be with you. And I know there's a Heaven somewhere, and maybe there we can talk more, like the trees. But I'll leave this war and never forget you with a rifle in your hands and the wind blowing your hair around your body. Or now with your baby in your arms.''

I watched his eyes glaze with a hint of tears and thought, This is a strange man. If more Americans had his softness, maybe they would see the truth and leave. But he is right. I would like to know him better. I wished that my whole family could know at least this one American. But during this life, the evil of this war shall always stand as a barrier. We shall never know each other.

Then, feeling the touch of hostility again, I said, ''While you may remember this war with me on a hilltop in the middle of battle, I shall always remember it as a lost mother or a Vietnamese child floating facedown in the rice paddies shot by some American helicopter. But maybe someday I can remember you without the bitterness. Maybe someday the gift of my daughter will cause my heart to soften.''

''Let's go,'' he mumbled. He started the motor and quickly turned around. In the next minutes, I was watching, wide-eyed, countless American helicopters and buildings pass me by. We were in the middle of what he had called the Marble Mountain Airstrip. I had to wait with my child, but an hour later, he walked with me to board one of the airplanes. He smiled, as I sat down, and he tried to make sure that I was tied in, all the while assuring me that everything was ready.

Then after a few minutes, the roar of the motors lifted us off the metal landing strip into the sky. I clutched Xuan Hoa tightly to my breast. An American at the doorway had the same strange helmet covering his face and head as the one in the last helicopter ride on which I was taken. I looked at him as he watched over a machine gun, and wondered if he might be the same man. Occasionally, he turned his head in my direction, but I would glance at Collins and worry about what would happen next.

Somehow, I knew my hate was ebbing away—maybe forever—and I remembered Grandfather's words. I could

never hate so terribly again. Was it because of him, or
my baby? Or maybe because I had become too tired? I
didn't know. A slow relief eased its way into my being,
and I knew Van Thi's vision would come true.

The time quickly passed, and Collins touched my arm.
The noise was so loud I couldn't understand his words,
but he pointed down. I looked and there far below were
the rice fields and villages of my country. It was dizzying
to look down through the open doorway, and I pulled
back. Then his hand rested on my shoulder, and he urged
me to look again.

The mountains were close. He pointed in the direction
of a village. Then I knew it was An Bang. I could see
the stream; not far away, I saw the waterfall. For a moment, I thought of my friend, Xuan Hoa, and hoped she
was in good health. Then the ground was coming close
very quickly.

We landed with a jolt, and I held my daughter closely.
Collins jumped out first, helping me step down. Through
the wind and dust blown by the helicopter he rushed me
a short distance away. Then he stopped. An Bang was a
five-minute walk, and I glanced toward the village watching curious farmers. I turned then again to him.

He said, "My friend is yelling at me to hurry. I have
to go. Take care of yourself and your baby."

He started to turn and run but hesitated. He looked at
me and spoke loudly over the noise of the helicopter,
"Someday, Kim Lan, if our two countries can ever live
peacefully together, maybe I'll find a way to make it
back to find you. I'll pray for you."

He touched my cheek with his hand and turned to run
back and jump on the helicopter.

I shouted, "Collins."

He stopped one last time and turned. I shouted through
the wind, "Thank you, but if you ever come back it will
be to a free country, not the one you left."

Shaking his head, the serious expression that had
masked his face almost broke into a smile. Then he
waved, ran to the aircraft, and jumped in. The windstorm
from it now increased, rushing past and whipping around
me. I shielded my daughter, who began to cry, but my
eyes remained fixed on him. As they struggled into the

air and then started to fly away, I watched as he knelt in the doorway and waved again. Then they became smaller, disappearing finally as a small dot miles away. I felt no sadness at his departure nor any lingering hatred. There was only a funny kind of feeling growing in me that the past was past, and something new awaited. Still, I felt tears thinking of my husband. Then Xuan Hoa cried. I glanced down at my baby, and I felt Van Thi's vision.

I still had a small bag of a few things that I had managed to keep hold of when the Americans had dragged me from that hole. A paper had fallen out, and I picked it up. Unfolding it, I saw my crude drawing of our soldiers after the battle at the Ly Ly. Tears came to my eyes as I saw our wounded and torn men and women marching into the mountains carrying with them a brave spirit that I had so inadequately described. We were the people of Vietnam. Two thousand years of history surged through our blood. We had defeated the French, the Chinese, and the Mongols. Now we would defeat the Americans. The Heavens had made a special place for us on this land, and we would honor that commitment.

I walked toward the village but then stopped and glanced one more time into the empty skies. He was gone—maybe forever. But I thought to myself that if he ever came back, he would be one that would learn to understand our people. I would welcome him.

"Before the Buddha's altar they knelt down
to offer thanks for Kieu's return to life . . .

'I'm nothing but a fallen flower,' she said.
'I drank of gall and wormwood half my life.
An exile's destiny was mine, I thought:
to toss upon the waves, beneath the clouds.
I never hoped to see this joyous day,
yet I've survived to meet you all again
and quench the thirst that long has parched my soul . . .'

But now the mirror cracked is whole again—
Heaven has put her back where she belongs . . .
A karma each of us has to live out:
let's stop decrying Heaven's quirks and whims.
Within us each there lies the root of good:
the heart means more than all talents on earth.

May these crude words, culled and strung one by one,
beguile an hour of two of your long night."

from *The Tale of Kieu*,
Nguyen Du

BIBLIOGRAPHY

Brown, Holmes; and Luse, Don, *Hostages of War: Saigon's Political Prisoners* (Indochina Mobile Education Project, 1973).

Doleman, Edgar C., Jr., *Tools of War: The Vietnam Experience* (Boston, MA: Boston Publishing Company, 1985).

Doyle, Edward; and Lipsman, Samuel, *Setting the Stage: The Vietnam Experience* (Boston, MA: Boston Publishing Company, 1981).

Doyle, Edward; and Lipsman, Samuel; and Weiss, Steven, *Passing the Torch: The Vietnam Experience* (Boston, MA: Boston Publishing Company, 1981).

Doyle, Edward; and Lipsman, Samuel, *America Takes Over 1965–67: The Vietnam Experience* (Boston, MA: Boston Publishing Company, 1982).

Fenn, Charles, *Ho Chi Minh* (New York: Charles Scribner's Sons, 1973).

Maitland, Terrence; and Weiss, Steven, *Raising the Stakes: The Vietnam Experience* (Boston, MA: Boston Publishing Company, 1982).

Ngo Vinh, *Before the Revolution: The Vietnamese Peasants under the French* (Cambridge, MA and London, England: The MIT Press, 1973).

Nguyen Du, *The Tale of Kieu*; Translated and annotated

by Huynh Sanh Thong (New York: Random House, 1973).

Nguyen, Phut Tan, *A Modern History of Viet Nam (1802–1954)* (Saigon, Vietnam: Nha sach Khai-Tri, 1964).

Nguyen Thi Dinh, *No Other Road to Take: Memoir of Mrs. Nguyen Thi Dinh*; Translated by Mai Elliott (Ithaca, NY: Data Paper Number 102, Southeast Asia Program, Department of Asian Studies, Cornell University, June 1976). Recorded by Tran Huong Nam (Hanoi, Vietnam: Nha Xuat Ban Phu Nu, 1968).

Salzburg, Joseph S., *Viet Nam: Beyond the War* (Hicksville, NY: Exposition Press, 1975).

Shulimson, Jack, *U.S. Marines in Viet Nam: An Expanding War 1966* (Washington, D.C., History and Museum Division, Headquarters, USMC, 1982).

Sully, François, *We the Vietnamese: Voices from Viet Nam* (NY, Washington, and London: Praeger Publishers, 1971).

Telfer, Major Gary L., USMC; and Rogers, Lt. Col. Lane, USMC; and Fleming, V. Keith, Jr., *U.S. Marines in Viet Nam: Fighting the North Vietnamese 1967* (Washington, D.C.: History and Museum Division, Headquarters, USMC, 1984).

Tran Mai Nam, *The Narrow Strip of Land*; Translated by Robert C. Friend (Hanoi, Vietnam: Foreign Languages Publishing House, 1969).

Webb, Kate, *On the Other Side: 23 Days with the Viet Cong*, (NY: Quadrangle Books, 1972).

Weinstein, Franklin B., *Viet Nam's Unheld Elections* (Ithaca, NY: Data Paper Number 60, Southeast Asia Program, Department of Asia Studies, Cornell University, July 1966).

ABOUT THE AUTHOR

Larry Vetter now calls the Texas hill country home, but from 1964 to 1970, his haunt was the US Marine Corps. Within a year of graduating from Texas A&M and the Aggie Corps of Cadets, he shipped out for Vietnam as a lieutenant in the engineers attached to the 7th Marines. Later he extended his tour of duty to serve as a patrol leader in the Third Reconnaissance Battalion. Within two years he was back in-country again. This time he served as an infantry company commander in the 26th Marines. It was then that he met the woman about whom this book is written. His words below describe their encounter and his promise.

In the summer of 1969, I sat on the beach near the South China Sea holding the hand of a woman who was pregnant and suffering labor pains. The place was about twenty miles south of Da Nang. I was a Marine captain; she was Viet Cong. Her man lay screaming in pain not far away, and it was obvious that he had thrown his body over a grenade to save her. Even though contractions continually gripped her body, she never uttered a sound. However, her eyes burned holes into my soul. All the fear, anger, and hatred within her lashed out through her dark eyes and held me. I sent her back by helicopter to the American hospital in Da Nang, but before I did I made her a promise. That promise is finally fulfilled in this book.